Train Your Brain fo
German Garcia-Fre

C000148989

TRAIN YOUR BRAIN FOR SUCCESS

HOW A HEALTHY BRAIN IS THE KEY TO HAPPINESS AND BETTER HEALTH

GERMAN GARCIA-FRESCO, PH.D

Dedication

To my wife, Diana, for her love, trust, and ceaseless emotional support; and to our sons, Lukas and Mateo.

To my parents, Stella and Roberto, whose love and guidance set me on the path to success.

To my best friends and partners, Mike and Tai, for giving me their generous support and mentorship throughout the years.

Contents

About Doctor Fresco

As director of the Adaptive Neuroscience Research Institute (ANRI), Dr. German Garcia-Fresco helps people explore and enhance their own potential. The mission of ANRI is to collaborate with some of the world's leaders in a variety of fields, including finance, neuroscience, psychology, nutrition, and business, using the latest technology available today.

As a scientist, Doctor Fresco's research has led to advances in the field of neurobiology, contributing to mechanisms involved in neurodegenerative diseases. His work has been featured in top scientific journals as well as *The New York Times* and several news channels around the world.

Recently, he has been focused on the behavioral aspects of brain functioning, specifically decision making, emotional control, and creative enhancement. He is currently trying to develop techniques to increase neuronal performance and developing health and educational brain programs for children and adults.

Asides from his scientific interests, he is an avid entrepreneur and successfully operates a variety of companies in the United States. He's the owner of Xtreme Park Adventures in Durham, North Carolina, which among other skill-building activities focuses on team building—a group effort in which all members of a team work together to achieve one goal in common. The group works in sync, combining their different abilities and strengths to focus all their energy and achieve their goals.

Dr. Fresco obtained his BA/MS in organic chemistry/molecular biology from Purchase College, SUNY (Sigma Xi honor society). He earned his Ph.D. in molecular neurobiology at the University of North Carolina, with a focus on the interactions of proteins between myelin and the axon in rodents. He has received numerous awards, including the President's Award for excellence in genetics and biochemistry.

Preface

Growing up in Argentina, like many children I was very energetic. I could not stop talking or moving, and when given a task could stay on it for only a few minutes before racing off to do something else. Back in those days, attention deficit hyperactivity disorder (ADHD) was not a common diagnostic for children. Although the condition was known among medical professionals, I can't remember a single classmate who was identified to the other children as having ADHD.

Children like me were simply said to be "difficult." My poor mom had to be in school every week to talk with either a teacher or the principal for something I had done.

Part of me is glad that I was never diagnosed, since I grew up without taking medication.

The other part of me wishes that these conditions had been more well known so that teachers could better understand and help their students. Throughout my childhood, I heard the authoritative pronouncements, "He will never make it," "He will never go to college," and "Who knows how he's going to end up in life." But my precious mother knew better. She was an educator and understood that my brain was just operating at a higher temperature than those of most other children. In fact, my mom took me to psychologists and even had me take an IQ test, and I was well above average. She knew the world was not ready for individuals like me. The school system was too rigid. A teacher once told my mom, "Your son is like a little pebble in someone's shoe." My mom did her best to help me out with school by training and encouraging me to try new things all the time to keep my brain active.

As I grew older, I learned to manage my attention deficiencies. When I was twelve, I was sent to the Liceo Aeronautico Militar in the city of Funes, province of Santa Fe. Life at the Air Force high school was quite different from my previous schools. I was forced to control my deficiencies, and I did because I loved my school, and I did not want to be expelled from it, but something really interesting happened then. In the military, order and perfection are a must, and this organization and order triggered a passion to the point of an obsession, which led to my obsessive compulsive disorder (OCD). I had no idea what was happening—I just felt so compelled and excited to be *organized.*

Having trained my brain to succeed, I finally graduated from the academy as a lieutenant and went on to college.

One day I was talking to a counselor at my university and the topic came up of my obsession with organization. When I mean "obsessed," I am talking about such things as when I had to measure the distance between the hangers in my closet or that my books had to be two inches from the edge of the shelf and organized from tallest to shortest from left to right. Crazy, right?

The counselor started talking to me about OCD, which at the time I had no idea what it even meant. She started describing behaviors to me, and they all matched with things I did and felt. I couldn't believe it. I thought I had a mental illness! A condition, a disorder. How could that happen? Fortunately, I considered myself a strong-minded person, and I made it my mission to conquer my so-called disorder. Within a few years, I was able to keep it under control and without any medication. Now bear in mind that I also had ADHD, which no one had yet diagnosed, but after going to school and graduating, and then going for my Ph.D. in neuroscience, based on my previous symptoms I was able to conclude that I probably did have ADHD when I was growing up.

You should understand that ADHD and OCD are mirror images of each other. ADHD is that part of me that just wants to procrastinate, be messy, and have no patience to sit in a class, while OCD is telling me the complete opposite. OCD tells me, "You better not miss any little piece of information from that class! Make sure you take notes, record the information precisely, take photos, and make a copy of *everything* in case you lose it."

Two very opposing forces acting at the same time.

This condition was both a curse and a blessing. I was able to take the power of both conditions to shape my life in a way that made me who I am today. I was valedictorian at my university, graduated with highest honors, and received the president's award for academic achievement. Not bad for someone with ADHD, right?

I became a certified brain health coach for Amen Clinics, a great training tool for professionals in my industry. Dr. Amen has revolutionized the way we look at people's mental conditions by using brain SPECT scans (a type of nuclear imaging test using a radioactive substance and a special camera to create amazing 3-D pictures) and natural ways to heal them. I was so intrigued by his methods that I decided to get my own brain scanned to see if there were any underlying conditions that could be fixed or help explain some of my behaviors.

Images 1 and 2 are the actual results of my scans at a resting and nonresting state. The information from the scans was amazing. Many of the behaviors and problems I had to deal with in life can be seen in just a snapshot of my brain!

The red and white areas you see on the brain scan are areas with overactivity in regions that control impulsivity, such as the anterior cingulate gyrus and the basal ganglia system. This could also create the feeling of being anxious or nervous. There are even depressions in my parietal lobes that you can see on my surface scan that are highly correlated with problems in directional orientation. All my life I have struggled with having the worse sense of direction! All my friends and family always make fun of me about this particular issue, and now I understand why.

Why did I have those problems? Was I born with these issues? Did something happen to me when I was growing up? Thankfully, some of those answers came to light as I was doing some background research of my life and past experiences.

For instance, my OCD could have been triggered by a strep infection. In fact, when I started becoming obsessive, I was also suffering from chronic strep throat infections. It was so bad that I had to get my tonsils removed when I was fifteen years old.

My temporal lobes show slight damage, which can explain some anger issues I had when I was younger. But *how* were my temporal lobes damaged? When I was a child, I was twice hospitalized for cracking my head open from falls while I was playing. I also played contact sports and was a gymnast, which caused many falls and blows to my head. The ridges of my bones within my skull could be the culprit of having a damaged temporal lobe or the parietal lobe, impairing my sense of direction.

Why am I telling you my brain's life story? Because I have firsthand personal experience with my brain (as you do too!) and, being a neuroscientist, I have been able to look "under the hood" (so to speak) and learn how my own brain functions. I was amazed, and you would be too if you could see how your brain's physical condition affects your life.

I chose to write this book to let you know and help you understand that your brain is the most precious equipment that you have, and the sooner you understand how it works, what may be wrong with it, and what it needs, the faster you will build your Three Pillars of Life: health, relationships, and wealth. Thanks to those brain scans, I can now tackle my conditions more efficiently using cognitive therapy, healthy supplements, and medication (if I should ever need it). I am ahead of the curve because knowledge gives me the power to act immediately.

I've been able to *train my brain for success*. Knowledge is power—and I want you to know your brain, train it, and be able to achieve your dreams!

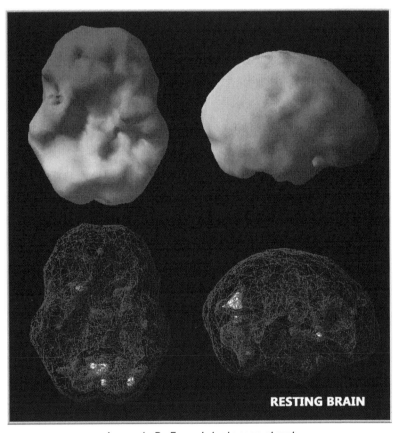

Image 1. *Dr. Fresco's brain scan at rest*

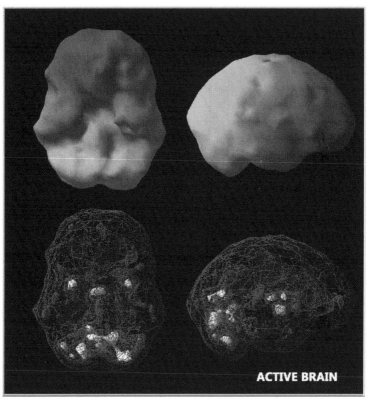

Image 2. *Dr. Fresco's brain scan after being active performing a cognitive task*

Introduction

You've just walked into an office for a job interview. With a better salary, more prestige, and more responsibility, this position could change your life. As you introduce yourself to the interviewer, you feel your armpits perspiring and your heart beating faster. As you sit down, you look at the interviewer for visual cues—is she making eye contact? Does she seem interested in you or bored? You note that she's wearing a very subtle and agreeable perfume, which is a relief, because in an office there's nothing worse than someone using an overpowering scent.

The interviewer asks you detailed questions about technical aspects of the job. You know you're being tested, but you've had the necessary experience, and your memory is good. As you speak, you're unsure of what to do with your hands, so you place them both lightly on the edge of her desk—confident but not too aggressive! After a conversation, during which you note the interviewer is being careful to withhold any emotional response, she closes her folder, looks you in the eye, extends her hand, and smiles broadly. Suddenly, you feel encouraged. As you shake hands—her grip is firm but not crushing—she says she'd like you to come back in a few days and meet the team. You agree.

As you leave the office, you feel elated—your years of hard work are paying off!

This everyday scene, which lasted only a few minutes, demonstrates the incredible complexity and power of the human brain. *Your* brain. Think about all the things that your brain did in that short amount of time. The list is impressive. Your brain directed the complex actions of your body, received and processed visual and other sensory data, monitored your emotions, verbally communicated with another person, accurately retrieved important memories, made judgments about the progress of the interview, evaluated the chances of success, and made projections about the future based on past and current events.

Not bad for a three-and-a half pound lump of water, fat, and protein.

This book is about your amazing brain. It's the most complex object in the known universe, and you have one. You can't buy a working brain at any price; you received yours at no charge, just for being born. Of course, your brain took a long time to get "up to speed"—for the first two years of your life, you didn't even know how to talk! And once your brain is fully mature, if it's healthy it never stops learning—it's always storing away new memories and thinking of new things for you to do.

You depend on your brain for everything you do in life, which leads us to two important questions:

Are you taking care of your precious brain so that it will last a lifetime?

Are you *training your brain for success*?

The second question is just as important as the first, which is why this book introduces the Three Pillars of Life: health, relationships, and wealth. Your brain, which directs your life, can be trained for success in all three areas, or it can lead you astray. What you do with this precious gift is up to you, and there's no reason why with diligence and self-awareness you can't stand high on your Three Pillars of Life.

While many factors can influence how you build your Three Pillars of Life, including genetics, the circumstances of your birth, and your susceptibility to disease, by an overwhelming margin your destiny is determined by how well you Train Your Brain for Success.

Having a healthy brain increases your chances of a successful and productive life. In this book, I'll reveal the secrets of brain health and offer a path toward true happiness.

I'll start with how your brain works—the nuts and bolts, so to speak. It's all about your roughly eighty billion neurons, which are connected to each other and to other cells, forming trillions of connections in your brain. It's amazing that we even know this because for most of human history—many thousands of years— no one had a clue as to how the brain worked. The brain was linked to human emotion and mood, which contributed to the enduring theory of the four humors—melancholy, phlegmatic, sanguine, and choleric. As I'll reveal, this ancient system lingers today in the areas of personality profile research.

Your brain can either malfunction or operate irrationally in many different ways. I'll discuss how we're influenced by hormones, the drugs in our bloodstream, our feelings and emotions, and physical defects or imperfections in our brains, all of which affect our decisions. We have biases, we imagine threats that don't exist, and we ignore threats that do exist. As we build our Three Pillars of Life, we need to constantly strive to put aside our preconceptions and biases and see life as it really is and not as we imagine it to be.

Emotional intelligence is important. It refers to your capability to recognize your own and other people's emotions, and manage your emotions to achieve your goals. A key element of emotional intelligence is empathy, which is your ability to place yourself in someone else's shoes and feel what they are feeling.

The world is perceptible to your brain through your five senses: sight, hearing, touch, smell, and taste. Every decision you make is weighed against the data distilled from your current and previous sensory input. Of your five senses, your sense of smell has the most power to directly affect your emotions and consequently the choices you make.

You have a unique personality, but can you measure it? Can you change or alter it? Many scientists believe the answers to these questions are both "yes." I'll show you many of the most prominent and popular personality assessment tests, which can help you gain insight into your personality type and help you improve any difficult areas. These include the Myers-Briggs Type Indicator and the HEXACO Personality Inventory-Revised (HEXACO-PI-R). We'll also look at the Dark Triad, a subject in psychology that focuses on three overlapping destructive personality traits: narcissism, Machiavellianism, and psychopathy.

Everything your brain does is the result of biochemical action, and external chemical and physical forces can alter your brain's functioning. These include the use of narcotic drugs or anything else that may be delivered to your brain by your bloodstream and which pass through the blood-brain barrier (BBB), a highly selective semipermeable membrane barrier that separates the circulating blood from the brain and extracellular fluid in the central nervous system.

Any restriction or loss of blood flow to the brain is a serious problem, including a stroke, which is diminished blood flow to all or part of the brain. Traumatic brain injury (TBI) is a major cause of death and disability in the United States, and if head injuries are repeated over time, the person's condition can morph into chronic traumatic encephalopathy (CTE), a degenerative disease found in people who have suffered repeated blows to the head. We'll talk about brain safety and why you should wear a seat belt, use child seats, wear a helmet when riding a bike, and slip-proof your house, especially as you get older.

As you Train Your Brain for Success and build your Three Pillars of Life, lifelong learning is important. Learning involves the actual growth of new cells called dendrites, but brain fibers can only grow from existing brain fibers. To learn something new, you must build on information that is already stored in your brain. Concentration and focus are very important cognitive abilities, and learning is a result of paying attention to what is being taught as well as making use of our senses. As you build your Three Pillars of Life, your ability to focus, learn, and remember are critically important.

I'll reveal the importance of getting a good night's sleep. If you live a life of constant sleep deprivation, your judgment is affected, reaction times slowed, mood soured, and body chemicals thrown out of balance. As you build your Three Pillars of Life, getting plenty of shut-eye is an important part of the process.

For millions of baby boomers and their families, Alzheimer's disease has become a serious health issue, which I discuss in detail. As of this writing, an estimated 5.5 million Americans of all ages have Alzheimer's disease. Sadly, the exact cause of Alzheimer's disease is currently unknown, and there is no cure. The best you can do to reduce the risk is by keeping your brain healthy, challenged, and engaged. Regular exercise directly benefits brain cells by increasing blood and oxygen flow in the brain, and may be a beneficial strategy to lower the risk of Alzheimer's and vascular dementia.

This book is about taking action to keep your brain healthy, and it begins with what you eat. I believe no one should be on a "diet"—we should have healthy eating habits for a lifetime of better health, not just for weight loss. When given the choice between real food and processed food, always choose real food because processed food causes inflammation, cancer, diabetes, and cardiovascular diseases.

Your body converts carbohydrates to glucose, your main source of energy. The glycemic index (GI) ranks dietary carbohydrates based on their overall effect on blood glucose concentration after the consumption of a meal. I'll show you how your diet should emphasize low and intermediate glycemic foods, and how to read food labels to make the best choices.

As a practical path toward healthy eating, I present Dr. Fresco's Plate—an easy-to-follow guide that will help keep you on a balanced diet and on track toward building your Three Pillars of Life, one delicious meal at a time.

To stay healthy and grow properly, your brain and body need five specific types of organic and inorganic molecules: carbohydrates, fats, proteins, vitamins and minerals, and water. With Dr. Fresco's Plate, your meals consist of lean proteins, low-carb vegetables, whole grains, low-glycemic fruits, and water or tea (not sugar-filled tea). Vegetables and fruits are also the main source for most of your micronutrients (vitamins and minerals). Fats are also an essential part of a healthy diet—they provide essential fatty acids, keep your skin soft, deliver fat-soluble vitamins, and are a great source of energizing fuel. Carbohydrates, which like fats have recently gotten much "bad press," are the main source of the energy for your trillions of cells. You'll see that my dietary recommendations are filled with delicious carbohydrates—but you need to avoid high fructose corn syrup, which is the number one cause of metabolic syndrome diseases.

This practical and easy-to-read book leads you to the ultimate goal: to Train Your Brain for Success and build of your Three Pillars of Life, allowing you to attain both happiness and a life of meaning. Both can be achieved through conscious effort and both are important—while it's good to feel happy, it's also important to have a deeper sense that your life has meaning, which transcends the more transitory experiences of either sadness or happiness.

Your path is your own. Happiness and meaning come in many colors, shapes, and forms. No one sees the world the same way you do, and no one has the same goals and aspirations. The guiding force of your life—the captain of your ship and the pilot of your plane—is your brain.

If you take care of it, it will take care of you!

Ready to Train Your Brain for Success? Let's get started!

1. Welcome to Your Brain!

Think for a moment about all the things you do every day.

You wake up in the morning, and when you remember it's the weekend, you feel happy.

The dream you had last night seems so vivid and so real, but soon it slips from your mind, forgotten like all the others.

At breakfast, you skillfully prepare an omelet, and the smell of freshly brewed coffee is reassuring—all is right with the world.

The phone rings. It's your partner calling with a question about the down payment on the house you're buying. She doesn't bother to introduce herself—of course, you recognize her voice. Without using a calculator, you figure out 20% of the sales price. You agree to meet at noon at the bistro downtown. You know exactly where it's located. You glance at the clock. The meeting is in three hours. No problem.

On the news, the topic is the trade deficit. You're irritated because the dollar has gotten stronger, making your export business more difficult because your goods now cost more overseas. You remind yourself to write a letter to the editor of the economics magazine to which you've been a subscriber for more than a decade.

You look in the mirror. You ask yourself, "Have I gained a few pounds?" Your clothes suddenly seem boring and frumpy. Time to go shopping.

Someone knocks on the front door. You glance out the window. The person is unknown to you. They're not wearing a delivery uniform. They seem to be nervously looking around. You pick up your phone and call your partner. When she answers, you keep her on the line as you cautiously answer the door. "Yes?" you say. The guy offers to patch your driveway. The blacktop is cracked, he says. You say, "No thank you," as you close the door and lock it. After saying goodbye to your partner, you call the police to report a scam artist.

All this happens in the first hour of a typical day in the life of your brain. You'll be awake for another fifteen hours, and during that time your brain will be making millions of calculations. It will retrieve thousands of memories—some of which you thought you had forgotten!—while storing away thousands more. Just like with the guy at the door, it will make threat assessments. It will respond with happiness when you see your partner enter the bistro. It will plan ahead into the future and look back into the past. It will tell you when a mosquito has alighted on your arm and needs to be swatted, and at dinnertime it will choose between the salmon or the steak.

Oh, and it will also ensure your heart keeps beating and you keep breathing, even while you're asleep.

Not a bad day's work for a three-pound hunk of mostly water and fat!

Into Uncharted Territory

Even though we humans (or, strictly speaking, the *Homo sapiens* species) have been living on earth in our modern form for two hundred thousand years, it's only in the past century that we've been able to develop much credible information about this amazing organ.

In ancient times, the brain could not be studied in its living state, and its function was debated. In Egypt, from the late Middle Kingdom onward, in preparation for mummification the brain was regularly removed and discarded, for the heart was assumed to be the seat of intelligence. The brain was one of the few organs the Egyptians did not preserve for use in the afterlife. They weren't sure what it was for, but they assumed you wouldn't need it in the Kingdom of the Dead.

The ancient Greeks, perhaps benefiting from observations made of soldiers who had received head injuries that seemed to change their behavior, were the first to connect the brain with "thinking." In the total absence of microscopes and electromagnetic imaging of the living brain, which wouldn't come along for another two thousand years, the ancient Greeks didn't do a bad job of deducing some basic truisms about the brain.

In the sixth and fifth centuries BCE, Alcmaeon of Croton was the first recorded philsopher to consider the brain to be where the mind was located. According to ancient authorities, "he believed the seat of sensations is in the brain. This contains the governing faculty. All the senses are connected in some way with the brain; consequently, they are incapable of action if the brain is disturbed . . . the power of the brain to synthesize sensations makes it also the seat of thought: The storing up of perceptions gives memory and belief, and when these are stabilized you get knowledge."

Hippocrates, who lived between 460 and 380 BCE, got it right when he wrote this about the brain: "Men ought to know that from nothing else but thence come joys, delights, laughter and sports, and sorrows, griefs, despondency, and lamentations. And by this, in a special manner, we acquire wisdom and knowledge, and see and hear, and know what are foul and what are fair, what are bad and what are good, what are sweet and what unsavory. Some we discriminate by habit, and some we perceive by their utility. By this we distinguish objects of relish and disrelish, according to the seasons; and the same things do not always please us. And by the same organ we become mad and delirious, and fears and terrors assail us, some by night, and some by day, and dreams and untimely wanderings, and cares that are not suitable, and ignorance of present circumstances, desuetude, and unskillfulness. All these things we endure from the brain, when it is not healthy, but is more hot, more cold, more moist, or more dry than natural, or when it suffers any other preternatural and unusual affliction."

Not a bad assessment! But what affected the brain? What made it function well or function poorly? Hippocrates and other ancient philosophers subscribed to the theory that human behavior was governed by each of the four humors: blood (sanguine), yellow bile (cholera), black bile (melancholy), and phlegm. Each humor was linked with one of the four elements of earth, air, fire, and water, as well as two of the qualities of hot, cold, wet, and dry. Therefore, a melancholic brain, associated with earth, was literally too cold and dry, while a sanguine brain, associated with air, was literally too hot and moist. Adjusting the heat/coolness and wetness/dryness of the brain would result in changes in behavior.

For most of human history, the brain's living activity couldn't be observed or recorded. In the 1880s, the very first experiments with neuroimaging were done by the Italian neuroscientist Angelo Mosso, who invented the "human circulation balance," which supposedly could noninvasively measure the redistribution of blood during emotional and intellectual activity.

In 1918, the American neurosurgeon Walter Dandy introduced the technique of ventriculography, whereby images of the ventricular system within the brain were obtained by injection of filtered air directly into one or both lateral ventricles of the brain via one or more small trephine holes drilled in the skull under local anesthesia.

In 1927, Egas Moniz, professor of neurology in Lisbon, introduced cerebral angiography, a medical imaging technique used to visualize blood vessels. This was done by injecting a radio-opaque contrast agent into the blood vessel and imaging using X-ray-based techniques, such as fluoroscopy.

By the way, you may be wondering about X-ray technology and its application to brain imaging. In 1895, German physics professor Wilhelm Röntgen discovered X-rays and the process whereby you could use them to make images of such things as the bones of your hand under the enclosing soft tissue. But the human brain is nothing but soft tissue, and ordinary X-rays don't show much of the brain—so the X-ray itself didn't help advance brain research.

It wasn't until the advent of computerized axial tomography (CAT or CT scanning) in the early 1970s that detailed anatomic images of the brain became available for diagnostic and research purposes. This revolutionary innovation enabled easy, safe, noninvasive, painless, and repeatable neuro-investigation. More or less concurrently, magnetic resonance imaging (MRI or MR scanning) was developed. Rather than using ionizing or x-radiation, MRI uses the variation in signals produced by protons in the body when the head is placed in a strong magnetic field.

These were all breakthroughs, but recent progress in brain science has come from the increasing power and speed of digital data analytics. Vastly increased processing power has spurred the creation of high-resolution brain maps along with the ability to analyze these maps over various periods of time and growth. It has been said that the human brain is the most complex entity in the known universe, and it's only with the aid of supercomputers that we, with our own brains, are able to manage and direct brain research as it moves into new frontiers.

The Basics

Because the human brain is the most complex entity in the known universe, to provide a full description of the anatomy and function of your brain would require a library full of books. While that's an impractical goal, I'm going to provide a very quick sketch of your brain and how it works.

In addition to water and fat (which I'll discuss later), your three-pound brain is composed of about one hundred billion cells. The most important cells are called neurons, and you have about eighty billion of them. They are very tiny: The diameter of an individual brain neuron is just four microns thick, and you could fit thirty thousand neurons on the head of a pin. Neurons are responsible for transmitting information from cell to cell. Each is like a tiny cable; the information starts on one end and travels as an electrical impulse to the other end, where it connects to another cable (another neuron), and the communication keeps going until it reaches its final target. This target can be a muscle you want to move, another cell group in your brain to let you come up with an idea, or a group of cells to release hormones that tell you to stop eating.

Remember, we're talking about *actual electrical impulses.* While you're awake, your brain generates nearly twenty-five watts of power, which is enough to light up a lightbulb.

Neurons have three main parts: the *cell body*, where the nucleus and all the DNA material is located; the *dendrites*, extruding from the main body; and the *axon*, which is a long branch that can extend up to three feet. Neurons communicate from the axon terminal to the dendrites of the next neurons (*Image 1*).

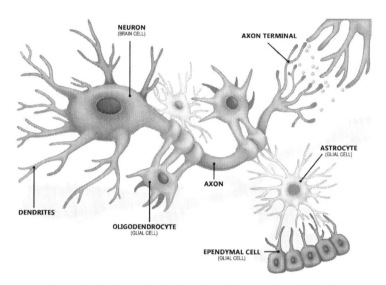

Image 1. *Anatomy of a brain cell and its supporting glial cells*

It's estimated that each of your brain's eighty billion neurons are connected to around ten thousand other cells, which creates close to one thousand trillion connections in your brain.

Your neurons are not the only cells in your brain; you have another large group that outnumber neurons fifty to one. These are called *glial cells* and are responsible for the support, protection, and maintenance of your neurons. They are like the "minions" of your brain.

This is where the subject of fat comes into play.

A large part of the "fat" in the brain is in the form of myelin, a fatty white substance that surrounds the axon of some nerve cells, forming an electrically insulating layer. It is essential for the proper functioning of the nervous system. The myelin is part of oligodendrocytes or Schwann cells, both of which are types of glial cells. Under a microscope, myelin looks like strings of sausages.

Myelinated axons are white; hence, the "white matter" of the brain. Myelin insulates axons from electrically charged atoms and molecules, which are found in the fluid surrounding the entire nervous system. Myelin decreases capacitance and increases electrical resistance across the cell membrane (the axolemma). Thus, myelination prevents the electric current from leaving the axon. This is no different from the insulation on copper wire in your home.

It has been suggested that myelin permits larger body size by maintaining rapid communication between distant body parts.

Cholesterol is an essential component of myelin, which is composed of about 40% water. The dry mass is composed of between 70% and 85% lipids and between 15% and 30% proteins.

Communication between neurons is by *synapse*. It is not by direct contact: there is a small space between the dendrites and the axon terminal called the *synaptic cleft (Image 2)*

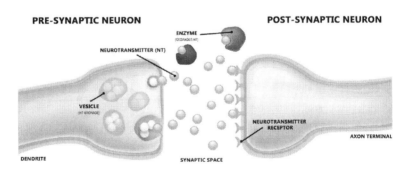

Image 2. *Anatomy of a synapse*

Here, neurotransmitters convey signals to excite or inhibit a neuron, and these signals are released into the synaptic cleft so they can reach the other side (the receiving dendrite) and bind to specific receptors to activate that cell, which, in turn, relays the message down to the next cell.

This process of communication between cells happens millions of times, over and over, for *everything* you do throughout your day. Your cells are constantly talking to each other, instructing your body what to do, storing memories, assessing threats, making calculations, and much more.

At the macro level, the three-pound brain is a spongy mass with the consistency of pudding. When you look at the brain, you can see lots of folds and grooves, which are there to increase the overall surface of the brain. These grooves, called *sulci*, divide our brains into four sections called *lobes*: the frontal lobes, the temporal lobes, the parietal lobes, and the occipital lobes (*Image 3*). These lobes make up our *cerebral cortex*, which is what allows us to rise above other animals in the animal kingdom. We have the most developed brain cortex in the world. The cortex is what gives us the ability to think and make rational decisions.

Two other sections are called the *cerebellum* and the *brain stem*. The cerebellum is involved in many processes, but its main role is for motor coordination. The brain stem is also referred to as the *reptilian brain*, due to its similarity to reptile brains. It provides all our basic functions and connects the brain to the rest of the body.

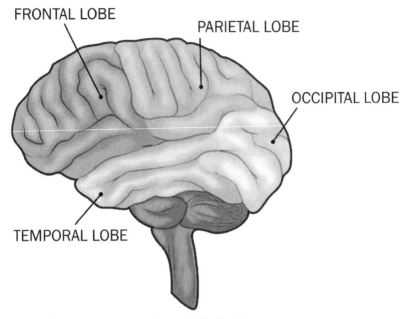

FRONTAL LOBE

PARIETAL LOBE

OCCIPITAL LOBE

TEMPORAL LOBE

Image 3. *Brain lobes*

There are many other structures within the brain; for our purposes, I will be mentioning the *limbic system*, as we will see that it is heavily involved in emotional processing, and the *hippocampus*, which is where our memory cells reside and our memories form.

It's also necessary to mention the brain's source of nourishment. A healthy brain depends on an adequate supply of oxygen and nutrients delivered through a dense network of blood vessels, which in the brain alone are roughly four hundred miles in length. That's the distance from Washington, D.C. to Boston, Massachusetts. Blood is supplied to the brain, face, and scalp through two major sets of vessels: the right and left common carotid arteries and the right and left vertebral arteries. Any interruption to the blood supply is a serious health problem.

The brain is often compared to a muscle, meaning the more you exercise it, the stronger and better it gets. One of the greatest discoveries in the last century was the notion that our brains can change over time. For many years, scientists thought that the brain was fixed and that neurons could not regenerate. While evidence pointing to the growth of new neurons in adults is elusive, it's clear that your existing brain can continue to learn new skills as long as you're alive and healthy, and even when you have a cognitive impairment, you can still learn new skills or get better. Exercise and diet have been shown to slow the effects of cognitive conditions, such as Alzheimer's disease or dementia. *Neuroplasticity* adapts neurons and networks to the changing sensory environment, allowing the brain to respond to new situations and changes. For instance, if you start playing the piano, you will notice that you are not very good at it, but with time and practice you get better, and it becomes more natural. This is because your brain has adapted to the new stimuli and changed according to your demand for playing the piano. This is neuroplasticity at its peak.

The Three Pillars of Life: Health, Relationships, and Wealth

While understanding how the brain is constructed and operates is very important, especially as you strive for good health and better nutrition, the important point is this: What has your brain done for you lately?

Having a brain is all well and good, but what's important is what you *do* with it.

Look at it this way: as long as we're here on earth and each of us is equipped with a marvelous brain (by virtue of evolution or as a gift from God—your choice), why not make the best of it? Why not strive to make our lives as happy, rich, and satisfying as possible, while helping those who are less fortunate? It seems an obvious path to follow, but in reality our brains, being supercomplex and imperfect, sometimes steer us off the path. I'll discuss what can go wrong with your brain in the next chapter; right now I'd like to focus on the *goal*. Unless we have a positive outcome clearly visualized, how can we know if we're off track?

What, then, do you want from life?

I don't mean specific consumer objects, such as a new car or a boat. I mean the bigger picture—those things that bring deep happiness and satisfaction year after year regardless of your spiritual beliefs, religion, creed, or political party affiliation.

I propose that there are Three Pillars of Life, each equally important, and each under the control of your brain. Once you understand and take control of all three pillars, you will reach a state of true and lasting happiness (*Image 4*).

Health

No one would dispute that good health makes living a full, rich life much easier and more rewarding. Most rational human beings would choose good health over bad health.

How much does your brain contribute to your good health?

Enough to make it worth serious consideration!

Yes, it's true that many aspects of your health are beyond the direct control of your brain.

If you were born with a birth defect, your brain had nothing to do with it.

If you were traumatized as a child by violence, it's not something you could have changed.

If you get an infectious disease, unless you were behaving recklessly (such as drinking unsafe water or using a dirty hypodermic needle), it may have nothing to do with your brain. Bacteria and viruses are nasty bugs that strike everyone at some time in their lives.

If you get cancer, it's likely your brain was not a causative factor.

Having said that, you'd be amazed at how much influence your mind has over your health.

Your brain, either trained or untrained, exerts its influence, for good or bad, in two ways.

The first is in the *choices* you make every day. You can choose to sit in front of the TV set, or you can go for a run around the block. You can choose to eat a jelly doughnut for breakfast, or you can eat an egg with whole-wheat toast. You can choose to smoke cigarettes, or you can make the effort to quit. While other forces—cultural, psychological, environmental—exert a pull on our decision making, we have enough free will to bend the arc of the health choices we make every day.

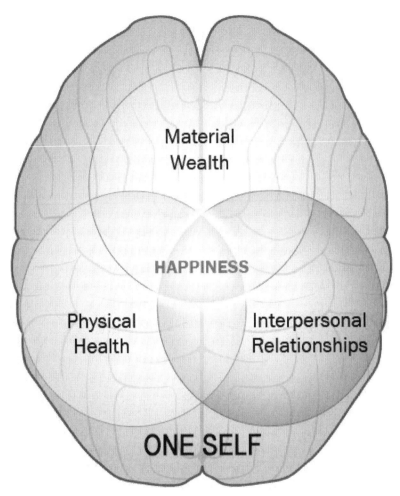

Image 4. *Representation of the pillars of life.*

Your brain, trained or untrained, also influences your health by virtue of your *attitude* toward life and adversity. It's not a myth that a positive outlook on life will make you physically healthier. Your mind has a tremendous influence over how you respond to illness or an accident when these things happen to you.

I once had a neighbor who was an elderly woman. Whenever I'd see her, she was cheerful. Nothing seemed to bother her. When I'd inquire about her health, she'd reply that she never felt better and that nothing was wrong. In fact, during her life she had been beset by a host of serious diseases, including cancer, which she survived. She was nearly blind and could barely hear, but if you talked to her, you'd never imagine that her health was anything less than wonderful. This was not because she was in denial (to be in denial about a health condition is not a good choice). It was because she didn't dwell on the diseases that afflicted her. When she got sick, she did what she was supposed to do to get better; and when she got better, she put the episode behind her. She had better things to do with her time than complain about her health.

My neighbor eventually passed away. She was in her nineties, I think—we were never quite sure of her exact date of birth. Up until the very end, she was alert and engaged. It was the power of her positive outlook on life—her positive brain—that helped her live to a ripe old age.

Relationships

Human beings are social animals. We function well in groups and depend on each other for protection and emotional support. To live in isolation is generally not good for your health.

There are certain places on earth where people live much longer than average. These are called "blue zones" and include such disparate places as Okinawa, Japan; Sardinia, Italy; and Loma Linda, California (a community that includes about nine thousand Seventh-Day Adventists). When you look at these communities and others where people live longer than average, what you *don't* see are exceptionally high expenditures for health care. These aren't places where there's a state-of-the-art hospital on every block. These people aren't being kept alive by prescription drugs and MRI machines.

What you *do* find is a sense of community, where people do things together, especially as they get older. Elderly people in

Okinawa have surprisingly low depression levels. On the streets of Okinawa, you see octogenarians riding motorcycles. They practice karate, walk several kilometers daily, and work in their vegetable gardens. They don't go to fitness gyms—there are no such things in Okinawa. Physical activity is not isolated but has an objective, making the elders feel they're active members of the community. Perhaps most importantly seniors are not shipped off to retirement homes. They remain part of a vibrant social network connecting them to the environment and their fellow citizens.

In Okinawa, people take care of each other, forming supportive links that sustain them through difficult times. They have a positive attitude toward life, which explains the extremely low levels of stress shown by Okinawan elders.

Can the opposite—loneliness and social isolation—make you sick? Absolutely. Loneliness is a serious health risk. Studies of elderly people and social isolation have shown that those without adequate social interaction are twice as likely to die prematurely.

Social isolation has measurable physical effects. It suppresses immune function and elevates inflammation, which can lead to heart disease, type II diabetes, and arthritis.

Scientific evidence indicates that strong, happy interpersonal relationships have a measurable positive effect on your health. Back in 1938 during the Great Depression, Harvard University began a study of the health of 268 Harvard undergraduates. Scientists hoped the study would reveal clues about how people can lead healthy and happy lives. As it turned out, researchers were able to follow the group of men (no women were yet enrolled at Harvard College) for eighty years as part of the Harvard Study of Adult Development, making it one of the world's longest studies of adult life.

As of April 2017, nineteen of the original subjects were still alive. In the meantime, the study was expanded to include the men's children, who number 1,300 and are themselves well into middle age. In the 1970s, 456 Boston inner-city residents were enlisted as part of another study, and as of April 2017 forty were still alive. Researchers began including wives of the participants in both studies.

"The surprising finding," said Robert Waldinger, director of the study, a psychiatrist at Massachusetts General Hospital and a professor of psychiatry at Harvard Medical School, "is that our relationships and how happy we are in our relationships have a powerful influence on our health. Taking care of your body is important, but tending to your relationships is a form of self-care too. That, I think, is the revelation."

More than money or fame, close personal relationships are what keep people happy throughout their lives. Those ties help delay mental and physical decline and insulate people from life's discontents, and they're better predictors of long and happy lives than social class, IQ, or even genes. That finding proved true across the board among both the Harvard men and the inner-city participants.

"When we gathered together everything we knew about them about at age fifty, it wasn't their middle-age cholesterol levels that predicted how they were going to grow old," said Waldinger in a popular TED Talk. "It was how satisfied they were in their relationships. The people who were the most satisfied in their relationships at age fifty were the healthiest at age eighty."

It must be noted that what we're talking about are real relationships between real people—not virtual online relationships. Ironically, the rapid expansion of social media hasn't lowered the rates of loneliness—it may have even made it worse. Studies of Facebook users have found that the amount of time you spend on the social network is inversely related to how happy you feel throughout the day. The more time you spend watching cute kitten videos, the less connected you are to real people.

These are choices you make with your brain. You can choose

to join a social group, or you can stare at a glowing screen. You can choose to eat lunch at work by yourself, or you can join your colleagues, even if you don't like all of them. You can choose to build and sustain relationships, and by doing so, you can choose to live a longer and happier life.

Wealth

Human beings are *consumers*. Each of us requires fuel, food, shelter, and all the things that sustain our unique form of life. In contrast, dolphins are not consumers. They only require fish to eat and a place to swim. They don't need houses or cars or clothing. They don't need high school diplomas, and they don't go to the movies.

Human beings need wealth because wealth buys the things we require. The only question is, how *much* do you need?

The answer is: Just as much as you need to live a comfortable and secure life.

Many people on earth—as in Okinawa, for example—lead relatively simple lives. They don't own much. They are very happy with what little they have.

Do you know what is the happiest nation on earth? Or, more precisely, the nation with the happiest people?

In March 2017, on the International Day of Happiness, the fifth *World Happiness Report* was published in support of the United Nations High Level Meeting on happiness and well-being. Edited by John Helliwell, Richard Layard, and Jeffrey Sachs, the report ranked 155 countries by their happiness levels. The data came from the Gallup World Poll, and rankings were based on answers to the main life evaluation question asked in the poll— the Cantril ladder: it asked respondents to think of a ladder, with the best possible life for them being a 10 and the worst possible life being a 0. They were then asked to rate their own current lives on that 0 to 10 scale.

In the 2017 *World Happiness Report*, Norway ranked as the happiest country, displacing the previous year's top-ranked Denmark, which had held the top spot for three out of the past four years. Rounding out the top ten in order were Denmark, Iceland, Switzerland, Finland, Netherlands, Canada, New Zealand, Australia, and Sweden. The United States ranked 14th, dropping down one spot from 2016.

Is Norway the richest country? No, but its economy is robust, with a gross domestic product per capita of $69,300, ahead of the United States, which according to the CIA *World Factbook* posts a per capita GDP of $57,300. Its main export is oil, and despite declines in oil prices, Norway has managed to avoid economic shocks.

"It's a remarkable case in point," said Professor John Helliwell of the University of British Columbia to the publishers. "By choosing to produce oil deliberately and investing the proceeds for the benefit of future generations, Norway has protected itself from the volatile ups and downs of many other oil-rich economies. This emphasis on the future over the present is made easier by high levels of mutual trust, shared purpose, generosity and good governance. All of these are found in Norway, as well as in the other top countries."

Happiness is certainly subjective, and in all fairness to Central America it's worth pointing out that according to the 2017 Gallup *Global Emotions Report*, the world's happiest country is not chilly Norway but steamy Paraguay, which placed first for the second year in a row.

It the *Global Emotions Report*, which asked respondents about their daily "positive experiences," the least happy country was Yemen, which also happens to have an adult life expectancy of only sixty-four years. At least it's a healthier place than lowest-ranked Chad, where the average lifespan is only fifty years, which is pretty much where it was in the Middle Ages.

Researchers conducted the survey over the phone or by face-to-face interviews with people ages fifteen or older. To learn about participants' positive experiences, pollsters asked people various questions, including whether they felt well rested, respected, and had enjoyed themselves the day before. For negative experiences, they asked about feeling physical pain, worry, sadness, stress, and anger the day before. Gallup used these results to formulate an index score for each country. Paraguay came out on top, with an index score of 84.

The United States, with an index score of 75, ranked 38th, tying with eight other countries: Luxembourg, Germany, Bolivia, Brazil, Austria, the United Kingdom, Mali, and South Africa.

That's right: the people of the United States, the world's wealthiest nation, are no more happier than those in Mali, which is one of the poorest nations on earth. And Paraguay, the happiest nation, is no Shangri-La; it's beset by poverty and income inequality.

Does money buy happiness? As we'll see in the pages ahead, the answer is mixed. The American Psychological Association's 2015 *Stress in America* survey showed that stress about money and finances is prevalent in the richest nation on earth. In fact, regardless of the economic climate, money has consistently topped Americans' list of stressors since the first *Stress in America* survey in 2007. Here are highlights noted in the report:

- Seventy-two percent of adults report feeling stressed about money at least some of the time, and twenty-two percent say that they experience extreme stress about money.
- Twenty-six percent of adults report feeling stressed about money most or all the time.
- Thirty-two percent of adults say that their finances or lack of money prevents them from living a healthy lifestyle.

This ties back to the importance of relationships—not only

close personal relationships but also the broader ties that bind a society together. Immense wealth is not the answer.

Exactly how much wealth do you need to be happy? A study conducted by Princeton economist Angus Deaton and psychologist Daniel Kahneman at Princeton University's Woodrow Wilson School found that money does indeed make people increasingly happy—but only up to about $75,000 a year. Above that there's little added benefit. As you might expect, the lower you are below that threshold, the more likely you'll report feeling unhappy. But no matter how much *more* than $75,000 people make, they don't report any greater degree of happiness.

The study notes there are actually two types of happiness: your variable, day-to-day mood—whether you're upbeat or melancholy at any particular moment—and the deeper satisfaction you feel about the way your life is going in the long run. While having an income above the magic line of $75,000 doesn't seem to affect your daily emotional mood—you'll still snarl in the morning before you've had your coffee—with greater wealth, you're more likely to feel an overall sense of security and satisfaction.

Why is $75,000 the magic threshold? This might change according to your region; an income of $75,000 per year in midtown Manhattan is a pittance compared with the buying power of $75,000 in, say, Indianapolis. Researchers found that lower income did not itself cause sadness but made people feel more stressed by the problems they already had. For example, the study found that among divorced people about 51% who made less than $1,000 a month reported feeling sad or stressed the previous day, while only 24% of those earning more than $3,000 a month reported similar feelings.

Past research on money and happiness has also revealed that it's not absolute wealth that's linked with happiness but *relative* wealth or status—that is, how much money you have compared with your neighbors. If you live in a neighborhood where everyone belongs to the fancy country club but you don't because you can't afford to pay the entry fees, feeling excluded will affect your happiness.

The point is that you need wealth to live a life free of everyday worries about how you're going to survive. How much wealth you need is up to you. The key factors are the *actual amount* of wealth you have now and *how much you need* to sustain the lifestyle you want. If they're in alignment, you're probably happy. If they're not in alignment, you won't be happy, even if you're a millionaire.

More than any other single thing, how much wealth you can acquire is a factor of how you use your brain. Get an education, work hard, save your money—those are all choices made by your brain.

Decision-Making

Every day we make choices.

Eat a sugary donut or take the whole-wheat toast?

Go into debt to buy an expensive sports car or stick with an affordable sedan?

Get angry at the clumsy waiter who spills your drink or brush it off?

Stay glued to social media every night or enroll in a college extension course?

Your ability to build your Three Pillars of Life depends upon the decisions you make every day. In fact, you make decisions constantly, from the moment you wake up and decide if you'll hit the "snooze" button, if you'll wear a shirt or a blouse, if you should eat bacon or drink a shake, or if you should walk or take the bus. Researchers estimate you make about thirty-five thousand significant decisions every day, so imagine the cumulative effect of all those decisions. If you could go back through time and change them, there would be millions, if not billions, of possible outcomes every single day!

Every day your life depends on your decisions to move ahead, finish a task, engage in a conversation, or ace a test. There are successful and unsuccessful people in life, and the difference between them is the sum total of all their decisions. We do need to compare apples to apples. We can't really compare the choices made by an Ivy League graduate working on Wall Street with a child born in a rural village with no electricity. You can only make decisions based on the choices available to you. For a child in a poor village, simply going to school every day may be a difficult but admirable life decision.

If we compare two average-income families in the United States, each with a boy or a girl attending similar schools and having similar opportunities, and one child manages to success-fully achieve a life where all his or her pillars are growing and the other's pillars are weak and crumbling, rest assured that the difference was their respective abilities to make good decisions.

I have known people—and I'm sure you have too—who seem to make terrible decisions over and over again. No matter how hard they try, they end up drawing the short straw, while others navigate through life with ease and enjoy great success. And no, it's not that one person was lucky and one was unlucky. It's all in their ability to train their brains to make the best choices. To me, when the "unlucky" people make bad decisions, it's as if they're out of sync or off the beat of the flow of life. I think of the anal-ogy of a dancer at a club who is completely off rhythm, and the way he tries to dance looks terrible, and he does it consistently. He's *always* off the beat of the music. He's not listening to the music and letting it flow through him; he's insisting on following his own drummer. The same applies to people who constantly make bad decisions. No matter what their choice, it's always the wrong one. Always offbeat.

The difficulty with such people is that once in a while they do make the right choice, but it's purely by chance. If you repeatedly have choices A or B, eventually you're going to hit the right choice. When that happens, these people mistakenly believe their ability to decide is terrific.

I confess I have a few relatives who live like that, and it pains me to see them fail over and over. I have seen people start a business, and it succeeds for a while, but then they make bad choices, and it fails. So they start a new one, but in their new business they use the same principles as the first one because they remember their brief period of success, and they believe their failure wasn't their fault. It was the bad economy, or the stupid customers, or no one appreciated their amazing product. Then they fail again, and they keep trying the same formula over and over again and failing over and over, not realizing that the first case was a fluke! The first brief success set up a pattern in their brains that dictates the rest of their lives. I have seen this happen. I have a friend who has been failing for nearly a decade, and no matter what you tell him he thinks the next venture will succeed if he applies the same principles he has been applying, which have always led to disaster. It's mind-boggling!

We all make bad decisions once in a while. The trick is to *learn* from them and then use that knowledge to make better choices. That's one way to Train Your Brain for Success. To avoid making the same mistakes over and over again, be sure to follow these guidelines when making major decisions that will affect your life.

Put your emotions aside. The vast majority of the decisions we make are based on our emotions, which means if you don't have a clear understanding of how your emotions work, as well those of others, you'll have a hard time deciding correctly. The fact that some people are so quick to decide, especially under emotional stress, is a recipe for disaster. They are relying on their primitive reptilian brain to take over and decide. This is how a person can kill a loved one while enraged or why someone loses their home on a bad business deal.

The more emotionally charged your decision, the more your neural pathways to the prefrontal cortex, where decision-making takes place, are disconnected. When cool thinking is required, you can't let the reptilian brain take over. Those types of decisions are good only for immediate life or death situations, such as when a wolf is coming at you, when a bus is about to run over your child, or when you wake up at night and smell smoke. Not when you want to decide what you are going to do with your life or what career path to follow or what house to buy. Those decisions need to be more carefully considered. You need to let your frontal cortex talk to the rest of the brain.

Know your subject. Another reason why people fail to decide properly is from a lack of knowledge. The less you know about something, the less you can make an educated decision and the more your emotions take over. For instance, let's say you want to buy a new car, and you're determined to get the new luxury model you saw advertised on television. Without bothering to learn about auto finance and how to get the best deal, you hurry to the dealership, ready to buy. Your "happy emotions" are thinking for you, and all you care about is leaving the dealership with a cool car. The problem is that three months down the road you'll realize how dumb you were to agree to lots of expensive options and to sign a car loan with a hefty interest rate. Now your cool car is costing you more than you can possibly afford.

You should have gone to the dealership armed with the right knowledge and questions to ask. Your rational brain should have been in control, but since you were uninformed because you were hasty, emotions ruled your decision.

Unfortunately, the bank doesn't care about your happiness—only about receiving your car payment on time!

Take care of yourself. Stress, lack of sleep, and poor food choices can affect the way you decide. The more you're deprived of your most basic needs, the more your brain turns into primitive mode to get what *it* needs. For example, if you're overtired from lack of sleep, your brain may shut down and go into sleep mode *while you're driving your car at seventy miles an hour on the highway!* (This is no joke. The National Highway Traffic Safety Administration estimates that in 2013 driving while drowsy was responsible for 72,000 crashes, 44,000 injuries, and 800 deaths.)

If you're sleep deprived, you may make the poor choice to take stimulants, such as caffeine or even amphetamines, which can cloud your judgment. A diet that includes too much sugar can make you jittery besides putting on excess pounds and raising your risk of diabetes. Remember that many substances can cross the blood-brain barrier and affect your thinking—so be sure to eat properly and get enough rest so you won't need stimulants.

Be aware of cognitive biases. Too often we cannot admit our own preconceptions. We think we see the world objectively when in fact we unconsciously allow our ingrained beliefs to color our judgments. This happens all too often in politics, where the candidate who can superficially validate our preconceptions about the world is the one for whom we'll vote—even though there may be a hundred rational reasons why this candidate would be a horrible choice. Or we limit ourselves. For example, you may have an unpleasant memory of high school that prevents you from enrolling in an adult education class that could really benefit you.

Question the status quo. People who are intellectually lazy tend to accept their circumstances in life and say, "This is just the way things are. I have no control over what happens to me, so why bother?" For them, it's easier to lie back, chill out, and not make waves.

In contrast, people who are actively engaged in building their Three Pillars of Life look to the future and say, "My life *could* be better—and I'm going to *make* it better!" They're capable of objectively looking at their situation and visualizing a better future, and then taking action to make it a reality.

It's also about having empathy and being able to see how the lives of other people could be made better. Even though it's the wealthiest nation in history, in many parts of the United States, the status quo means high unemployment, high crime, low education, and poor health. A characteristic of the advanced brain is the ability to say, "While my life is comfortable and I wouldn't change it, the status quo for other people is unacceptable, and I can help change that."

Summary

- Your brain is the most advanced and complex object in the known universe. Weighing just three pounds and composed mostly of water, fat, proteins, and trace minerals, the work of your brain is done by eighty billion neurons.

- Neurons have three main parts: the *cell body*, where the nucleus and all the DNA material is located; the *dendrites*, extruding from the main body; and the *axon*, which is a long branch that can extend up to three feet. Neurons communicate from the axon terminal to the dendrites of the next neurons.

- Your neurons are connected to each other and also to around ten thousand other cells. All in all, there are about one thousand trillion connections in your brain. These connections are electrical, and your brain generates enough electricity to power a twenty-five-watt lightbulb!

- Across the span of thousands of years of human history, it's only been in the past few centuries—in fact, the past few decades—that scientists have been able to describe the workings of the brain and see it function. As recently as a century ago, it was impossible to observe the brain—a fragile structure solidly encased in your skull—in action. In ancient times, people didn't understand the significance of the brain, probably because the heart, which could be observed beating and circulating blood, seemed to be the most important organ of the body. Therefore, the influence of the brain could only be inferred from observing human behavior.

- For most of human history, the brain was linked to human emotion and mood, and ancient observers saw how a head injury could alter someone's personality. This contributed to the enduring theory of the four humors—melancholy, phlegmatic, sanguine, and choleric. In fact, this system lingers today in the personality profile research done by Hans Eysenck and Jeffrey Alan Gray.

- Thanks to advanced imaging technology, today we're beginning to understand how the brain works and to appreciate its immense power as well as its vulnerabilities. Increasingly, scientists are discovering that in many ways you can Train Your Brain for Success! While your body is important and needs to be kept healthy, your brain makes all the decisions, both life altering and trivial. As you go about your daily activities, your brain calls the shots. It chooses to have you jump out of an airplane, watch a kitten video, apply for a job, vote for a political candidate, have a hamburger for lunch, scratch your left ear because it itches, buy a house—everything you say and do is controlled by your brain.

- As a human being, you seek happiness and fulfillment. To achieve this, you need to build your Three Pillars of Life, which are your health, relationships, and wealth. While many factors can influence your success in building your three pillars, including genetics, the circumstances of your birth, and your susceptibility to disease, by an overwhelming margin what determines your destiny is *your brain*.

- Since your brain is the guiding force in your life, it makes sense to learn as much as you can about it. You need to know how it works, how to care for it, and how to *train it for success.* After all, if you own a home and it's your only shelter from the elements, I'll bet you know how it works and how to take care of it. If the roof leaks or the wiring is not up to code, you'll take steps to fix the problem. Your brain is more important than your house! That's why this book was written—to help you understand and Train Your Brain for Success.

- Your brain is the "decider" in your life—and to build your Three Pillars of Life, you need to be able to make decisions that are objective, empathetic, and make your life better.

2. The Ways Your Brain Can Malfunction

The human brain is capable of both amazing achievements and dismal failures. It can soar to the skies, and it can fall flat. It can be healthy or diseased.

How many times have you said to yourself:

"What was I thinking about when I made that poor choice?"

"I wish these negative thoughts and emotions would go away!"

"Because my mind dwells on how I've been insulted by my boss, I can't seem to concentrate on my job."

"I'm trying to learn this new skill, but I just can't get a handle on it."

"I keep forgetting important dates and appointments."

Sometimes a problem with our brain is just the by-product of the fact that we're imperfect creatures, and even the most robust and healthy brain makes mistakes. Plus, our emotions are important in our everyday behavior, and with emotions comes the possibility of irrational choices. The alternative would be to live as Mr. Spock from *Star Trek*—perfectly rational, unmoved, and unfeeling.

In other cases, a continued problem may represent a real disease or defect. Sometimes it's something that we just have to live with, while at other times it may be a treatable disease.

Here are just a few of the many causes for suboptimal brain performance.

Genetics

We cannot choose our parents. Each baby born is a participant in the vast global game of genetic roulette. From your parents, you get all the physical attributes that make you who you are—your race, your skin color, your ethnic history, and, at least initially, your place on the socioeconomic ladder.

Even if you can't change your DNA, knowledge is always a good thing, at least so we can properly diagnose the source of a disease. As science progresses, it may be possible to exert more influence over our genetic predisposition; but as we know, such progress will raise tangled ethical issues that are beyond the scope of this book.

An inherited brain disorder is caused by a variation or a mutation in a gene. (A *variation* is a different form of a gene, while a *mutation* is a change in the gene itself.)

Some genetic brain disorders are due to random gene mutations or mutations caused by environmental exposure, such as cigarette smoke. In other words, they are not disorders that you inherit directly from your parents but are caused by something happening during the period when the fetus is growing into a baby. Other disorders are inherited, which means that a mutated gene or group of genes is passed down through a family. Brain disorders can also be due to a combination of both genetic changes and other outside factors.

Some examples of genetic brain disorders include the following:

Leukodystrophies

These are a group of rare, progressive, metabolic, genetic diseases that affect the brain, spinal cord, and often the peripheral nerves. Each type of leukodystrophy is caused by a specific gene abnormality that leads to abnormal development or destruction of the myelin sheaths of the brain. Each type of leukodystrophy affects a different part of the myelin sheath, leading to a range of neurological problems. Leukodystrophy can cause problems with hearing, balance, memory, behavior, movement, vision, ability to eat, and thought processes. Leukodystrophies are progressive diseases, meaning that the symptoms of the disease tend to get worse over time.

Treatment of most leukodystrophies is supportive and symptomatic. For spasticity and motor difficulties, physical therapy and medications may be helpful. Anti-epileptic medications should be provided for seizures, and burning paresthesia (a sensation of burning or prickly skin) from peripheral neuropathy may respond to medications for neuropathic pain.

Phenylketonuria

Commonly known as PKU, this is an inherited disorder that increases the levels of a substance called phenylalanine in the blood. Phenylalanine is a building block of proteins (an amino acid) that we get from the food we eat. It is found in all proteins and some artificial sweeteners. If PKU is not treated, phenylalanine can build up to harmful levels in the body, causing intellectual disability and other serious health problems.

Tay-Sachs Disease

A child who inherits a defective gene from both parents will develop Tay-Sachs disease. The disease shows itself when an enzyme that helps break down fatty substances is absent. Left unchecked, these fatty substances—called lipids—then build up to toxic levels in the child's brain and affect the nerve cells. At about six months old, an affected baby will begin to show symptoms. As the disease progresses, the child's body loses function, leading to blindness, deafness, paralysis, and death. There is currently no cure for Tay-Sachs disease, and death usually results by age five.

Wilson Disease

This is an inherited disorder caused by a mutation in a gene in which excessive amounts of copper accumulate in the body, particularly in the liver, brain, and eyes. In individuals diagnosed with Wilson disease, psychiatric or nervous system problems are often the initial features. Signs and symptoms of these problems can include tremors, impaired thinking ability, speech problems, depression, anxiety, clumsiness, difficulty walking, and mood swings.

Huntington's Disease

A progressive brain disorder that causes uncontrolled movements, emotional problems, and loss of thinking ability (cognition), Huntington's disease may trigger changes in personality and a decline in thinking and reasoning abilities. Individuals with the adult-onset form of Huntington's disease usually live about fifteen to twenty years after signs and symptoms begin. The juvenile form, which also involves movement problems and mental and emotional changes, begins in childhood or adolescence. School performance declines as the disease becomes emotionally disruptive. Additional signs of the juvenile form include slow movements, clumsiness, frequent falling, rigidity, slurred speech, and drooling.

Because these conditions and others are genetic, their causes are hardwired into the patient's genetic programming. For this reason, most genetic disorders cannot be cured. The available treatments help manage the diseases, while the treatments themselves and their efficacy vary from one type of disorder to another. Genetic researchers, however, are increasingly optimistic about gene therapy, which has shown promising results in clinical trials but not yet on the general population. Gene therapy is hoped to cure or reduce the effects of genetic disorders by replacing the malfunctioning or mutated gene, manipulating or turning off the gene causing the disease, or stimulating other bodily functions to fight the disease.

Other brain diseases are thought to have a genetic component. For example, the cause of Alzheimer's disease is poorly understood. A significant amount of the risk is believed to be genetic, with many genes usually involved, while other risk factors include a history of head injuries, depression, or hypertension. While no treatments currently stop or reverse its progression, some may temporarily improve symptoms. Mental and physical exercise, good eating habits, and a lower body mass index may decrease the risk of Alzheimer's.

If you happen to have an inherited genetic brain disease, yours is a valiant and never-ending battle to overcome the effects of the disease and live a normal productive life.

Acquired Mental Disorders

For thousands of years, medical professionals have wanted to be able to point to a genetic cause of mental illness and deficiency. Indeed, in many industrialized democracies, such as the United States, as well as dictatorships, including Nazi Germany, the sterilization of "mentally inferior" people was practiced routinely in the belief that society didn't want their bad genes to be passed on.

As usual, reality is much more stubbornly complex. Even before the Human Genome Project concluded in April 2003, scientists were striving to find the genetic component responsible for alcoholism, Alzheimer's, schizophrenia, autism, ADHD, depression, and other ailments that were assumed to be caused by a genetic flaw. But proof has been elusive, and many neuropsychiatric ailments that scientists traditionally thought had a major genetic component don't seem to have one.

More than a decade after the sequencing of the human genome, there is still no reliable genetic test for schizophrenia, Alzheimer's, autism, or any other major neuropsychiatric disorder except for Huntingon's disease. Scientists have consistently failed to find genes for schizophrenia, depression, and other major mental disorders. For example, among identical twins, if one becomes schizophrenic, the risk to the other is on average less than 50%, suggesting environmental influences. Similar findings have been observed with depression and other mental disorders.

Thanks to the growing synergy between epidemiology and molecular biology, the role of the environment in the etiology of mental illness has become more clear. Environmental threats to mental health include infectious agents; pollutants, such as environmental lead; and other exogenous factors that influence an individual's physical surroundings. These traditional parameters, along with nutritional deficiencies, injuries, and pharmaceutical and illicit drugs, also include psychosocial conditions that relate to the individual's perceptions of the social and physical world.

Here are a few examples of acquired mental diseases.

Post-Traumatic Stress Disorder (PTSD)

Commonly associated with frontline military personnel, this ancient disorder has historically been known under various terms, including "shell shock" and "combat neurosis." PTSD is a mental health problem that some people develop after experiencing or witnessing any life-threatening event, such as combat, a natural disaster, a car accident, or sexual assault. PTSD symptoms usually start soon after the traumatic event but may not appear until months or years later. They also may come and go over many years. They may include violent thoughts, feelings, or dreams related to the events, attempts to avoid trauma-related cues (such as loud noises or flashing lights), mental or physical distress to trauma-related cues, alterations in how a person thinks and feels, and the permanent presence of the fight-or-flight response.

Adverse Childhood Experiences (ACEs)

A close cousin to PTSD, adverse childhood experiences (ACEs) are stressful or traumatic events, including direct abuse and indirect household dysfunction, such as growing up with family members who have substance use disorders or witnessing domestic violence. The term was coined in 1995, when physicians Vincent Felitti and Robert Anda launched a large-scale epidemiological study that probed the child and adolescent histories of seventeen thousand subjects, comparing childhood experiences to adult health records. They found—and many other researchers have confirmed—that like PTSD, ACEs can result in actual physiological changes to the brain and a permanent elevation of the "fight or flight" response. Researchers have discovered that when the developing brain is chronically stressed, it releases a hormone that actually shrinks the size of the hippocampus, an area of the brain responsible for processing emotion and memory and managing stress. Because of these and other changes to the brain, ACEs are strongly related to the development and prevalence of a wide range of health problems throughout a person's life span, including those associated with substance misuse.

The best hope for treating both ACEs and PTSD is a combination of therapy and medication. By working with a healthcare professional, individuals can resolve their triggering factors and learn ways of coping with the stress of the past trauma. Therapies that have shown to be effective include psychotherapy, group therapy, cognitive behavioral therapy, and hypnotherapy. A combination of one or more therapeutic approaches may best meet the needs of the individual patient. No single approach works for every patient, and some individuals respond better to certain treatments than others.

Cerebral Palsy

Caused by brain injury or brain malformation that occurs before, during, or immediately after birth while the infant's brain is under development, cerebral palsy can affect the child's reflexes, balance, muscle tone, muscle control, muscle coordination, and posture. It can also affect a child's ability to speak, gross motor skills, and fine motor skills. The growing brain sometimes compensates for defects, in essence, by "rewiring" to bypass or compensate for damaged areas. For this reason, early diagnosis and beginning treatment are recommended. Treatments need to be tailored to the patient and encompass short-term and management approaches to all the specific conditions that a child may face. The treatment plan could involve medications, physical therapy, surgery, and more.

Epilepsy

A brain condition that causes repeated, sudden, brief changes in the brain's electrical activity, epilepsy can cause a variety of symptoms, including seizures or convulsions. During a seizure, brain cells fire uncontrollably at up to four times their normal rate. Seizures temporarily affect the way a person behaves, moves, thinks, or feels. There are many possible causes, including brain injury, either before or after birth; brain tumors; infections, especially meningitis and encephalitis; genetic conditions, abnormal blood vessels in the brain, and lead poisoning.

In most cases, treatment includes one of many antiepileptic medications. In serious cases, surgery may be offered, but brain surgery can cause permanent alteration to brain function, and therefore the risks of surgery have to be balanced against the benefits.

Many other diseases and conditions can attack and impair your brain, including brain tumors, concussions from sports or accidents, strokes, and a host of syndromes. If you suspect you've had a brain injury, seek professional medical attention as quickly as possible.

The Reptilian Brain

Your brain governs a wide range of behaviors, responses, and everyday mundane tasks. It makes choices based on available information, it controls many bodily functions without your conscious direction, it responds reflexively when presented with a threat, and it dreams of new inventions and works of art. These activities, and many more, would be overwhelming if controlled by one, fully conscious, self-aware apparatus. For example, would you want to be required to regulate your own heartbeat, breathing, and digestion during every waking moment? No, you wouldn't—the job would be maddening and leave you no time to do anything else.

Fortunately, your brain's functions are apportioned into three areas: the reptilian, the emotional, and the rational (*Image 1*).

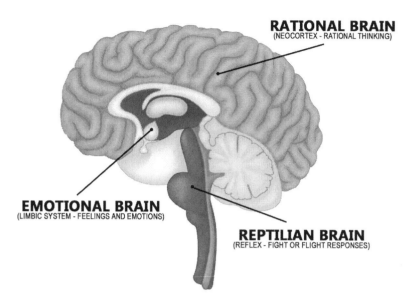

Image 1. *The 3 brains*

The triune brain is a model of the evolution of the vertebrate forebrain and behavior originally proposed by the American physician and neuroscientist Paul D. MacLean. Detailed in his 1990 book *The Triune Brain in Evolution*, MacLean described the brain in terms of three distinct structures that emerged along an evolutionary path. Although this model is a highly simplified explanation of brain activity and organization, it provides an easy-to-understand approximation of the hierarchy of brain functions.

The reptilian complex, also known as the R-complex or reptilian brain, was the name MacLean gave to the *basal ganglia*, structures derived from the floor of the forebrain during development. The term derives from the idea that the forebrains of reptiles and birds were dominated by these structures. MacLean proposed that the reptilian complex was responsible for species-typical instinctual behaviors involved in aggression, dominance, territoriality, and ritual displays.

This portion of the brain is also responsible for the most basic survival functions, including breathing, body temperature, heart rate, and orientation in space. Functions such as heart rate and breathing are extremely important, and the control mechanisms in this part of the brain must be reliable and consistent. In fact, the functions of this part of the brain will normally supersede all other brain activity. For example, if you try to hold your breath, which is a conscious activity initiated by the prefrontal cortex, you will find that as carbon dioxide builds up in your bloodstream, your reptilian brain will take command and make you breathe again. While through training you may be able to increase your resistance to the basic urge to breathe, inevitably you will eventually give in and take a breath.

That's a good thing, because your reptilian brain is putting your survival at the forefront. But your reptilian brain can be programmed to mistake unhealthy choices as necessary for survival. For example, take eating. In the past, our primitive reptilian brain motivated us to find as much food as possible and protect our territory from unwanted intruders. When food was available, you ate it because it might be scarce in the days ahead.

While technology has progressed at a rapid rate, our reptilian brains still live in the past. The basal ganglia still lives in the savannah, chasing antelope and running from lions. It's still motivating us to act as if our basic needs are scarce. But in most industrialized nations, food is everywhere, and calories are more than abundant. Historically, the most scarce and precious nutrients for survival have been salt, sugar, and fat. These were foods that you didn't get very often, so when you did, you didn't hesitate to consume them.

Guess what's weighing down our supermarket shelves and fast-food restaurants today? Salt, sugar, and fat. These three ingredients still excite our taste buds. They optimize our palate because of the feedback loop between our behavior and the reward mechanisms, including dopamine, our behavior triggers. As a result, the reptilian brain will often direct us to consume them as much as possible.

The behavioral influence of the reptilian brain—for both good and bad—is moderated by our large prefrontal cortex, which provides consciousness and self-awareness. It can introduce the power of rational choice and give us the ability to say to ourselves, "It may feel good to eat this double chocolate doughnut now, but in the long run it's going to be bad for me, so I won't do it."

Cognitive Bias

The previous examples are disorders that are measurable and can be diagnosed. They often reveal themselves in medical imaging technology and may involve an actual change to the structure of the brain. They can lead to illness and to sub-optimal brain performance, and prevent you from achieving the Three Pillars of Life.

In everyday life, however, people with perfectly healthy brains sometimes make choices that are irrational and not in their best interest. It's like when you do something and then later you say, "What was I thinking? How could I have been so foolish?"

This happens because in the assembling and weighing of the evidence on both sides of a question—such as, "Should I open the door for the strange man who's knocking?"— your brain can give too much weight to some factors and not enough to others.

This is called *cognitive bias*. In 1972, Amos Tversky, Daniel Kahneman, and their colleagues introduced the theory of cognitive biases as an outgrowth of their experience of people's innumeracy, or the inability to reason intuitively with the greater orders of magnitude. They demonstrated several replicable ways in which human judgments and decisions differ from rational choice theory.

More often than not, cognitive biases are related to our memories; and because our memories are not complete representations of all the events that took place at a particular moment in time, we are inclined to fill the gaps in the missing memories. We fill in the gaps incorrectly, so we make mistakes that lead to biased thinking and decision-making errors.

In other cases, cognitive biases may be related to problems of attention that arise due to our inability to be aware of everything that comes across our path. Thus, our brain is always filling the gaps with pre-assumed pieces of information. All these deficiencies that we encounter in our thinking and decision-making processes influence the way we see and think about the world around us. Our brains, in a sense, are a little bit lazy. Brain processing consumes a lot of energy, and by creating shortcuts and filling in the blanks, when making decisions the brain saves a lot of time and energy.

Trying to simplify the information around us, however, can lead to errors in our thinking process. Sometimes we err on the side of safety, while at other times we disregard obvious warning signs and expose ourselves to risk. Teenagers, who think they'll live forever, routinely ignore cautionary information much to the horror of their parents!

The non-teenage brain is wired to pay more attention to negative situations than positive ones. While both positive and negative emotions have an impact on our brain to avoid repeating the situation, negative situations use a different pathway in our brains that overrides everything else.

For instance, if you're driving down the road by yourself in the middle of the night and you suddenly notice that the car behind you has made two or three of the same turns you made, a cognitive bias might make you think you are being followed, and therefore you decide to take a different route to your house. In fact, the person making those same turns as you could have been a neighbor who happened to be out at the same time as you, but because the other option—someone following you—could be a dangerous situation, your brain leans toward getting you out of that scenario.

There are hundreds of cognitive biases. Below are twelve of the most common ones that affect us on a daily basis.

Reward Bias

This is perhaps the most powerful bias that influences human behavior. Our brain is wired to crave immediate rewards, leading us to choose lesser immediate benefits over greater long-term benefits. Children are particularly susceptible to this type of bias. You can see it in the experiment called the marshmallow effect, where the child is offered the choice to eat the marshmallow immediately or wait five minutes to get two.

Reward bias can be very dangerous, since it is the basis for addictive personality. Delayed gratification is the ability to resist the temptation for an immediate reward and wait for a later reward. This requires a more sophisticated thinking pattern and self-control.

Anchoring Bias

We are usually influenced by the first piece of information that we hear, which then affects any future information related to the first piece of information. Hence, the first piece of information acts as an *anchor* for the others to follow. This bias is heavily used by marketers to anchor a specific price point for a product they are trying to sell. eBay is a great example to see anchoring in action: the "buy it now" item serves as an anchor price for the same item you might be trying to bid on. In politics, we see it when a candidate attempts to "brand" his or her opponent early in the campaign, creating an indelible negative image the opponent must constantly battle.

Hindsight Bias

This bias is also known as the "knew it all along effect" and involves the tendency to see situations as more predictable than they really are. We tend to look back at events and assume that we knew all along what was going to happen. A clear example of this bias is when investors believe they could have predicted which company stocks performed better than others.

Confirmation Bias

This very common bias is the tendency to selectively filter only evidence that confirms our existing beliefs or theories. Rather than consider all the facts in a logical and rational manner, we tend to listen to the information that confirms our own beliefs and discount evidence to the contrary. This bias is even more prominent in groups of people. We simply look to reinforce our beliefs, which is why we tend to surround ourselves with people who have similar thoughts or beliefs to our own.

Misinformation Effect Bias

This bias happens when a person's recall of episodic memories (memories of biographical events occurring at a particular time and place) become less accurate because of post event information. Information presented early is influenced by information that occurs later on, thus affecting the ability to retain accurate information. Essentially, the new information that a person receives works backward in time to distort the memory of the original event. For instance, you might witness a crime and the faces that you are shown to identify the offender affect the original face you have in your memory. Sometimes we believe that we are 100% sure about an event, but the truth is that our memory is very susceptible to subtle influences.

The Authority Bias

This is the tendency to accept the opinion of someone who we believe is an authority on the subject. We usually tend to attribute greater accuracy to the opinion of an authority figure, and we are more influenced by that opinion. Part of this bias has been rooted in the authority we give our parents, from the time we are born all the way to adulthood. This bias is very commonly used in health product commercials, where you see an expert, either a doctor or a very fit personal trainer, recommending the product for you to buy. Sometimes people tend to overvalue the opinion of experts, which can be a risky thing to do.

Self-Serving Bias

We tend to give ourselves credit for success while blaming others or external factors for our failures. For example, when you do well on an exam, you praise yourself for studying hard. If you fail the exam, you might blame the teacher because that person didn't explain things thoroughly or your friends because they distracted you when you were trying to study. This bias is important because it allows us to preserve our own self-esteem.

Gambler's Fallacy

We tend to put a tremendous amount of weight on previous events, believing that they will influence future outcomes. The most common example is when you're flipping a coin. Let's say you get "heads" six times in a row. Your inclination is to predict that the next toss will be tails, but the likelihood of either heads or tails on the next toss is still fifty-fifty. It does not change.

Stereotyping Bias

As the name implies, this bias occurs when we expect a group or a person to have certain qualities without having specific information about them. For instance, we may assume that all police officers are racist and aggressive, or when seeing a man wearing a *keffiyeh* we may assume he is a terrorist. This bias can be useful since it allows us to quickly identify strangers as friends or enemies—the problem is that we tend to overuse and abuse it.

Placebo Effect Bias

This bias happens when we believe that something will have a certain effect on us, and we behave as if it really did. This bias is commonly used in the medical testing world, where the "control" subjects are given inert pills, while others are given the actual drug. Placebo effects can be very powerful to the point of causing physiological changes in your body.

Overconfidence Bias

Some people are too confident about their abilities. This bias causes them to take greater risks than they normally would. Experts are usually more prone to this bias than laypeople because they are more convinced that they are right and that they can do it because of their "expertise." For example, a pilot may take his plane up in bad weather because he's confident in his abilities, or a doctor might give you the wrong diagnosis because he or she feels confident that they know what they're talking about.

Blind Spot Bias

I like this one because this is the bias of not realizing you actually have a bias. Failing to recognize your own cognitive weakness is a bias itself. We tend to notice other people's biases, especially when they're wrong, more often than we notice our own.

Procrastination

It cannot be denied that while the brain can malfunction in the sense that it makes poor decisions—such as choosing to ride a motorcycle without a helmet or deciding that robbing a bank is a good idea—it can also malfunction by making no decision and taking no action when both are necessary. This can put you further away from the Three Pillars of Life.

We all know what it's like to put off or postpone painful choices.

Perhaps we know that our boss is a jerk, but we delay reporting his behavior to human resources because we want to avoid conflict.

We need to lose weight, and we say, "I'll start my diet tomorrow. Today is not a good day to do it."

We want to go back to college and get our degree, but things always seem to get in the way, and the decision keeps getting pushed back.

Every day most of us not only push away painful decisions, but we also—paradoxically—postpone things that are obviously good for us, such as cleaning the spoiled food out of the refrigerator or getting our annual flu shot. (Have you had *your* flu shot? If not, why not? They're free just about everywhere and can make a big difference to your health!)

Why do we put off doing things we need to do?

There are six common reasons why we procrastinate.

1. The task itself is unpleasant. It's true that cleaning out the cat's litter box is not pleasant and never will be. Seeing an overdue bill arrive in the mail and reading it rather then shoving it under the pile can be difficult. Scheduling a potentially life-saving colonoscopy is not everyone's first choice of fun things to do. One way you can complete your unpleasant tasks on time is by dividing and conquering. Instead of focusing on the big scary goal, design a series of easy-to-complete, intermediate tasks. Another strategy is to form an if-then plan to automate goal striving—for example, "If I go online, I'm first going to check my student loan account to make sure my payments are up to date." And, as we'll see in other examples below, often the solution is to be able to do what the human brain is uniquely capable of: visualize the future reward, and commit to reaching it despite the lack of immediate gratification.

2. Easily available alternatives. When a tough choice looms, it's often easy to find some other seemingly productive activity that provides the illusion of getting something done. When your work environment is structured, you have fewer ways to escape. For example, if you work on an assembly line, the work comes at you whether you're ready or not, while in many office environments the lack of imposed direction can contribute to the increase in procrastination. It's easy to look busy by checking Facebook rather than writing the challenging sales report. One solution is to design your environment in a way that makes your desired task more difficult to avoid and puts the "fun stuff" further out of reach.

3. The time gap between the task and the reward. To use the example of the colonoscopy, it's difficult for many people to associate the task (getting the colonoscopy) with the distant reward (catching a possible case of colon cancer early before it gets dangerous). Hopefully, this is one of the earliest lessons we learn as children: that rewards come in the future, and we need to take action now to ensure rewards will come. A long temporal gap between task and reward can produce internal conflict between future and present interests. Because the reward is difficult to visualize, a smoker can spend months saying they'll quit tomorrow. The solution is to find a way to make long-term goals feel more within reach and adjusting your expectations so that you're not worried if you don't see or feel a reward immediately.

4. Fear of failure. This point is particularly important. Its source is a lack of self-confidence and the fear of consequences if we fail. For many people, failing presents such a significant psychological threat their motivation to *avoid failure* exceeds their motivation to *achieve success*, causing them to unconsciously sabotage their chances of success.

Sometimes this fear can be rational; for example, if you're planning to scale the Half Dome in Yosemite National Park without a safety rope, where a single mistake could result in your death, then it's understandable if you postpone the climb until conditions are perfect. Putting off a low-risk activity because you're afraid to fail isn't rational, though, and has its roots in a poor sense of self-esteem. In fact, failure, criticism, and rejection often provide you with the opportunity to grow and develop your life and career. Failure, criticism, and rejection are outcomes. You can't take them personally. They are a result of things you have *done*, not who you *are*.

When difficulties arise, people with weak self-confidence easily develop doubts about their ability to accomplish the task at hand, while those with strong beliefs are more likely to continue their efforts. When low self-confidence causes people to avoid activities, they miss opportunities to acquire new knowledge and skills.

5. The excitement of a looming deadline. Some people believe they function better when under pressure and their hormones provide a feeling of urgency. There's actually a scientific basis for this belief. Dopamine is a neurotransmitter in the brain that affects your productivity, motivation, and focus. Some even call it the "motivation molecule" because it boosts your drive and concentration while helping you resist negative impulses.

This may be true, but getting "amped up" and beating the deadline is not the best way to accomplish a task; research has shown that last-minute completions are more likely to be slipshod or have mistakes.

Why do people wait until the last minute? Causes include a strict upbringing in which putting things off until the last minute becomes a form of rebellion, inherited personality traits, and a fear of failure—or even a fear of success and its resulting increase in responsibilities. There's also the illogical perception of time, which we tend to see in big chunks, such as semesters, seasons, or quarters. A deadline of six months from now seems so far away—unless your project requires six months of preparation, in which case you'd better get started!

6. Information overload. In the era of big data, "complexity paralysis" is becoming increasingly common. Information overload is when your brain exceeds its processing capacity and leaves you feeling bewildered, not unlike when your computer runs out of RAM and crashes. It can also destroy your concentration, leaving you more susceptible to making poor decisions. As a result, you're more likely to overload yourself from other sources of information as a means of procrastinating on important tasks. We live in a world where the Internet provides such a tsunami of dopamine-triggering information that we can even become desensitized to its effects over time, making it much harder for us to achieve optimum happiness and build our Three Pillars of Life.

Education and Past Experience

Every one of us has been influenced by the culture in which we were raised and the type of education we received. Our ingrained beliefs help shape our perceptions of the world around us and the decisions we make.

For example, consider the worldview of the child who has been caught up in a nasty divorce, and in the process of separation one parent has actively trained the child to reject the other parent. *Parental alienation syndrome* (PAS) is a term coined by child psychiatrist Richard A. Gardner in the early 1980s to refer to what he described as a disorder in which a child, on an ongoing basis, belittles and insults one parent without justification, due to a combination of factors, including indoctrination by the other parent, almost exclusively as part of a child custody dispute. While PAS can't be defined as a mental disorder because it's not a mental health issue contained within one individual but rather a relationship dysfunction between the two parents and then the child and parent, for the purposes of this book, it's very real. The effect of PAS—regardless of whether you believe it's a disease—is that it makes an individual see the world not as it is but through a distorted lens, leading to negative choices with no basis in reality. It can certainly stand in the way of an individual successfully building the Three Pillars of Life—health, relationships, and wealth.

Similarly, if a child is educated in a religious sect or cult that teaches an apocalyptic view of the world or that other religions are evil and must be exterminated, then that child is likely to grow up with those beliefs and hold a distorted worldview that will lead to bad decisions.

Children who are taught that they have no free will and that it's pointless to try to better yourself in an unfair world may grow up to be procrastinators who avoid responsibility because they don't see any benefit in taking action.

You also have the familiar archetype of the spoiled wealthy child who grows up believing that work is what other people do, and that personal income is something that is deposited into one's bank account every fiscal quarter by the family trust fund. Just like the person growing up in an impoverished and dysfunctional family, the wealthy freeloader will face greater challenges in building the Three Pillars of Life.

These examples aren't traditional adverse childhood experiences because there's no shock to the system and no triggering of the fight-or-flight response leading to permanent hormonal changes. In fact, there's an aspect of subjectivity to all of them, meaning that from the perspective of an adult who's guiding the child, the adult's worldview may be seen as being perfectly normal. To the adult in a cult, the decision to withdraw from the world and follow an apocalyptic path may seem to be a perfectly rational and logical choice.

It's also important to remember that every child needs to raised within a framework of supporting values and traditions. This framework is typically based upon family customs, political alignment, and religious viewpoints. For example, at least superficially, a child raised in a staunchly Protestant Republican household is going to see the world through a different lens than a child who's raised in an agnostic Democratic household. A young person raised in a violent slum will view his or her future prospects differently from someone brought up in a comfortable Fifth Avenue apartment. A child in the United States will look forward to October 31 as being an exciting and important holiday, whereas to a child in China it's just another normal day. Scientific studies have shown that children raised in households where adults smoke cigarettes are far more likely to smoke than those raised in a nonsmoking environment.

Even birth order makes a difference. First born? Parents tend to hold up their firstborns as role models for younger siblings, which can create a lot of pressure. Adults take firstborns seriously and invest more in them, which can create a self-image of leadership. When parents fawn over every firstborn "first," it motivates the oldest child to achieve. Middle child? They respond to what they see happening to the older sibling. Once a role is defined by the firstborn, the second-born will often seek out a role that's completely the opposite. Middle children tend to be agreeable, diplomatic, and compromising, and they handle disappointment well. The youngest child? By the time they've had a couple of children, parents tend to be more relaxed when the last one comes along. They don't feel compelled to invest as much. As a result, last-borns are often left alone, and they slide by "under the radar." They shoulder less responsibility, so they tend to be more carefree, easygoing, fun-loving, affectionate, and sociable. They often like to make people laugh, because when you're the littlest kid in the group being funny is often the best way to get approval from the giants looming over you.

These examples are just generalities. The human mind is an amazing instrument, capable of astonishing feats of self-examination and self-improvement. Many children emerge from nasty divorces with level heads, others escape cultlike environments to lead productive lives, and some who are raised in the lap of luxury become motivated, hardworking adults. An important key to building the Three Pillars of Life is self-awareness, which is the subject of the next chapter.

Summary

- It would be nice if everyone's brain worked perfectly all the time (especially the brains of your teenaged son or the crazy lady who lives next door!), but your brain can malfunction or operate irrationally. We are influenced by hormones, the drugs in our bloodstream, our feelings and emotions, physical defects or imperfections in our brains—all these and more affect our decisions.
- Your brain's growth and formation is directed by the DNA passed down from your parents, which can create built-in thought patterns as well as physical defects or abnormalities. Mental disorders can also be acquired in the form of trauma, adverse childhood experiences, epilepsy, and cerebral palsy. Some can be treated and even overcome.

- Sometimes the line between mental illness and genius is hard to define! Consider these words of the great writer Leo Tolstoy, who suffered from classic melancholia, which he wrote in *A Confession and Other Religious Writings:* "Today or tomorrow sickness and death will come (they had come already) to those I love or to me; nothing will remain but stench and worms. Sooner or later my affairs, whatever they may be, will be forgotten, and I shall not exist. Then why go on making any effort? How can man fail to see this? And how go on living? That is what is surprising! One can only live while one is intoxicated with life; as soon as one is sober it is impossible not to see that it is all a mere fraud and a stupid fraud! That is precisely what it is: there is nothing either amusing or witty about it, it is simply cruel and stupid." And yet Tolstoy persevered.

- We are all subject to imperfections of our brains. We have biases, we imagine threats that don't exist, and we ignore threats that do exist. As you Train Your Brain for Success and build your Three Pillars of Life, you need to constantly strive to put aside your preconceptions and biases and see life as it really is and not as you imagine it to be.

- Procrastination can be a problem for anyone! When facing an important task, your brain can malfunction by making no decision and taking no action, when both are necessary. There are six common reasons why we procrastinate:

1. The task itself is unpleasant.
2. Easily available alternatives.
3. The time gap between the task and the reward.
4. Fear of failure.
5. The excitement of a looming deadline.
6. Information overload.

- Our parents, families, communities, and peers influence our outlook on life and our decisions. For example, parental alienation syndrome is a disorder in which a child, on an ongoing basis, belittles and insults one parent without justification. The child didn't invent this; it's primarily due to indoctrination by the other parent, almost exclusively as part of a child custody dispute. If you believe that your opinions have been unfairly shaped by a childhood authority figure impeding your progress toward your Three Pillars of Life, you might want to consider seeking help from a therapist. It could be a very positive decision!

3. Understanding Yourself and Others

Each of us views life through a unique lens that's been formed by our genetics and upbringing. This is perfectly normal, and in the West we tend to celebrate these differences because we believe they are a source of strength in a society. In contrast, look at a regimented society, such as North Korea, where individuality is repressed, and all citizens are pushed toward having the same thoughts, feelings, and beliefs as everyone else. In North Korea, "understanding yourself" means aligning your mind and heart with the nationally approved program. In the West, the word we use to describe this is "brainwashing."

The key to achieving the Three Pillars of Life lies not in abandoning your individuality to conform to some artificial standard or ideal. It's in knowing who you are and understanding both yourself and others.

Note that this is a two-part process. Understanding yourself is one part, while the second, and equally important is understanding others.

Emotional Intelligence (EQ)

Aside from an actual disease of the brain, the most powerful force acting upon our thoughts and decisions is our emotions. When faced with a decision—which car to buy, which job to take, which political candidate to vote for—while we may spend time weighing the facts and trying to be objective, our final decision will often depend on how our choice makes us *feel*.

Our decision-making abilities are inexorably linked to our emotions. While we may think that our decisions arise from a rational thinking process, the truth is that most of the decisions we make are influenced by our emotions as well as our past experiences. There's nothing wrong with this, as long as we take a balanced approach and have highly developed sense of *emotional intelligence*.

The term first appeared in a 1964 paper by Michael Beldoch, and subsequently gained popularity in the 1995 book *Emotional Intelligence* written by the author, psychologist, and science journalist Daniel Goleman. Emotional intelligence (known by either the literal acronym "EI" or the one that suggests it's the flip side of IQ, namely "EQ") refers to the capability of individuals to recognize their own and other people's emotions, discern between different feelings and label them appropriately, use emotional information to guide thinking and behavior, and manage their emotions to adapt to environments or achieve a goal.

Each of us can determine how to control and moderate our emotions. It is not an easy task, but it is doable.

Emotional intelligence can be defined and described in many ways that need not concern people who aren't mental health professionals. Here's the "mixed model" that Goleman proposed, which provides a good foundation for discussion.

Goleman's model outlines five main EQ constructs:
1. Self-awareness—The ability to know one's own emotions,

strengths, weaknesses, drives, values and goals, and recognize their effect on others while using instinctive feelings to guide decisions.

2. Self-regulation—Involves controlling or redirecting one's disruptive emotions and impulses and adapting to changing circumstances.

3. Social skills—Managing relationships to move other people in a desired direction.

4. Empathy—Considering other people's feelings, especially when making decisions.

5. Motivation—Being driven to achieve for the sake of achievement.

Our emotional perception of and subsequent responses to events and situations are deeply dependent on how the brain and body respond to each other.

Since this book is about your brain, let's begin by examining how the brain senses, creates, and stores emotions. The key region in our brain responsible for emotions is the *amygdala*, a collection of almond-shaped structures buried inside the medial temporal lobes, which are especially important in consolidating memories of emotional experiences. The amygdala is also connected to the hippocampus, where long-term memories are stored.

Emotional intelligence (either EI or EQ) is the capacity for individuals to be able to recognize their own and other people's emotions. Emotional intelligence also allows us to discriminate between different emotions and label them appropriately. We can then use other people's emotional information to adjust our own emotions to influence them and achieve our goals. The higher your EQ, the higher your ability to control your and other people's emotions.

Being "smart" and having a high IQ have little relationship to your emotional intelligence. Research has shown that most successful people have a high emotional intelligence independent of their IQ. In fact, some people with a low IQ but a high EQ tend to be more successful than people with a high IQ but a low EQ. People with high EQ usually have greater mental health, higher job performance, and greater leadership skills.

In concurrence with many other researchers, I can confidently say that your success in life is mainly rooted in your emotional intelligence.

Most people who fail to achieve the Three Pillars of Life do so mainly as a result of their inability to make the best decisions for themselves. Your decision-making ability requires not only experience and knowledge but also understanding your and other people's emotional states. At first, one might think that decision-making only happens in our cerebral cortex, where higher brain functions take place. The truth is that effective decision-making is not possible without the motivation and meaning that is provided by emotional input.

If our emotional centers were not involved in our decision-making process, our ancestors would not have been able to survive. For example, imagine if a caveman encounters a bear, and in response he decides to rationally think of his options. By the time he's done thinking, the bear will have had him for dinner! Our emotional centers have developed to ensure our survival. When something is highly emotionally charged, our higher brain functions are circumvented. They're sidelined so that we can be ready for our fight-and-flight response.

In our modern world, the threats we face are not the same ones we faced thousands of years ago, but our brains still react the same way to emotional events. This is why the decision-making process can be very hard at times. It is very important for us to understand and be able to take control of our emotions so that we can make the best decisions possible.

I have met people for whom everything seems to go wrong. I have come to realize that not everything is actually wrong; it's just that their decision-making process is defective. They have no idea how to decide correctly. Their emotional control and impulsive behavior limit them from making rational decisions. The only solution such people have is to take control of themselves and understand how their emotions work so that they can see themselves from an outside perspective and be able to make better decisions in their lives.

Can you improve your emotional intelligence?

Yes, you can—and you should.

Hundreds of studies have shown that boosting emotional intelligence improves relationship satisfaction, leadership ability, entrepreneurial potential, career success, and overall happiness. It is also the best antidote to work stress; and because most jobs involve dealing with people, and people with higher EQ are more rewarding to deal with, it can bring greater career success.

Many coaching interventions strive to enhance some aspect of EQ, usually under the name of interpersonal, social, or "soft skills" training. Do these programs really work? For example, if you've been told you need to be a better listener, show more empathy for others, or keep your temper under control, what are the odds you can really improve? How do you know if your efforts will pay off and which interventions will be most effective?

Here are a few key points to consider.

1. You can boost your EQ. While our ability to identify and manage our own and others' emotions is fairly constant over time, having been grounded in our genetics and early childhood experiences, long-term improvements are possible with dedication and guidance. Some people are certainly just naturally more insecure, shy, or self-centered, while other people are born with natural positivity, composure, and people skills. One factor is that EQ tends to increase with age, even without deliberate interventions. In plain English, most people mature with age, especially as hormones that propel the sex drive—a major source of emotional stress—tend to wane.

2. Quality coaching programs can be effective. While no program can transform the Wicked Witch of the West into the benevolent Glinda, a professional coaching intervention can achieve measurable improvements. Studies suggest that the most coachable element of EQ is interpersonal skills—that is, common etiquette and knowing how to relate to other people on a basic level. Stress management programs can be effective, and even empathy can be trained in adults. This is all thanks to the neuroplasticity of the brain, which I'll discuss in greater depth in the pages ahead.

3. Get objective feedback. This is the hardest part because it involves emotional contact at exactly the points where you may be the most sensitive. If you're in a structured program run by a professional, you'll be appropriately prepared, and negative opinions will be presented in a way that's as nonthreatening as possible. Feedback is valuable because most of us are generally unaware of how others see us, and this especially true for managers. Too many intelligent, highly motivated, and outwardly responsible people rarely pause to contemplate their own behaviors, or when they do, they do it to reassure themselves that other people are wrong because they don't embrace everything the person says.

A major reason for our inability to be objective about ourselves is often wishful thinking or overconfidence, but in some cases it may be the opposite: an ingrained belief that because no one listens to *what* we say, *how* we say it doesn't matter. Any intervention with the goal of increasing EQ must begin by helping people understand their real strengths and weaknesses.

There is an old joke about how many psychologists it takes to change a light bulb. The answer is just one—provided the light bulb *wants* to change. Be the light bulb that wants to change!

Empathy

The cornerstone of emotional intelligence and our ability to build lasting relationships with other people—an important part of the Three Pillars of Life—is empathy. This is the experience of understanding another person's condition from their perspective. You place yourself in their situation and feel what they are feeling.

In his 1980 paper "Interpersonal Reactivity Index" (IRI), Mark Davis, professor of psychology at Eckerd College, suggested that there are four important types of empathy.

1. The perspective taking (PT) scale measures the reported tendency to spontaneously adopt the psychological point of view of others in everyday life ("I sometimes try to understand my friends better by imagining how things look from their perspective").

2. The empathic concern (EC) scale assesses the tendency to experience feelings of sympathy and compassion for unfortunate others ("I often have tender, concerned feelings for people less fortunate than I am").

3. The personal distress (PD) scale taps the tendency to experience distress and discomfort in response to extreme distress in others ("Being in a tense emotional situation scares me").

4. The fantasy (FS) scale measures the tendency to imaginatively transpose oneself into fictional situations ("When I am reading an interesting story or a novel, I imagine how I would feel if the events in the story were happening to me").

Empathy can be measured in the brain. In a 2013 study published in the *Journal of Neuroscience*, researchers at the Max Planck Institute for Human Cognitive and Brain Sciences identified that while the tendency to be egocentric is innate for human beings a part of your brain called the right supramarginal gyrus recognizes a lack of empathy and can make the correction. Located approximately at the junction of the parietal, temporal, and frontal lobe, the supramarginal gyrus is part of the cerebral cortex. This area of the brain helps us to distinguish our own emotional state from that of other people and is responsible for empathy and compassion. When the right supramarginal gyrus doesn't function properly or when we have to make snap decisions, researchers found our capacity for empathy is dramatically reduced.

The research team headed by Tania Singer said, "When assessing the world around us and our fellow humans, we use ourselves as a yardstick and tend to project our own emotional state onto others. While cognition research has already studied this phenomenon in detail, nothing is known about how it works on an emotional level. It was assumed that our own emotional state can distort our understanding of other people's emotions, in particular if these are completely different to our own. But this emotional egocentricity had not been measured before now."

The right supramarginal gyrus helps us set aside our natural egotistical perception of ourselves and experience empathy for others. When during the research the neurons in this part of the brain were disrupted, the participants found it difficult to stop from projecting their own feelings and circumstances onto others. The participants' assessments were also less accurate when they were forced to make particularly quick decisions.

No matter what form it takes, the ability to empathize is critical to building the Three Pillars of Life. There's the obvious empathic concern of seeing someone injured by the side of the road, stopping, and calling for an ambulance. If you do something like this, you'll build up positive energy in your mind because you will have the satisfaction of knowing you've done something good—you've helped to relieve the suffering of other people.

But empathy can appear in situations where you might not expect it.

In business, if you can empathize with the needs and desires of your customers, you'll be more successful in selling your product or service. At the customer service level, you—or your reps—must learn to listen actively to customers when they are speaking. If the customer is angry, pay specific attention to the details. A customer may be angry at the lack of attention given to them by a previous associate, which can be a bigger problem that actually having an issue with the product or service. Apologize even if you think it's not necessary, and express a sincere desire to help the customer and solve their problem.

Empathy is necessary at the highest levels too. Here's a story that might surprise you. Mike Markkula was one of the first investors in Apple, and in the early days he wrote "The Apple Marketing Philosophy," a memo that represents the fundamental DNA of Apple over three decades. As reported by Walter Isaacson in his biography of Steve Jobs, Markkula set down three principles:

The first was *empathy*, an intimate connection with the feelings of the customer: "We will truly understand their needs better than any other company."

The second was *focus*: "In order to do a good job of those things that we decide to do, we must eliminate all of the unimportant opportunities."

The third and equally important principle was *impute*. It emphasized that people form an opinion about a company or product based on the signals that it conveys. "People *do* judge a book by its cover," he wrote. "We may have the best product, the highest quality, the most useful software, etc. If we present them in a slipshod manner, they will be perceived as slipshod; if we present them in a creative, professional manner, we will impute the desired qualities."

If you're able to put yourself in your customers' shoes and understand their expectations, you'll make more sales and strengthen your Three Pillars of Life. Empathy is also a critical skill for you to have as a leader. It contributes to an accurate understanding of your employees and how they view themselves and their jobs. It also bolsters your communication skills because you can sense what others want to know and if they're getting it from you.

Given the growing diversity in today's workplace, an especially good way to develop empathy is to have traveled or worked in multicultural environments. By exposing yourself—and your brain—to the ways and customs of other people, you can learn that the way they see and experience things is not as unlike your own as you might have imagined.

Here's a statistical correlation that's worth pondering.

Numerous studies—by Gallup and others—have been taken to determine the happiest states in America. That is to say, the states with the happiest residents. Typically, Hawaii tops the lists, followed by such states as Colorado and California.

The interesting thing is that studies have also been done to rank the states according to the per capita ownership of *passports*. That's right—the states with the most international travelers or at least those who aspire to travel beyond our borders. The top states are predictably New Jersey (where over 68% of the population hold a passport), California, and New York.

The striking thing is the list of states at the *bottom* of the number of passport holders per capita. I won't name them, but these states, whose inhabitants tend not to travel abroad and who have a more provincial view of the world, also tend to be at the bottom of the happiness surveys. On average, their residents are further away from achieving the Three Pillars of Life, and they also happen to see no need for or have little opportunity to travel abroad and experience foreign cultures and lifestyles.

How We're Tested Every Day

When I say, "You need to know yourself," the response of most readers might be, "Well, duh, of course I know myself!"

Really? While you may *think* you know yourself, your opinions and beliefs—even bedrock values—are under constant assault, primarily by marketers who want to sell you something and whose first job it is to convince you that you need what they're selling.

Persuasion marketing is the art and science—to use the terms loosely—of getting you to agree with what the salesperson is telling you. Here, imitation is the most sincere form of flattery at least according to advocates of the "mirror technique."

While maintaining casual conversation, by mirroring your physical posture and gestures, the salesperson can develop an unspoken bond with you, making you feel the two of you are "in sync." Then, the superclever salesperson will introduce a gesture of her own, and if she sees you copy her gesture, she knows she's gone from following you to leading you. Now she can interject her own ideas into the conversation, hopefully extracting from you the response of "That's just what I was thinking—I'll buy it right now!" The theory seems dumb except for one thing: people are more likely to trust someone who's like them and who shares their viewpoint. This is the key to peer-to-peer selling, such as Tupperware and Avon practice. A Midwestern suburban house-wife is more likely to buy perfume from another Midwestern suburban housewife than from a man with a foreign-sounding accent.

Consider the pharmaceutical companies that run ads on TV introducing a disease, telling you how horrible it is, and then suggesting you see your doctor and telling him or her you might need the medication for the disease you hadn't heard of. Here's an example. In 2013, the drug giant Cephalon announced it had produced a drug to cure "shift work disorder" (SWD). The premise of so-called shift work disorder was that the fatigue you feel when you stay up all night working a night shift is actually a *disease* requiring chemical intervention. You're not simply tired because you're sleep deprived or out of sync with your body's natural rhythms: you're tired because you have a medical disorder! And unless you take the new drug Nuvigil, which has serious side effects, including "serious rash or a serious allergic reaction that may affect parts of your body such as your liver or blood cells, and may result in hospitalization and be life-threatening," you'll never be cured.

If you're a shift worker and you feel tired—understandably so!—you need to be pretty secure in your knowledge of yourself and the reality of your situation to resist such blandishments.

The ultimate example of an external persuader convincing you to change your mind about something is when police or other authorities convince someone to confess to a crime they didn't commit. The process has been replicated by researchers. In January 2015, British researchers Julia Shaw and Stephen Porter published their study entitled, "Constructing Rich False Memories of Committing Crime." They wrote in the paper's abstract, "Memory researchers long have speculated that certain tactics may lead people to recall crimes that never occurred, and thus could potentially lead to false confessions. This is the first study to provide evidence suggesting that full episodic false memories of committing crime can be generated in a controlled experimental setting. With suggestive memory-retrieval techniques, participants were induced to generate criminal and noncriminal emotional false memories. . . ." The researchers got "confessions" from a full 70% of their college-aged subjects by using a blend of real facts and invented fiction. From parents or a guardian, and with the approval of an ethics committee, Shaw and Porter first acquired a few facts about the subject's teen years, such as the name of her best friend and hometown. Then, during three interviews of just forty-five-minutes each, Shaw extracted information from the students about one true experience (which they remembered) and one fabricated experience (of which she convinced them).

After a few hours of feeding the students tidbits of the verified info, she added them up to equal her fabricated crime—and most students were persuaded: They were criminals. "In such circumstances," Shaw told *Science Daily*, "inherently fallible and reconstructive memory processes can quite readily generate false recollections with astonishing realism. In these sessions we had some participants recalling incredibly vivid details and re-enacting crimes they never committed."

Sadly, such cases have happened in real life—perhaps most notoriously in the case of the Central Park Five. On the night of April 19, 1989, Trisha Meili, a female jogger, was brutally attacked in Manhattan's Central Park. Five juvenile males were quickly arrested and tried variously for assault, robbery, riot, rape, sexual abuse, and attempted murder. They were convicted and received sentences ranging from five to fifteen years, and each spent between six and thirteen years in prison.

They were convicted on the basis of their confessions, extracted after hours of interrogation by police. Analysis of the DNA collected at the crime scene did not match any of the suspects—it had come from a single, unknown person. Although four of the suspects had confessed on videotape in the presence of a parent or guardian, they retracted their statements within weeks, claiming that they had been intimidated, lied to, and coerced into making false confessions.

In 2002, Matias Reyes, who had been a juvenile at the time of the attack, confessed to raping the jogger, and DNA evidence confirmed his involvement in her rape. Reyes also said he committed the rape alone, and his description of the act matched every detail. At the time of his confession, Reyes was a convicted serial rapist and murderer serving a life sentence.

Every day, in ways both great and small, external forces are at work on us with the goal of getting us to change our minds, see something differently, or even accept what we know to be patently untrue. You and your brain must be constantly vigilant and let nothing lead you away from your Three Pillars of Life.

Your Environment Affects the Decisions You Make

As human beings, we're born into a world that's perceptible to us through our five senses: sight, hearing, touch, smell, and taste. Our sense receptors—eyes, ears, skin, nose, tongue, as well as the millions of nerves inside our body—are constantly receiving information and passing it along to the brain, where it's processed, evaluated, acted upon if necessary, and stored away as memories for future reference. Every decision we make is weighed against the data distilled from our current and previous sensory input.

Let's say you're at home and out of the corner of your eye you glimpse a small creature moving across your floor. Your brain instantly judges this new visual information to be an anomaly: small creatures are not supposed to be moving across your floor. This needs to be investigated! You stand up and move closer. Direct visual contact is made. The creature has a small compact body and a number of roughly equal legs. How many legs? Your memory informs you that insects have six legs, while spiders have eight. The creature pauses in its ambling. You count the legs: eight! Your memory sounds the alarm: Spiders are venomous and likely to bite you if they think you're getting too close. This spider cannot be allowed to remain in the room.

Now let's say that your previous experiences with spiders have been negative, either because you've actually been bitten or when you were a child you heard scary stories about how horrible spiders were. Your decision might then be to get a rolled-up magazine and swiftly whack the spider, killing it. With the threat removed, your fight-or-flight hormones, which have surged, can settle back to their baseline level. Whew!

But perhaps, like myself, your previous experiences with spiders have been innocuous, and in fact you love all creatures great and small. You stay quite calm and your fight-or-flight hormones don't elevate. You decide not to kill the spider but relocate it. So you quickly get a small jar, and using a piece of paper coax the little fellow into the jar. You take the jar outside and release the spider in the bushes, where he'll enjoy more profitable hunting than would be available in your house. In fact, rather than being relieved that you've just escaped a painful death from a spider bite by killing the creature, you feel good about yourself for having done the little critter a favor.

This is just one example of the many thousands that occur every day in which an immediate sensory input is combined with our memories and values to produce a decision and an action.

Everything we see, hear, smell, feel, and taste is compared with the "control" group in our memory. It's how we judge threats versus opportunities.

When you go to the store to buy bananas, you look at the bananas on display and compare them to the bananas in your memory. You might decide the store bananas are more green than you think is acceptable. Based upon this information, you've decided to look elsewhere, when your friend says, "It's okay if they're green. All bananas are green. You just put them in a paper bag and close the bag. They'll ripen more quickly, and you can eat them sooner." Now you have another decision: Is your friend an authority on bananas? Can she be believed, or is she just repeating nonsense? You decide that your friend is believable; and anyway, it would be emotionally awkward to decline her advice. So you decide to take a chance and buy the bananas.

The Power of Smell

Of our five senses, which one do you think has the most power to directly affect our emotions and consequently the choices we make?

It's our sense of smell.

You catch a whiff of freshly baked bread, a new vinyl LP, Play-Doh, or even that strangely pungent floor cleaner the school janitor used, and suddenly you're enveloped in a flood of vivid memories, often from your childhood. More than anything else, smells can trigger memories so strong and real it feels like you've been transported back in time.

It's known as "odor-evoked autobiographical memory" or the Proust phenomenon, after French writer Marcel Proust. In his novel *In Search of Lost Time* (previously also translated as *Remembrance of Things Past*), the narrator dips a madeleine cookie into a cup of tea and is transported back in time as long-forgotten memories of his childhood come flooding back.

Why does this happen? It's because our olfactory nerves are "hot-wired" directly to the brain. Incoming smells are first captured by the olfactory receptor neurons in the upper part of the nose, which generate an impulse that is passed to the brain along the olfactory nerve to the olfactory bulb. It processes the signal before passing information about the smell to other areas closely connected to it, collectively known as the limbic system. Located just beneath the cerebrum on both sides of the thalamus, the primary structures within the limbic system include the amygdala, hippocampus, thalamus, hypothalamus, basal ganglia, and cingulate gyrus. It has also been referred to as the paleomammalian cortex.

The limbic system is responsible for not only our emotional

lives but also many higher mental functions, such as learning and forming memories. The amygdala is the emotion center of the brain, while the hippocampus is essential in the formation of new memories about past experiences. It is often regarded as being the old, or primitive, part of the brain because these same structures were present within the brains of the very first mammals (*Image 1*).

In contrast, visual, auditory, and tactile information does not pass directly through these brain areas. For example, visual information follows a much more complicated path. Data from the retina is relayed through the lateral geniculate nucleus of the thalamus to the primary visual cortex, located in the occipital lobe in the back of the brain. The primary visual cortex is densely packed with cells in many layers, which respond to different types of visual information; for example, different cells respond to edges at different angles or edges moving in a particular direction. Although the visual processing mechanisms are not yet completely understood, recent findings suggest that visual signals are fed into at least three separate processing systems.

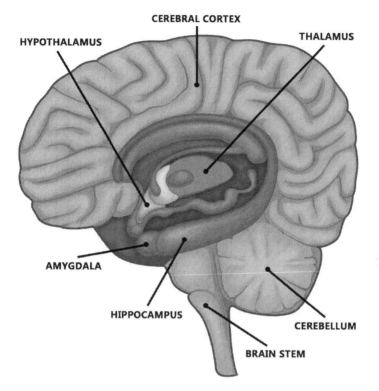

Image 1. *The Limbic System*

One system appears to process information mainly about shape; a second, mainly about color; and a third, movement, location, and spatial organization. All these systems work together to produce the vivid images of solid objects that we perceive. Meanwhile, the brain extracts biologically relevant information at each stage and associates firing patterns of neuronal populations with past experience.

That's a lot of information processing! This may be why olfaction, more than any other sense, is so successful at triggering emotions and memories, and why smells trigger more vivid emotional memories and are better at inducing that feeling of "being brought back in time" than images. They can also influence the decisions we make with our brains. Smells have the power to drive our behavior on an instinctive and subconscious level. Smell is often the first warning of safety or danger, friend or foe. Smells can be used to affect your buying decisions. One study in Sweden sought to determine whether consumers became more focused on advertising signs when exposed to different scents.

The researchers recruited one hundred people on Kungsgata Street in Stockholm and equipped them with special eye-tracking glasses. This enabled the researchers to see exactly what caught their eyes. The participants were unaware that some were exposed to a vaporizer that pumped out the smell of chocolate chip cookies as they strolled past a Stockholm café.

Analyses of data from the eyeglasses showed what the participants looked at and for how long. Sure enough, participants who were exposed to the smell were 50% more aware of the café signs than those who hadn't been exposed to the enticing smell. Their inclination to buy something at the café rose 40% compared with the control group who were not exposed to the scent. "Café-related scents drew attention to the café and increased recollections of the sight," said Poja Shams, one of the researchers. "This in turn raises the intention to buy."

Is this a bad thing? Maybe, maybe not, but it's certainly valuable to know that as you Train Your Brain for Success and build your Three Pillars of Life, the choices you make are under constant pressure—from your own memories and expectations as well as from savvy marketers who know how to subconsciously influence your choices.

Summary

- Not only is your brain the center of your ability to make decisions but it's also the center of your emotions, which can be very powerful and exert tremendous influence on the choices you make. This is why it's important to Train Your Brain for Success by having a well-developed *emotional intelligence* (EQ).

- The term first appeared in a 1964 paper by Michael Beldoch and subsequently gained popularity in the 1995 book *Emotional Intelligence* written by the author, psychologist, and science journalist Daniel Goleman. It refers to the capability of individuals to recognize their own and other people's emotions, discern between different feelings and label them appropriately, use emotional information to guide thinking and behavior, and manage their emotions to adapt to environments or achieve a goal.

- A key element of emotional intelligence is *empathy*. This is the ability of primates to experience and understand a peer's condition from their perspective. You place yourself in their shoes and feel what they are feeling. Being empathetic does not mean being a doormat; on the contrary, research has found that people who are empathetic often achieve extraordinary results across a wide range of industries.

- The extent to which we truly know ourselves is tested—even assaulted—every day, particularly by marketers who want to sell us something and whose first job is to convince us that we need what they're selling. They're very good at it, and as you build your Three Pillars of Life it will often take a great deal of self-confidence to say, "I don't need what you're selling!"

- The world is perceptible to us through our five senses: sight, hearing, touch, smell, and taste. Our sense receptors—eyes, ears, skin, nose, tongue, as well as the millions of nerves inside our body—are constantly receiving information and passing it along to the brain, where it's processed and evaluated. Every decision we make is weighed against the data distilled from our current and previous sensory input. Let's say you hear the sound of heavy metal music coming from a car on your street. The sound may provoke you to run outside and join the fun, or it may provoke you to call the police—it all depends on your brain's prior association with heavy metal.

- Of our five senses, our sense of smell has the most power to directly affect our emotions and consequently the choices we make. It's known as "odor-evoked autobiographical memory" or the Proust phenomenon, after French writer Marcel Proust. In his novel *In Search of Lost Time,* the narrator dips a madeleine cookie into a cup of tea and is transported back in time as long-forgotten memories of his childhood come flooding back. There's a scientific reason for this. It's because our olfactory nerves are "hot-wired" directly to the brain. Information about incoming smells is sent directly to the limbic system, which is not only responsible for our emotional lives but also many higher mental functions, such as learning and formation of memories.

4. Know Your Personality

Everybody says such things as, "I like Jim. He's got a great personality."

Or, "I wish my personality were more outgoing. I'm too shy."

Or, "She's got a really abrasive personality."

We talk a lot about personality—but what does it mean?

The word "personality" itself stems from the Latin word "*persona*," which referred to a theatrical mask worn by performers to either project different roles or disguise their identities. Today, personality is commonly defined as a set of individual differences that are affected by the development of an individual: values, attitudes, personal memories, social relationships, habits, and skills. There are many more definitions; for example, Jess Feist, Gregory J. Feist, and Tomi-Ann Roberts say in their book *Theories of Personality*, "Although no single definition is acceptable to all personality theorists, we can say that personality is a pattern of relatively permanent traits and unique characteristics that give both consistency and individuality to a person's behavior."

Since the dawn of history, natural philosophers have observed and theorized about human personality. Analysis of individual differences started with the ancient Greek physicians Hippocrates and Galen. The concept of the four humors held that a person's temperament was based on the balance of bodily humors: yellow bile, black bile, phlegm, and blood. Choleric people were characterized as having an excess of yellow bile, making them irascible. High levels of black bile were believed to induce melancholy, signified by a somber, gloomy, pessimistic outlook. Phlegmatic people were thought to have an excess of phlegm, leading to their sluggish, calm temperaments. Finally, people thought to have high levels of blood were said to be sanguine and were characterized by their cheerful, passionate dispositions.

The interaction of the four humors explained differences of gender, emotions, age, and disposition. The influence of the humors changed with the seasons and times of day and with the human life span. Heat stimulated action, while cold depressed it.

In the absence of scientific evidence, these beliefs persisted well into the modern era. In the *Castel of Helth*, published in 1541 by Tudor humanist Thomas Elyot, sickness is described as an imbalance—or distemperature—in the quantity or quality of one of the four bodily humors. In his 1639 book *Optick Glasse of Humors*, University of Cambridge cleric Thomas Walkington promised greater self-knowledge through understanding the role of the four bodily humors in determining individual human behaviors and overall disposition. "Temperament"—what we would call personality—was literally a matter of bodily temperature, the result of the action of cold, hot, wet, and dry in governing behavior.

Fast-forward to today. Thanks to scientific methodologies, we have more effective tools to reveal and classify the basic types of human personality, and develop a greater and more accurate level of self-awareness. This can lead us to make better decisions and bring us closer to the Three Pillars of Life.

The Lexical Hypothesis and the Big Five Personality Traits

Nearly every personality test relies upon language and specifically the use of words to identify or describe various personality traits. This idea was first explored in 1884 by Sir Francis Galton in his book *Measurement of Character*. His approach was both simple and laborious, as he wrote: "I tried to gain an idea of the number of the more conspicuous aspects of the character by counting in an appropriate dictionary the words used to express them." The concept slowly developed over the next century. In 1936, Harvard University researchers Gordon Allport and Henry S. Odbert used *Webster's New International Dictionary* as their source. From the dictionary's list of approximately 400,000 words, Allport and Odbert identified 17,953 unique terms used to describe personality or behavior.

Despite some variation in its definition and application, the lexical hypothesis is generally defined by two postulates. The first states that those personality characteristics that are most important in people's lives will eventually become part of their language. The second follows from the first, stating that more important personality characteristics are more likely to be encoded into language as a single word.

The Big Five personality traits, also known as the five-factor model (FFM), is a model based on common language descriptors of personality. When the statistical technique of factor analysis is applied to personality survey data, some words used to describe aspects of personality more often appear to be associated with the same person. For example, someone described as "generous" is more likely to also be described as "empathetic" rather than "uncaring."

The five factors—which are really just five collections of

associated words that we believe correspond to personality traits—are these:

Openness to experience (inventive/curious vs. consistent/ cautious). Openness reflects a person's degree of creativity, intellectual curiosity, and preference for fresh ideas. It may be reflected in an appreciation for adventure, curiosity, the arts, emotion, and variety of experiences. It is also described as the extent to which a person is imaginative or independent and depicts a personal preference for a variety of activities over a strict routine.

Since every positive trait has a negative flip side, high openness can also be perceived as shallowness, unpredictability, or lack of focus. Those with low openness seek to gain fulfillment through perseverance and are characterized as pragmatic and data-driven but can also be perceived as dogmatic and close-minded.

Conscientiousness (efficient/organized vs. easygoing/careless). This is a tendency to show self-discipline, aim for achievement, be dependable and organized, act dutifully, and prefer planned rather than spontaneous behavior. High conscientiousness is often perceived as stubbornness and obsession.

While low conscientiousness is associated with flexibility and spontaneity, it can also appear as sloppiness, poor focus, and lack of reliability.

Extraversion (outgoing/energetic vs. solitary/reserved). This is characterized by positive emotions, sociability, personal energy, assertiveness, talkativeness, and the tendency to seek stimulation in the company of others. High extraversion is often perceived as attention seeking and domineering.

Low extraversion causes a reserved, reflective personality, which can be perceived as unconcerned, aloof, or self-absorbed.

Agreeableness (friendly/compassionate vs. challenging/detached). This is a tendency to be cooperative and compassionate toward others rather than suspicious and antagonistic. It is also a measure of one's helpful and trusting nature, and whether a person is generally well tempered or easily irritated.

On the negative side, high agreeableness can be seen as naiveté or submissiveness. Someone who is persistently agreeable is easily manipulated.

Low agreeableness personalities are often challenging or competitive people, which can be seen as being argumentative or untrustworthy.

Neuroticism (Sensitive/nervous vs. secure/confident). This is the tendency to often experience and express negative emotions, such as depression, anxiety, anger, and vulnerability. Neuroticism also refers to the degree of emotional stability and impulse control, and is sometimes referred to by its low pole, "emotional stability." A high need for stability manifests itself as a calm and stable personality, but can also be seen as uninspiring and unconcerned. A low need for stability causes a reactive and unpredictable personality. These are often very dynamic individuals, but they can be perceived as insecure and unstable.

People who don't exhibit a clear tendency toward one of these Big Five are considered moderate, adaptable, and reasonable personalities—but the opposite is that they can be perceived as inscrutable, unprincipled, and calculating.

Here are some of the most widely used personality tests. If you take them in the right spirit—as being quick snapshots of a moment in time rather than any kind of in-depth long-term analysis—they can serve as useful tools as you Train Your Brain for Success and build your Three Pillars of Life.

The Big Five Personality Test

If you go online, you'll find many sites offering personality tests based on the Big Five. They are generally free because they want your responses for research, or they want to you sign up for paid services.

One site is Truity at www.truity.com. It's free and takes fifteen minutes. I took it, and the test consisted of the usual personality statements ("I like going to art museums") to which you respond by choosing an agree/disagree response on a Likert scale of one to five (such as "disagree strongly" or "neutral/no opinion"). The next section asked many political questions, such as whom I voted for in the 2012 presidential election. This made me think Truity was collecting political data on its respondents. OK, fair enough. The next page asked me if I wanted to create an account to view my results. I clicked "No thanks, I'll just view the results." The next page showed me my results: highest in Openness, with various levels in the other four categories and explanations of what it meant. The page asked me if I wanted to "register now to save your results." I didn't save them and didn't register.

Then I went to the Big Five Personality Test offered by *Psychology Today* at https://www.psychologytoday.com/tests/personality/big-five-personality-test.

It's free, and before you begin they say, "After finishing this test you will receive a FREE snapshot report with a summary evaluation and graph. You will then have the option to purchase the full results for $6.95." Hey, they tell you up front what to expect—can't complain about that. I took the test, which was the same multiple-choice format as the Truity test. It took about two minutes. On the results page, they gave me a partial "teaser" result with this message: "Would you like to learn more about the different traits that make up your personality? Curious as to what makes you who you are? The full test report shows your scores and interpretation for 5 personality factors as well as helpful advice on how to reach your full potential." To obtain the full report would cost me $6.95.

That's what it's all about: from you they want either data or money or both.

The Myers–Briggs Type Indicator (MBTI)

Constructed by Katharine Cook Briggs and her daughter, Isabel Briggs Myers, in 1944, the Myers-Briggs Type Indicator is an introspective self-report questionnaire that aims to indicate psychological preferences in how people perceive the world around them and make decisions.

The MBTI is based on the typological theory proposed by Carl Jung, who had speculated that humans experience the world through four principal psychological functions: sensation, intuition, feeling, and thinking. They are grouped in pairs: The two *perceiving* functions are sensation (usually called sensing in MBTI writings) and intuition. The two *judging* functions are thinking and feeling.

According to Jung's typology model, each person uses one of these four functions more dominantly and proficiently than the other three; however, all four functions are used at different times depending on the circumstances.

If you recall the example of the spider, your response is a combination of perceiving ("It's a spider!") and judging (either "It's an awful thing that needs to be killed!" or "Poor little creature—he needs to be outside where he belongs.").

Jung's typology theories further postulated that each of the four cognitive functions has one of two polar orientations "extraversion" or "introversion," giving a total of eight dominant functions. The MBTI is based on these eight hypothetical functions.

The Jungian notions of extraversion and introversion are a bit different from what most people think as "extroverted" and "introverted." Extraversion means literally "outward turning" and introversion, "inward turning." The preferences for extraversion and introversion are often called "attitudes." People who prefer extraversion draw energy from initial action: they tend to act, then reflect, then act further. Conversely, those who prefer introversion prefer to reflect, then act, then reflect again. To rebuild their energy, introverts need quiet time alone away from activity.

Back to the spider, the extraverted person might perceive the spider and immediately take action (kill it or throw it outside), while the introverted person might pause and think, "What's that spider doing in here? Is it posing a danger to me? How did it get inside? Is it better to squish it or capture it?"

As the MyersBriggs.org website says, "The essence of the theory is that much seemingly random variation in behavior is actually quite orderly and consistent, being due to basic differences in the ways individuals prefer to use their perception and judgment. Perception involves all the ways of becoming aware of things, people, happenings, or ideas. Judgment involves all the ways of coming to conclusions about what has been perceived. If people differ systematically in what they perceive and in how they reach conclusions, then it is only reasonable for them to differ correspondingly in their interests, reactions, values, motivations, and skills."

In other words, if you perceive spiders to be ugly, nasty creatures, your judgment of them will carry over into related areas. For example, you may not be as sympathetic to concerns about the environment and the effects of insecticides. You may not be comfortable going on a camping trip to the Amazon, where you might encounter really humongous spiders. You may not want to take a job caring for insect displays at the local zoo.

The Myers-Briggs testing process leads to your being assigned to one of sixteen personality types on the MB "type table." Eight are introverted types, and eight are extraverted types.

For example, the ISTJ (introversion + sensing + thinking + judging) type is described thusly:

"Quiet, serious, earn success by thoroughness and dependability. Practical, matter-of-fact, realistic, and responsible. Decide logically what should be done and work toward it steadily, regardless of distractions. Take pleasure in making everything orderly and organized—their work, their home, their life. Value traditions and loyalty."

In contrast, here's the ENTJ (extraversion + intuition + thinking + judging) type:

"Frank, decisive, assume leadership readily. Quickly see illogical and inefficient procedures and policies, develop and implement comprehensive systems to solve organizational problems. Enjoy long-term planning and goal setting. Usually well informed, well read, enjoy expanding their knowledge and passing it on to others. Forceful in presenting their ideas."

The goal is that you can use the results to make informed decisions in various aspects of your life and help you build your Three Pillars of Life. These include:

Relationships: While there's no correlation between your type and a successful relationship with another—any two types can be attracted to each other—type differences in relationships can be a source of either growth or conflict. If you're experiencing a conflict, understanding and applying type theory to your relationship can enhance communication and provide you and your partner with a better understanding of how you deal with conflict.

Spirituality: Because people of different types are drawn to various spiritual practices and have various ways of expressing their understanding of spirituality, you may find your type provides a way of understanding your spiritual path and development. If you tend toward introversion, for example, you might be more drawn to solitary or reflective practices, while if you're drawn to extraversion you might be more attracted to group or active spiritual practices.

Careers and the workplace: Research has revealed that you're more likely to perform well in a career that allows you to make use of your natural type preferences. Your type can also help you develop your leadership capabilities by highlighting areas where you have particular strengths. If you manage employees, the natural diversity in types is healthy and stimulating, but it can also lead to misunderstandings and friction in the workplace. Understanding and applying type to the workplace can result in increased communication, more effective teams, and more satisfied employees and customers.

Education: Your type can reveal how you prefer to learn. For example, if you're naturally extraverted, you may prefer learning situations that allow you to talk with others and become physically engaged with the environment. If you're inclined toward introversion, you may prefer learning environments that allow you to engage in quiet reflection, where you can process your thoughts internally until they are more developed.

The key to exploring your type is to remember that no one type is any "better" than any other. Every type has the same opportunity to build the Three Pillars of Life and find fulfillment and happiness.

Although it is not the official testing website for the Myers-Briggs test, you can get an idea of which of the sixteen personalities you have at www.16personalities.com. It's free and gives you a close representation of your personality type. If you want the full version of the Myers-Briggs test, you can get the assessment done by a certified Myers-Briggs practitioner, which I am one.

HEXACO

Proposed in 2004 by Michael C. Ashton and Kibeom Lee, et al., in their paper "A Six-Factor Structure of Personality-Descriptive Adjectives: Solutions From Psycholexical Studies in Seven

Languages" published in the *Journal of Personality and Social Psychology*, the HEXACO model of personality structure is a six-dimensional model of human personality based on findings from a series of lexical studies involving several European and Asian languages. The six factors, or dimensions, are:

1. Honesty-Humility (H): Persons who score high on the Honesty-Humility scale avoid manipulating others for personal gain, feel no special entitlement to elevated social status, are not interested in lavish wealth and luxuries, and feel little temptation to break rules.

Conversely, persons with very low scores on this scale are motivated by material gain, are inclined to break rules for personal profit, feel an exaggerated sense of self-importance, and will deceive others to get what they want,

2. Emotionality (E): Those who score high on the Emotionality scale feel empathy and sentimental attachments with others, experience anxiety in response to life's stresses, feel a need for emotional support from others, and experience fear of physical dangers. Conversely, those who score low on this scale feel emotionally detached from others, feel little worry even in stressful situations, are not deterred by the prospect of physical harm, and have little need to share their concerns with others.

3. Extraversion (X): Persons with high scores on the Extraversion scale experience positive feelings of enthusiasm and energy, enjoy social gatherings and interactions, feel confident when leading or addressing groups of people, and feel positively about themselves. Conversely, those who score low on this scale feel less lively and optimistic than others do, are indifferent to social activities, and may consider themselves unpopular and feel awkward even when they are the center of social attention.

4. Agreeableness (A): People who score high on the Agreeableness scale can easily control their temper, are willing to compromise and cooperate with others, forgive the wrongs they suffered, and are lenient in judging others. Conversely, those who score low on this scale feel anger readily in response to mistreatment, are stubborn in defending their point of view, are rather critical of others' shortcomings, and hold grudges against those who have harmed them.

5. **Conscientiousness (C):** Those who score high on the Conscientiousness scale think carefully when making decisions, strive for accuracy and perfection in their tasks, work in a disciplined way toward their goals, and organize their time and physical surroundings. Conversely, those who score low on this scale make decisions on impulse or with little reflection, are satisfied with work that contains mistakes, avoid difficult tasks or challenging goals, and tend to be unconcerned with orderly surroundings or schedules.

6. **Openness to Experience (O):** People with a high score on the Openness to Experience scale use their imagination freely in everyday life, take an interest in unusual ideas or people, become absorbed in the beauty of art and nature, and are inquisitive about various domains of knowledge. Conversely, the low scorer on this scale is rather unimpressed by most works of art, feels little intellectual curiosity, avoids creative pursuits, and feels little attraction toward ideas that may seem radical or unconventional.

Together, they comprise the acronym HEXACO.

Each of the six factors is composed of four facets with characteristics indicating high and low levels of the factor:

Honesty-Humility (H): Sincerity, fairness, greed avoidance, modesty

Emotionality (E): Fearfulness, anxiety, dependence, sentimentality

Extraversion (X): Social self-esteem, social boldness, sociability, liveliness

Agreeableness (A): Forgivingness, gentleness, flexibility, patience

Conscientiousness (C): Organization, diligence, perfectionism, prudence

Openness to Experience (O): Aesthetic appreciation, inquisitiveness, creativity, unconventionality

Each of the twenty-four facets has a detailed description. For example, here's the description of the Sincerity scale within the domain of Honesty-Humility:

"The Sincerity scale assesses a tendency to be genuine in interpersonal relations. Low scorers will flatter others or pretend to like them in order to obtain favors, whereas high scorers are unwilling to manipulate others."

This one is for the Unconventionality scale within the domain of Openness to Experience:

"The Unconventionality scale assesses a tendency to accept the unusual. Low scorers avoid eccentric or nonconforming persons, whereas high scorers are receptive to ideas that might seem strange or radical."

You take the HEXACO Personality Inventory-Revised (HEXACO-PI-R) online at hexaco.org. The site says that to complete the inventory, which consists of one hundred questions, you will indicate your agreement or disagreement with various statements of the kind, "I like to watch television" or "I often go for walks." It usually takes about fifteen minutes to complete the inventory itself plus some additional research questions and some (optional) demographic questions about gender, age, and education.

The results computed from your responses will be provided after you have finished. Your responses are then combined with those of many other respondents and used for research that will be published in scientific journals and other sources.

Your participation is completely voluntary, anonymous, and confidential.

After you take the test, you're shown the results. For each of the twenty-five scales, on a bar chart you're shown your score, the median score of everyone else—i.e., "Canadian university students (men and women) who provided self-reports while participating in academic research studies"—and a larger shaded area showing the middle 80% of everyone's scores (10th to 90th percentiles). Basically, you see how you land relative to other people. You can see, for example, if you have more or less "social self esteem" or "inquisitiveness" than the general sample.

Here's the big question: What should you conclude from your results? The HEXACO website says, "Your profile of results is meant to give you some insight into your basic personality dispositions. But you shouldn't overinterpret your results or treat them as a kind of 'prophecy' for your future. If you're disappointed with your score for a certain trait, you can still try to change some of your attitudes and behaviors related to that trait, and you can still find ways to make your level of this trait less of a problem for you (or for others)."

You can take the HEXACO test here: http://hexaco.org/hexaco-online.

The Dark Triad

No, this is not the name of the next installment of the *Star Wars* movie franchise.

The dark triad is a subject in psychology that focuses on three overlapping personality traits:

Narcissism. Characterized by grandiosity, pride, egotism, and a lack of empathy, narcissism is the pursuit of gratification from vanity or egotistic admiration of one's own attributes. It's the tendency to seek admiration and special treatment. The term originated from Greek mythology, where the young Narcissus fell in love with his own image reflected in a pool of water. Narcissism is not the same as egocentrism. A person who is egocentric believes they are or should be the center of attention, but unlike a narcissist does not receive emotional gratification from that attention.

Machiavellianism is characterized by manipulation and exploitation of others, a cynical disregard for morality, and a focus on self-interest and deception. Named after the philosophy espoused by Niccolò Machiavelli in *The Prince*, people who score high on this trait are cynical (in an amoral self-interest sense), unprincipled, believe in interpersonal manipulation as the key for life success, and behave accordingly.

Psychopathy is characterized by continuing antisocial behavior, impulsivity, selfishness, callousness, and remorselessness. Because the psychopath can appear normal, even charming, psychopathy is among the most difficult disorders to spot. Underneath, the person lacks conscience and empathy, making them manipulative, volatile, and often (but by no means always) criminal. Adult psychopathy is largely impervious to treatment, though programs are in place to treat callous, unemotional youth in hopes of preventing them from maturing into psychopaths.

A spectrum disorder, psychopathy can be diagnosed only using the twenty-item Hare Psychopathy Checklist. (The bar for clinical psychopathy is a score of thirty or more.) Brain anatomy, genetics, and a person's environment may all contribute to the development of psychopathic traits.

Research on the dark triad is used in applied psychology, especially within the fields of law enforcement, clinical psychology, and business management. People scoring high on these traits are more likely to commit crimes, cause social distress, and create severe problems for an organization, especially if they are in leadership positions. People who exhibit traits of psychopathy and Machiavellianism can cause you harm, but many narcissists only harm themselves.

While all three dark triad traits are conceptually distinct, empirical evidence shows them to be overlapping. The long-debated "nature versus nurture" issue has been applied to the dark triad, and empirical studies have been conducted in an effort to understand the relative contributions of biology (nature) and environmental factors (nurture) in the development of dark triad traits.

Until recently, the only way to capture the dark triad in the lab was to administer lengthy tests measuring each personality trait separately. With the development of the "Dirty Dozen" scale, however, psychologists Peter Jonason and Gregory Webster (2010) are now making it possible to spot these potentially troublesome traits with a simple twelve-item rating scale.

If you're curious about yourself, here's where you can take a free test: http://personality-testing.info/tests/SD3/

This is an interactive version of the Short Dark Triad, developed in 2011 by Delroy Paulhus and Daniel Jones to provide a more uniform assessment and also to trim down the total length.

The test consists of twenty-seven statements that must be rated on how much you agree or disagree with them. The test should not take most people more than five minutes.

The website advises that your use of this assessment must be strictly for educational purposes. It cannot be taken as psychological advice of any kind. If you are interested in anything more than learning about the dark triad of personality and how it is assessed, do not take this test. Your answers will be recorded and possibly used for research and/or otherwise distributed in an anonymous fashion.

In fact, the Personality Testing website is replete with a wide variety of personality tests that you can take for your own amusement and information (not as a diagnosis!). They include:

Big Five Personality Test: As we saw earlier in this chapter, this measures the "five fundamental personality traits" ("big five"). This test uses public domain scales from the International Personality Item Pool.

Evaluations of Attractiveness Scales—Male / Female: The EMAS and EFAS measure individual differences in preferences for the looks of men and women respectively.

Generic Conspiracist Beliefs Scale: A measure of belief in conspiracy theories.

Multifactor General Knowledge Test: A test of general knowledge measuring four facets of general knowledge.

Musical Preferences Test: Rate clips of music to calculate your preferences for musical styles. Why anyone would need this test is puzzling—for example, if you're a fan of death metal, you don't need to be informed of this fact.

Nonverbal Immediacy Scale: This scale measures individual differences in the use of body language in communication.

Open Extended Jungian Type Scales: A version of the Briggs-Meyers test that weighs sixteen personality types on the basis of four dichotomies.

Right-Wing Authoritarianism Scale: The RWAS scale was developed as part of the study of authoritarian and fascist regimes that became popular after World War II.

Rosenberg Self-esteem Scale: Developed in the 1960s by Morris Rosenberg for a study of adolescent self-image, the RSES has become the most widely used general purpose measure of self-esteem in psychological research.

Woodworth Psychoneurotic Inventory: Often cited as the first personality test, the WPI was developed by the United States military during World War I to screen for recruits at high risk of developing shell shock.

All these tests are provided for educational and entertainment uses only. They are not clinically administered, and as such the results are not suitable as a rationale for important life decisions. These tests are also not infallible, and if the results say something about you that you don't think is true, you are right and they are wrong, but they can be useful as you build your Three Pillars of Life.

The Enneagram Tests

The Enneagram of Personality, or simply the Enneagram (from the Greek words *"ennéa,"* meaning "nine" and *grámma*, meaning something "written" or "drawn"), is a model of the human psyche that is principally understood and taught as a typology of nine interconnected personality types. Although the origins and history of many of the ideas and theories associated with the Enneagram of Personality are a matter of dispute, contemporary Enneagram understandings are principally derived from the teachings of Oscar Ichazo and Claudio Naranjo. Naranjo's theories were partly influenced by the teachings of the early twentieth century Armenian mystic and philosopher G. I. Gurdjieff.

The Riso-Hudson Enneagram Type Indicator is a popular Enneagram-based test that uses 144 paired statements. The test takes about forty minutes to complete. It was developed by the Enneagram Institute, formed in 1997 by Don Richard Riso and Russ Hudson, with the goal to further research and development of the Enneagram, claimed to be a powerful and insightful tool for understanding ourselves and others.

Here are the nine personality types. Remember that each one can either express itself in a positive or a negative way, depending upon the individual. Therefore, for example, the Leader could be either Franklin D. Roosevelt or Adolph Hitler:

One—Reformer: principled, orderly, perfectionist, self-righteous

Two—Helper: caring, generous, possessive, manipulative

Three—Motivator: adaptable, ambitious, image conscious, hostile

Four—Individualist: intuitive, expressive, self-absorbed, depressive

Five—Investigator: perceptive, original, detached, eccentric

Six—Loyalist: engaging, committed, defensive, paranoid

Seven—Enthusiast: enthusiastic, accomplished, uninhibited, manic

Eight—Leader: self-confident, decisive, dominating, combative

Nine—Peacemaker: peaceful, reassuring, complacent, neglectful

These nine "characteristic roles" are each composed of nine attributes, which occur in varying degrees. A person's personality manifestation may change according to the conditions of the moment; for example, someone classed as a Reformer may begin to think, feel, and act more like an Individualist when stressed or an Enthusiast when relaxed.

1. Ego fixation
2. Holy idea
3. Basic fear
4. Basic desire
5. Temptation
6. Vice/Passion
7. Virtue
8. Stress
9. Security

But as the old saying goes, *caveat emptor*: let the buyer beware. The Enneagram has been criticized as being pseudoscience and subject to interpretation, making it difficult to test or validate scientifically, with little demonstrated reliability or validity. The scientific skeptic Robert Todd Carroll wrote in his book *The Skeptic's Dictionary: A Collection of Strange Beliefs, Amusing Deceptions, and Dangerous Delusions* that the Enneagram is an example of a pseudoscientific theory that "can't be tested because they are so vague and malleable that anything relevant can be shoehorned to fit the theory."

As you build your Three Pillars of Life—health, relationships, and wealth—the use of self-administered personality tests can be useful as long as you remember that no matter what a personality test reveals to you about yourself, you need to believe that you are in charge of your personality and the decisions you make! With self-awareness and discipline, you can steer your personality in the direction you want to go.

Here's just one example. I've met many businesspeople who began their careers seeing themselves as introverted and reluctant to do what every business leader must eventually do: give a presentation or a speech in front of an audience. Yet they saw this limiting aspect of their personality and decided to change it, and to embrace the idea of standing up in front of people and giving a presentation. Many have been helped by joining an organization such as Toastmasters International. This global organization has more than 352,000 members who seek to improve their speaking and leadership skills by attending one of the 16,400 clubs in 141 countries that make up its global network of meeting locations. By regularly getting up in front of their peers and giving speeches and gaining feedback, members learn to overcome an undesirable personality trait and help build stronger Pillars of Life.

Similarly, if you have an addiction to alcohol—which can seriously damage your Three Pillars of Life—an organization such as Alcoholics Anonymous, with its structure of peer support, can help you change this negative part of your personality and get you on the road to health and happiness.

Summary

- Each of us has a unique personality. The word "personality" itself stems from the Latin word *"persona,"* which referred to a theatrical mask worn by performers to either project different roles or disguise their identities.

- Nowadays, personality is commonly defined as a set of individual differences that are affected by the development of an individual: values, attitudes, personal memories, social relationships, habits, and skills. Every culture has its own viewpoint on personality; for example, Buddhism teaches that from the ethereal Prakriti spring the three primary *gunas* (qualities): *tamas* (darkness), *rajas* (activity), and *sattva* (beingness). All three are always present in all beings and objects but vary in their relative amounts. Humans have the unique ability to consciously alter the levels of the *gunas* in our bodies and minds, thus molding our personalities.

- One theory of personality is the lexical hypothesis, which is defined by two postulates. The first states that those personality characteristics that are most important in people's lives will eventually become part of their language. The second states that more important personality characteristics are more likely to be encoded into language as a single word.

- The model of the Big Five personality traits, also known as the five-factor model (FFM), is based on common language descriptors of personality. They are:

1. Openness to experience (inventive/curious vs. consistent/cautious)
2. Conscientiousness (efficient/organized vs. easygoing/careless)
3. Extraversion (outgoing/energetic vs. solitary/reserved)

4. Agreeableness (friendly/compassionate vs. challenging/ detached)
5. Neuroticism (sensitive/nervous vs. secure/confident)

- Truly knowing yourself is a powerful key to happiness and success. A great many self-administered personality tests, while not clinically valid, can help you gain insight into your personality type and help you improve any difficult areas. If you go online, you'll find many sites offering personality tests based on the Big Five. They include Truity.com and the test at *Psychology Today*. Other specialized tests include your preferences for musical styles, your tolerance for right-wing authoritarianism, and how much you're inclined to believe in conspiracy theories.

- The Myers-Briggs Type Indicator is an introspective self-report questionnaire that aims to indicate psychological preferences in how people perceive the world around them and make decisions. It's based on the typological theory proposed by Carl Jung, who had speculated that humans experience the world through four principal psychological functions: sensation, intuition, feeling, and thinking. The Myers-Briggs testing process leads to your being assigned to one of sixteen personality types on the MB "type table." Eight are introverted types, while eight are extraverted types.

- The HEXACO model of personality structure is a six-dimensional model of human personality based on findings from a series of lexical studies involving several European and Asian languages. Each of the six factors is composed of four facets with characteristics indicating high and low levels of the factor:

1. Honesty-Humility (H): Sincerity, fairness, greed avoidance, modesty
2. Emotionality (E): Fearfulness, anxiety, dependence, sentimentality
3. Extraversion (X): Social self-esteem, social boldness, sociability, liveliness
4. Agreeableness (A): Forgivingness, gentleness, flexibility, patience
5. Conscientiousness (C): Organization, diligence, perfectionism, prudence
6. Openness to Experience (O): Aesthetic appreciation, inquisitiveness, creativity, unconventionality

You take the HEXACO Personality Inventory-Revised (HEXACO-PI-R) online at hexaco.org. To complete the inventory, which consists of one hundred questions, you'll indicate your agreement or disagreement with various statements, and the results are tallied.

- The Dark Triad is a subject in psychology that focuses on three overlapping destructive personality traits: narcissism, Machiavellianism, and psychopathy. People scoring high on these traits are more likely to commit crimes, cause social distress, and create severe problems for an organization, especially if they are in leadership positions.

5. Your Brain: A Complex Biochemical Machine

I know what you're thinking about self-administered personality tests: "Can't they be manipulated by the subject? Wouldn't a Machiavellian personality seek to portray himself as a trustworthy Boy Scout, thereby subverting the value of the test?"

The answer is "yes," which is why such tests are generally not clinically accepted and useful only for informational purposes or as just one part of a broader, multifaceted approach.

But think about this: Why is a Machiavellian personality the way it is? Or a shy and withdrawn personality? While the brain is incredibly complex, it's not magical, and over the long term doesn't act randomly. That's why the word "personality" has validity. We can say with great assurance that if a human being exhibits certain behaviors and patterns of decision-making today that person will likely exhibit the same behaviors and patterns of decision-making tomorrow, next month, and next year. There is observable consistency.

We also know that external chemical influences can alter behavior. If you give a person heroin and then a week later administer methamphetamine, the differences in his behavior will be obvious and will be the result of the actions of two very different drugs in combination with his existing personality.

Consequently, you'd think it would be valuable to be able to draw conclusions about a person's personality not only from subjective tests but also from objective measurement of the real, physical characteristics that influence how we behave.

If this sounds medieval, maybe it is. As we learned earlier, for centuries natural philosophers theorized that human behavior was governed by the four humors, which produced four personality types: sanguine (enthusiastic, active, and social), choleric (short-tempered, fast, or irritable), melancholic (analytical, wise, and quiet), and phlegmatic (relaxed and peaceful). By making adjustments to these humors (by bleeding, for example) and altering the person's environment by making them hotter, colder, wetter, or dryer, you could bring about a change in personality.

On a much more sophisticated level, the current study of brain biology and chemistry is leading us into a world where we can make conclusions about human behavior based on what we can uncover about a person's individual brain chemistry.

Some of the first credible biology-based personality theories were proposed by Hans Eysenck, a twentieth-century German-born English psychologist who spent his professional career in Great Britain, and Jeffrey Alan Gray, a British psychologist who was a student of Eysenck. Eysenck published a book in 1947 called *Dimensions of Personality*, describing two personality dimensions:

Extraversion. This is the degree to which people are outgoing and interactive with people, mediated by the activation of the reticular formation, which is a set of interconnected nuclei that are located throughout the brain stem. Its dorsal tegmental nuclei are in the midbrain, its central tegmental nuclei are in the pons, and its central and inferior nuclei are found in the medulla. It's responsible for somatic motor control (maintaining tone, balance, and posture; and breathing and swallowing), cardiovascular control, pain modulation, sleep and consciousness, and habituation (the process in which the brain learns to ignore repetitive, meaningless stimuli while remaining sensitive to unexpected stimuli).

Neuroticism. This is the degree of emotional stability and is associated with the limbic system, which is not really a "system" but a set of structures located where the subcortical structures meet the cerebral cortex. The primary structures within the limbic system include the amygdala, hippocampus, thalamus, hypothalamus, basal ganglia, and cingulate gyrus. These structures are involved in motivation, emotion, learning, and memory. It is highly interconnected with the nucleus accumbens, which is important in sexual arousal and the "high" derived from certain recreational drugs.

It is common practice in personality psychology to refer to the dimensions by the first letters, E and N. They provide a two-dimensional space to describe individual personality, much like latitude and longitude describe a point on the face of the earth. Eysenck noted how these two dimensions are similar to the four personality types first proposed by the Greek physician Hippocrates.

High N and high E = Choleric

High N and low E = Melancholic

Low N and high E = Sanguine

Low N and low E = Phlegmatic

Does this ancient method of classification look familiar? It should!

A third dimension, psychoticism (the degree of aggression and interpersonal hostility), was added to the model in the late 1970s, based upon collaboration between Eysenck and his wife, Sybil B. G. Eysenck.

Eysenck's student, Jeffrey Alan Gray, studied personality traits as individual differences in sensitivity to rewarding and punishing stimuli. He developed the Biopsychological Theory of Personality, a comprehensive alternative theoretical interpretation derived from the biological and psychological data studied by Eysenck that leaned more heavily on animal and learning models.

He hypothesized two systems controlling behavioral activity based on the hypothesis that there are two basic human and animal motivations: *Avoiding* punishment and negative experiences, and its opposite, *approaching and obtaining* rewarding experiences:

The behavioral inhibition system (BIS). This is a neuropsychological system that predicts an individual's response to anxiety-relevant cues in a given environment. It includes brain regions involved in regulating arousal: the brain stem and neocortical projections to the frontal lobe. BIS is responsive to punishment, novelty, uncertainty, and non-rewarding stimuli. It regulates avoidance behaviors and is often referred to as the punishment system. It's activated in times of punishment, boredom, or negative events. By responding to such cues as negative stimuli or events that involve punishment or frustration, this system ultimately results in avoidance of such negative and unpleasant events. Individuals with more active BIS may be vulnerable to negative emotions, including frustration, anxiety, fear, and sadness.

The periaqueductal grey, medial hypothalamus, amygdala, septo-hippocampal system, posterior cingulated, and prefrontal dorsal stream are believed to underpin this system.

The behavioral activation system (BAS). In contrast, this is based on a model of appetitive motivation and an individual's disposition to pursue and achieve goals. The BAS includes brain regions involved in regulating arousal, including the cerebral cortex, thalamus, and striatum. The system is responsive to conditioned and unconditioned reward cues, and is referred to as the reward system. The BAS is aroused when it receives cues corresponding to rewards, controls, and actions that regulate behaviors of approachment rather than avoidance. This system has an association with hope or expectation of a positive outcome. The BAS is sensitive to conditioned appealing stimuli and is associated with impulsivity. In general, individuals with a more active BAS tend to be more impulsive and may have difficulty inhibiting their behavior when approaching a goal.

Dopaminergic fibers ascending from both the substantia nigra and ventral tegmental area to innervate the basal ganglia, together with motor, sensorimotor, and prefrontal cortices, are assumed to underpin this system.

In 2000, Gray amended the Biopsychological Theory of Personality into the Reinforcement Sensitivity Theory (RST), based on the idea that there are *three* brain systems, each having its own way of responding to reward and punishment stimuli. To the behavioral inhibition system (BIS) and behavioral approach system (BAS), he added:

Fight-flight-freeze system (FFFS). This mediates the emotion of fear (not anxiety) and active avoidance of dangerous situations. The personality traits associated with this system are fear-proneness and avoidance. The periaqueductal grey, medial hypothalamus, amygdala, anterior cingulate, and prefrontal ventral stream are purported to underpin this system.

Phineas P. Gage

No discussion of the biological roots of human personality would be complete without mentioning the amazing story of Phineas P. Gage.

On September 13, 1848, Phineas P. Gage, then twenty-five

years of age, was directing a work gang blasting rock while preparing the roadbed for the Rutland & Burlington Railroad south of the town of Cavendish, Vermont. Setting a blast entailed boring a hole deep into an outcropping of rock, adding blasting powder and a fuse, and then using a three-foot iron rod called a tamping iron to pack ("tamp") sand into the hole above the powder. As Gage was tamping, the powder exploded, driving the iron rod upward, like a javelin. It entered the left side of Gage's face in an upward direction, just forward of the angle of the lower jaw. Continuing upward outside the upper jaw and possibly fracturing the cheekbone, it passed behind the left eye, through the left side of the brain, and out the top of the skull through the frontal bone. The rod damaged much of his left frontal lobe and possibly the right as well.

Gage, still very much alive, walked to an oxcart for the ride to town. Thirty minutes later a doctor named Edward H. Williams examined Gage. He wrote:

"When I drove up he [Gage] said, 'Doctor, here is business enough for you.' I first noticed the wound upon the head before I alighted from my carriage, the pulsations of the brain being very distinct. The top of the head appeared somewhat like an inverted funnel, as if some wedge-shaped body had passed from below upward. Mr. Gage, during the time I was examining this wound, was relating the manner in which he was injured to the bystanders. I did not believe Mr. Gage's statement at that time, but thought he was deceived. Mr. Gage persisted in saying that the bar went through his head. Mr. G. got up and vomited; the effort of vomiting pressed out about half a teacupful of the brain, which fell upon the floor."

By some miracle, Phineas P. Gage recovered and even held a few jobs before he died of an epileptic seizure at the age of thirty-six. Aside from the fact that he survived, physicians at the time took great interest in the fact that his personality changed. His hometown doctor, John Martyn Harlow, who was in charge of his treatment (such as it was in those days), wrote in 1869:

"The equilibrium or balance, so to speak, between his intellectual faculties and animal propensities, seems to have been destroyed. He is fitful, irreverent, indulging at times in the grossest profanity (which was not previously his custom), manifesting but little deference for his fellows, impatient of restraint or advice when it conflicts with his desires, at times pertinaciously obstinate, yet capricious and vacillating, devising many plans of future operations, which are no sooner arranged than they are abandoned in turn for others appearing more feasible. A child in his intellectual capacity and manifestations, he has the animal passions of a strong man. Previous to his injury, although untrained in the schools, he possessed a well-balanced mind, and was looked upon by those who knew him as a shrewd, smart business man, very energetic and persistent in executing all his plans of operation. In this regard his mind was radically changed, so decidedly that his friends and acquaintances said he was 'no longer Gage.'"

While it's true that much myth and supposition have grown up around the story of Phineas P. Gage, his was the first and certainly the most important case in modern history to reveal that some aspects of behavior and personality can be associated with specific regions of the brain. Despite the fog of legend, his story showed us that complex functions, such as decision-making and social cognition, are largely dependent upon the frontal lobes.

There are several contemporary versions of the Phineas P. Gage story.

In 1987, at the age of fourteen, Ahad Israfil, of Dayton, Ohio, was shot in the head at work when his employer allegedly knocked a firearm to the floor. The shotgun blast destroyed most of his right cerebral hemisphere. He was rushed to the hospital, and after a five-hour operation, doctors were amazed when he attempted to speak.

Surgeons used a silicon implant to fill the gaping hole in his skull where the brain had been and stretched his scalp over his new skull. Incredibly, not only did Ahad Israfil retain sufficient mental faculties to speak, walk, and live a normal life, but he also managed to earn his college degree.

Hemispherectomy

The story of Phineas P. Gage leads directly to another fascinating question: "Just how much of your brain can you lose and still be alive and functioning as a normal human being?"

The answer: More than you might imagine.

A hemispherectomy is a very rare neurosurgical procedure in which one cerebral hemisphere (half of the brain) is removed, disconnected, or disabled. This procedure is used to treat a variety of seizure disorders where the source of the epilepsy is localized to a broad area of a single hemisphere of the brain, notably Rasmussen's encephalitis.

The first hemispherectomy was performed on a dog in 1888 by German physiologist Friedrich Goltz. The first one on a human being was done by American neurosurgeon Walter Dandy in 1928 to treat glioblastoma multiforme, a form of brain cancer. In the 1980s, neurologist John M. Freeman and neurosurgeon Ben Carson (yes, that Dr. Ben Carson!) at Johns Hopkins Hospital revitalized hemispherectomy as a treatment for severely epileptic children. The goal was to reduce or eliminate epileptic seizures while providing hope for a normal life. The procedure is almost exclusively performed in children because their brains are capable of a high level of neuroplasticity, whereby neurons from the remaining hemisphere take over the tasks from the lost hemisphere. This likely occurs by strengthening neural connections that already exist on the unaffected side but which would have otherwise remained undeveloped in a normally functioning, uninjured brain. In one study of children under five who had this surgery to treat catastrophic epilepsy, 73.7% were freed of all seizures.

But the brain is a very complex and subtle instrument. While it's true that some people can sustain massive injuries to the brain—and even have portions removed—it's also true that relatively tiny anomalies or injuries can be highly injurious or even fatal.

Strokes

For example, consider a problem that's unfortunately all too common—stroke. In the previous discussions of massive brain injuries or partial brain removal, a common thread was that the blood flow to the remaining healthy brain was not interrupted, and the remaining healthy brain kept on functioning at an acceptable level. Recall that when the iron rod plunged through the head of Phineas P. Gage and destroyed part of his brain he never lost consciousness. After the accident, he was dazed and confused but conscious and able to walk and talk. We can conclude that by some miracle the blood flow to the undamaged portion of his brain was unimpaired. The doctor reported Gage didn't bleed very much, indicating the major arteries that supply blood to the brain were not punctured.

At any given time, the brain receives about 25% of the body's circulating oxygen, but it's used immediately and cannot be stored. To stay healthy and function properly, brain cells require a constant supply of oxygen. The brain is very sensitive to its vital supply of oxygen—for example, when you stand up too quickly and become dizzy, it's a symptom of a slight decrease of blood flow to the brain that can be sensed. Jet fighter pilots will lose consciousness if they're subjected to high G-forces, and they're trained to recognize the signs of oxygen deprivation to the brain, which include tunnel vision, loss of color vision, and "sparkly" peripheral vision. If they do black out, consciousness and vision return before motor control (remember, this is while they're flying a plane at 300 mph). Even once the pilot is able to move again, there's often a buildup in commands to the limbs that cascade together, causing the pilot to flail around for a second or two, which pilots call the "funky chicken."

By the way, the brain cannot store glucose (blood sugar) either—it needs a steady supply from the blood. Diabetics who give themselves too much insulin can drop their blood sugar level and faint, and without immediate glucose infusion the brain can die.

From the moment your heart starts beating in the womb (about seven weeks after conception) until the day you die (hopefully eighty or more years later), blood, which carries vital oxygen and glucose, must be supplied continuously to the brain. It must continue while you're asleep and if you're rendered unconscious. Life-giving blood is delivered to the brain through two main arterial systems:

The carotid arteries come up through either side of the front of the neck. (To feel the pulse of a carotid artery, place your fingertips gently against either side of your neck, right under the jaw.)

The basilar artery forms at the base of the skull from the vertebral arteries, which run up along the spine, join, and come up through the rear of the neck.

The restriction or loss of blood flow to the brain is a serious problem—potentially much more serious than the removal of part of the brain. A stroke can be caused by either a clot obstructing the flow of blood to the brain (called an ischemic stroke) or a blood vessel rupturing and preventing blood flow to the brain (called a hemorrhagic stroke).

Ischemic stroke occurs when a blood vessel carrying blood to the brain is blocked by a blood clot. This causes blood to not reach the brain. High blood pressure is the most important risk factor for this type of stroke. Ischemic strokes account for about 87% of all strokes.

An ischemic stroke can occur in two ways.

In an embolic stroke, a blood clot or plaque fragment forms somewhere in the body (usually the heart) and travels to the brain. Once in the brain, the clot travels to a blood vessel small enough to block its passage. The clot lodges there, blocking the blood vessel and depriving the downstream brain cells of oxygen.

A thrombotic stroke is caused by a blood clot that forms inside one of the arteries supplying blood to the brain. This type of stroke is usually seen in people with high cholesterol levels and atherosclerosis. The medical word for a clot that forms on a blood vessel deposit is thrombus.

The source of many clots that break free, as well as the constriction of blood flow in an artery, is plaque. It accumulates on the inner walls of your arteries and is made from various substances that circulate in your blood that include calcium, fat, cholesterol, cellular waste, and fibrin, a material involved in blood clotting. In response to plaque buildup, cells in your artery walls multiply and secrete additional substances that can worsen the state of clogged arteries.

The buildup of plaque in the internal carotid artery may lead to narrowing and irregularity of the artery's lumen, preventing proper blood flow to the brain. More commonly, as the narrowing worsens, pieces of plaque in the internal carotid artery can break free, travel to the brain, and block blood vessels that supply blood to the brain. This leads to stroke, with possible paralysis or other deficits.

A transient ischemic attack (TIA, or "mini stroke") is caused by a temporary clot. When that happens, part of the brain cannot get the blood and oxygen it needs, so brain cells quickly die.

Lacunar strokes, or lacunar infarcts, are a series of very tiny ischemic strokes. The symptoms are clumsiness, weakness, and emotional variability. They make up the majority of silent brain infarctions and are probably a result of chronic high blood pressure. They are actually a subtype of thrombotic stroke. They can also sometimes serve as warning signs for a major stroke.

To reduce your chances of having an ischemic stroke—and disrupting your efforts to build your Three Pillars of Life—make sure you control your weight, get plenty of exercise, don't smoke, and eat a healthy diet, all of which can reduce the buildup of dangerous plaque in your arteries.

Hemorrhagic strokes are less common but more serious; while only 15% of all strokes are hemorrhagic, they are responsible for about 40% of all stroke deaths. A hemorrhagic stroke is either a brain aneurysm burst or a weakened blood vessel leak. Blood spills into or around the brain and creates swelling and pressure, damaging cells and tissue in the brain.

There are two types of hemorrhagic stroke: intracerebal and subarachnoid.

Intracerebral is the most common and occurs when a blood vessel inside the brain bursts and leaks blood into surrounding brain tissue (intracerebal hemorrhage). The bleeding causes brain cells to die, and the affected part of the brain stops functioning properly. High blood pressure and aging blood vessels are the most common causes of this type of stroke.

Subarachnoid strokes involve bleeding in the area between the brain and the tissue covering the brain, known as the subarachnoid space. This type of stroke is most often caused by a burst aneurysm.

Learn the FAST Protocol

Stroke victims who are suffering from a diminished blood flow to all or part of the brain exhibit three classic symptoms that everyone should learn and be able to recognize: facial drooping, arm weakness, and speech difficulties. These, plus the fourth action item, time, form FAST, the acronym used as a mnemonic to help detect and enhance responsiveness to stroke victim needs. The acronym stands for:

Facial drooping: A section of the face, usually only on one side, that is drooping and unresponsive. This can be recognized by a crooked smile.

Arm weakness: The inability to raise one's arm fully.

Speech difficulties: An inability or difficulty to understand or produce speech.

Time: If any of the symptoms above are showing, time is of the essence; call emergency services or go to the hospital.

If you or a loved one shows these symptoms, the chance for a cure is very good—but you must act quickly. A clot-busting medication called tissue plasminogen activator (tPa) can be given to someone if they're having a stroke, potentially reversing or stopping symptoms from developing, but it has to be given within three hours of the start of symptoms.

The first thing you should do is call 911 and tell the dispatcher you think the person is having a stroke. After calling 911, write down what time they began showing symptoms of a stroke. This information will help emergency responders and the doctors determine appropriate treatment once the person arrives at a hospital or stroke center.

If the victim is conscious, don't encourage them to stand; lay them down on their side with their head slightly raised and supported.

Stroke victims sometimes feel sleepy and may express a desire to take a nap rather than call 911. Don't fall for this—call 911 right away.

Do not give them anything to eat or drink. Loosen any restrictive clothing that could cause breathing difficulties. If weakness is obvious in any limb, support it and avoid pulling on it when moving the person.

If they are unconscious, check their breathing and pulse, and put them on their side. If they do not have a pulse or are not breathing, start CPR straight away.

If you are unsure how to perform CPR, the ambulance call taker will give instructions over the phone. Better yet, go online and Google "how to perform CPR." You never know when you'll be called upon to save someone's life!

Years ago, strokes were difficult to treat and often resulted in death or long-term disability. Today, with prompt medical attention, having a stroke might be nothing more than a minor detour on your way to building your Three Pillars of Life—but you have to recognize the symptoms and act quickly!

Total Blood Stoppage

If the brain's blood supply suddenly stops, as in the case of sudden cardiac arrest, which completely stops all heart function and the victim stops breathing, then, without oxygen, irreversible brain damage starts to occur within three to five minutes.

After the heart stops or blood flow is totally cut off (as if someone is being strangled), the brain can survive for up to about six minutes; but without cardiopulmonary resuscitation (CPR), the brain then begins to die. CPR artificially pumps blood into the head, which can prolong brain life. That's why everyone should know CPR because you never know when you might have to use it.

Prompt resuscitation allows the physician time to assess and treat the damaged brain. Medication and mechanical ventilation permit tissue oxygenation, but severe brain damage or a prolonged period without oxygen or glucose will cause the brain to die.

By definition, "brain death" is when the entire brain, including the brain stem, has irreversibly lost all function. The legal time of death is that time when a physician has determined that the brain and the brain stem have irreversibly lost all neurological function.

But there are amazing exceptions to the six-minute rule. Most of them involve children drowning in cold water who are then successfully resuscitated.

As the *Seattle Times* reported in August 2011, twelve-year-old Charles "Dale" Ostrander fell into the Pacific Ocean near Long Beach. The water temperature was about fifty-six degrees. After being submerged for twenty-five minutes, he was pulled from the water, seemingly lifeless. After more than ten minutes of resuscitation efforts, his heart started beating. "His age protected him, significantly," said Dr. Michael Copass, medical director of the Seattle Medic One program, which provides emergency medical care in Seattle and King Counties. "And cold water protected him." In cold water, the body's metabolism slows, and the organs need less oxygen. It's called the diving reflex and has been studied in mammals, such as seals.

For reasons not well understood, children seem to have a greater ability than adults to survive nearly drowning in cold water. Scientists think it's akin to hibernation. Another factor that works in favor of children is their smaller body mass, which means an immersed child cools down faster than an adult.

Medical studies include cases of people surviving for forty-five minutes or more in cold water. The colder the water, in some cases, the greater the survivability. A number of studies have shown that hypothermia—reduced body temperature—is highly protective of the brain when it is starved for oxygen and blood flow. In the case of Dale Ostrander, the water that bathed him was certainly quite cold, and it's likely that his core body temperature dropped during his cardiac arrest event.

In fact, neurosurgeons are discovering that cooling parts

of the brain during brain surgery provides information about which areas of the brain are associated with speech and allows surgeons to do a better job of "mapping" the brain before, for example, removing a tumor. As reported in February 2016 in the journal *Neuron*, researchers have developed a technique for protecting brain function in conscious patients in the preliminary stage of neurosurgery by cooling small, localized brain regions to temporarily interrupt their workings and then map the areas required for word formation and the timing of speech. Developed by Michael Long of New York University's Langone Medical Center and his colleagues, researchers used a special device to cool, to about 10°C (50°F) each, selected brain regions that are implicated in speech production. Meanwhile, the fully conscious patients were asked to recite the days of the week or a simple string of numbers so that their speech function could be assessed while each region was cooled.

Cooling slows cellular activity, and in some cases the researchers found that it interfered with the patients' ability to speak, slowing and blurring their speech. But this effect was only temporary, and brain function returned to normal immediately after the cooling device was removed from the brain. "This study confirms that cooling is a safe and effective means of protecting important brain centers during neurosurgery," said Long. "It also represents a major advance in the understanding of the roles played by the areas of the brain that enable us to form words."

These examples—of brains being disabled by tiny clots that block blow flow as well as amazing cases of brain activity being restored after dramatic cooling—point to the incredible complexity of the brain and that it's both quite fragile and at the same time remarkably resilient. Later in the book, we'll take a closer look at the brain's amazing resilience, or neuroplasticity, and how it can help you Train Your Brain for Success and build your Three Pillars of Life.

Traumatic Brain Injury

The brain, by itself, is a vulnerable organ. After all, any entity incapable of motion and composed of mostly fat and water and having the consistency of butter doesn't have any natural defenses. It can be damaged very easily!

Luckily, the brain comes in a very handy transport case—your skull, or more precisely, the cranium, which is the part of your skull that encloses your brain. The cranium provides both support and protection, and in everyday life it does a pretty good job.

Within the cranium, your brain is swaddled in three layers of membranes called meninges; if the name sounds familiar, it's because of the serious infection called meningitis. The meninges form a flexible, structural, but semipermeable protective pad that completely surrounds the central nervous system. The brain is also cushioned and protected by cerebrospinal fluid that is produced by the choroid plexus tissue, which is located within the brain, and flows through a series of cavities (called ventricles) out of the brain and down along the spinal cord. The cerebrospinal fluid is kept separate from the blood supply by the blood-brain barrier. While this barrier prevents most blood-borne toxins from entering the brain, it's not an absolute barrier because molecules that are fat soluble can easily pass through. These include alcohol, nicotine, and anesthetics. The reason for that is because a cell's plasma membrane is made of phospholipids, and anything that is fat soluble (nonpolar) can still pass through.

The cerebrospinal fluid also brings nutrients from the blood to the brain and removes waste products.

In this book, I don't talk too much about the spinal cord, but it's a critical part of the system that exerts command and control over your body. The spinal cord is made up of bundles of nerve fibers that run down from the brain through a canal in the center of the bones of the spine. These bones protect the spinal cord.

Like the brain, the spinal cord is covered by the meninges and cushioned by cerebrospinal fluid.

Despite these layers of protection, the brain can be injured. Sometimes it's by actual penetration of the skull, as in the case of the unfortunate Phineas P. Gage, but more often injury is the result of an impact to the head that mashes the brain against its bony container and disrupts the normal function of the brain.

When the head has a rotational movement during trauma, the brain moves, twists, and experiences forces that cause differential movement of brain matter. This motion squeezes, stretches, and sometimes tears the neural cells.

Any time the brain suffers a violent force or movement, the soft, floating brain is slammed against the skull's uneven and rough interior.

Not all blows or jolts to the head result in a TBI. The severity of a TBI may range from "mild" (i.e., a brief change in mental status or consciousness) to "severe" (i.e., an extended period of unconsciousness or memory loss after the injury). Most TBIs that occur each year are mild, commonly called concussions.

According to the Centers for Disease Control and Prevention, traumatic brain injury is a major cause of death and disability in the United States. TBIs contribute to about 30% of all injury deaths. Every day, 153 people in the United States die from injuries that include traumatic brain injury. Those who survive a TBI can face effects that last only a few days or the rest of their lives. Effects of TBI can include impaired thinking or memory, movement, sensation (e.g., vision or hearing), or emotional functioning (e.g., personality changes, depression).

As of 2013, the most recent year for which the CDC has statistics, the number one cause of TBI is accidental falls, which account for 47% of all TBI-related emergency room (ER) visits, hospitalizations, and deaths in the United States. Those who are most likely to be injured in a fall are children and senior citizens.

The second leading cause of TBI is being struck by or against an object, accounting for about 15% of TBI-related ER visits, hospitalizations, and deaths in the United States.

Motor vehicle crashes are the third overall leading cause of TBI-related visits to the ER, hospitalizations, and deaths (14%).

When looking only at TBI-related deaths, intentional self-harm is the second leading cause (33%). Motor vehicle crashes are the third leading cause (19%).

According to the CDC, if the victim is conscious, symptoms of concussion fall into four broad categories:

	THINKING	PHYSICAL	EMOTIONAL	SLEEP
1.	Difficulty thinking clearly	Headache; fuzzy or blurry vision	Irritability	Sleeping more than usual
2.	Feeling slowed down	Nausea or vomiting (early on); dizziness	Sadness	Sleep less than usual
3.	Difficulty concentrating	Sensitivity to noise or light; balance problems	More emotional	Trouble falling asleep
4.	Difficulty remembering new information	Feeling tired; having no energy	Nervousness or anxiety	

Some of these symptoms may appear immediately after the time of the injury, while others may not be noticed for days or months later, as the person attempts to resume their everyday life. It's possible that the victim will not recognize or admit that they are having a problem. Observers, such as family members or colleagues, may not connect the behavior to the injury—if they're even aware of an injury.

People who may have a concussion need to be seen by a health care professional, so if you think you or someone you know has a concussion, contact one today.

Neuropsychological assessment is typically used to assess the functional impact of a mild brain injury, which is often initially diagnosed by evaluating the symptoms a person reports after sustaining the injury.

Actually *seeing* the damage from a TBI can be difficult. Due to the diffuse and varied nature of mild brain injury, typical neuroimaging (CT scans or MRIs) often show no evidence of injury. In part, this is because mild brain injury can often damage the white matter of the brain—the axons of neurons in the brain. This is much harder to capture or visualize using common types of brain imaging. Sometimes a doctor will order imaging tests, such as a CT scan or an MRI, to make sure the patient's brain is not bruised or bleeding.

Neuropsychological tests have become more widely used to diagnose a concussion. These tests are only one of many ways that the patient's physician can find out how well the person is thinking and remembering after an accident.

Newer, more sophisticated imaging technologies show promise in more effectively capturing the damage that occurs in a mild brain injury. These imaging technologies are currently much more expensive and are not as readily available.

If head injuries are repeated over time, a person's condition can morph into chronic traumatic encephalopathy (CTE), a degenerative disease found in people who have suffered repeated blows to the head. CTE is most commonly found in professional athletes participating in boxing, bull riding, rodeo riding, professional wrestling, American football, rugby, ice hockey, stunt performing, and other contact sports, and who have experienced repeated brain trauma, such as concussions, as well as blows to the head that do not produce concussions. It can affect high school athletes following just a few years of participation in sports. CTE can also be found in cases of prolonged domestic violence.

Unlike simple concussions, which may show no visible changes to the brain, the primary physical manifestations of CTE may include a reduction in brain weight associated with other changes, including atrophy of the frontal and temporal cortices and medial temporal lobe. Unfortunately, CTE cannot currently be diagnosed while a person is alive. It can only be definitively diagnosed by direct tissue examination *after death*, during the autopsy and immunohistochemical brain analyses.

Until medical technology becomes more advanced, the only way to diagnose CTE in a living patient is by observing the patient's behavior and through interviews.

CTE was originally observed in boxers in the 1920s and given the fancy Latin name "*dementia pugilistica.*" The seminal work on the disease came from British neurologist Macdonald Critchley, who in 1949 wrote a paper titled "Punch-drunk syndromes: the chronic traumatic encephaopathy of boxers." For decades, it was assumed that the "punch-drunk" syndrome was confined to boxers and others who took direct and repeated blows to the head—a niche demographic. But in the early 2000s, Dr. Bennet Omalu, a neuropathologist working at the Allegheny County Coroner's Office in Pittsburgh, worked on the case of American pro football player Mike Webster, who had died following unusual and unexplained behavior. He examined brain tissue from Webster and eight other NFL players. Although Webster's brain appeared normal at autopsy, Omalu conducted independent tissue analyses. Using specialized staining, Omalu found large accumulations of tau protein in Webster's brain, which would affect his mood, emotions, and executive functions similar to the way clumps of beta-amyloid protein contribute to Alzheimer's disease.

Tau proteins are complicated, but the quick overview is that cells are able to take up nutrients from their environment thanks to membrane-spanning transporter proteins. A cell's transport system is organized in orderly parallel strands resembling railroad tracks. Food molecules, cell parts, and other key materials travel along the "tracks." A protein called tau helps the tracks stay straight, but a cell's tau can collapse into twisted strands called tangles. In areas where tangles are forming, the tracks can no longer stay straight. They fall apart and disintegrate. When this happens to enough brain cells, the brain begins to malfunction.

In 2005, Omalu, along with colleagues in the Department of Pathology at the University of Pittsburgh, published his findings in the journal *Neurosurgery* in a paper entitled "Chronic Traumatic Encephalopathy in a National Football League Player." This was followed by a paper on a second case in 2006 describing similar pathology.

Investigations into the susceptibility of NFL players accelerated. Within ten years, it had become a matter of undisputed concern.

A study published in July 2017 in the *Journal of the American Medical Association (JAMA)* is the latest linking dangerous head injuries to football. Scientists examined the brains of 202 deceased football players to see if they showed the physiological signs of CTE. They also talked to relatives to gather more information about the players, including if they were known to have suffered head trauma in the past and to learn their athletic records.

The players had an average of fifteen years playing football, and the median age at death was sixty-six. The researchers found that the brain tissue of 87% of all players showed evidence of CTE. Breaking this down, this included 99% (110 of 111) of NFL players, 21% of high school players, and 91% of college players. The more professional games someone played, the more severe their head trauma.

The researchers cautioned that these results may be skewed to highlight brain injuries because all the brain tissue samples were donated by relatives of the deceased players, who may have done so because they suspected their loved ones had CTE from their football careers.

Researchers are also finding evidence of increased rates of CTE among combat veterans. Autopsies of four soldiers who served in the war in Afghanistan revealed similar signs of brain damage that has been seen in the NFL and other professional athletes with a history of head trauma,

Dr. Anne McKee, a neuropathologist at Boston University who serves as co-director of the Center for the Study of Traumatic Encephalopathy (CSTE), wrote in *Science Translational Medicine* that autopsies of the soldiers, who were an average age of thirty-two, showed evidence of CTE. McKee and her team found evidence of CTE in the brains of the soldiers, three of whom had mild traumatic brain injuries from a roadside bomb blast, while one had several concussions but none caused by a blast. McKee noted that while athletes with CTE typically display these abnormalities in the brain's frontal lobes—where helmeted heads collide—in the blast-injured veterans, the trauma was more evenly distributed.

Could the force of one explosion cause that much damage? Apparently so. "The force of the blast wind causes the head to move so forcefully that it can result in damage to the brain," Dr. Lee Goldstein, an associate professor of psychiatry and neurology at Boston University who co-led the research with McKee, said in a news release.

An army physician cautioned that in the three blast cases the soldiers had previous concussions from sports, fights, and accidents, making it more difficult to say that their military duty was the sole cause of their brain damage.

But no matter how you look at it, the brain is a sensitive and easily damaged organ. While most of us are not NFL football players or soldiers on patrol in Afghanistan, many of us engage in bicycle riding, skiing, skateboarding, and other activities that involve a risk of head injury. Many of us also have children who play sports and engage in risky behavior. As we build our Three Pillars of Life—both for ourselves and for the benefit of our children—it's good not to be sidelined by an avoidable brain injury! To stay safe, follow these guidelines:

Seat belts and child seats. In a motor vehicle, *always* wear your seat belt. Children should always sit in the back seat of a car and be secured in child safety seats or booster seats that are appropriate for their size and weight. Babies should be secure in an approved baby seat and facing to the *rear*, not forward.

Helmets. While riding a bicycle, skateboard, motorcycle, snowmobile, or all-terrain vehicle, you and your child should each wear a helmet. Also wear appropriate head protection when playing baseball or contact sports, skiing, skating, snowboarding, or riding a horse.

Alcohol and drug use. If you're impaired by alcohol or drugs, including prescription medications, don't drive any type of vehicle, including your boat. Alcohol abuse is the leading known contributing factor in fatal boating accidents.

Slip-proof your house. Especially as we get older, we're more likely to slip and fall. Make sure you have appropriate railings, your bathroom is safe, and your floors are unobstructed by toys or slippery throw rugs. Put a nonslip mat in the bathtub or shower. Keep your home well lit, and make sure your balance and vision are good.

You have only one brain—so take good care of it! It's the most important tool you have as you build your Three Pillars of Life.

Summary

- Barring the action of some supernatural unseen force, everything your brain does is the result of biochemical events. External chemical influences can alter your behavior. Heroin provokes a different brain response than alcohol or amphetamines. Accordingly, we can draw conclusions about a person's personality not only from subjective tests but also from objective measurement of the real, physical events inside your brain. The key thing to remember is that your brain is tractable. You can Train Your Brain for Success.

- The amazing story of Phineas P. Gage, who in 1848 suffered a massive brain injury and survived, was a milestone case in modern history that revealed some aspects of behavior and personality were associated with specific regions of the brain. His story showed us that complex functions, such as decision-making and social cognition, are largely dependent upon the frontal lobes.

- People can survive a hemispherectomy, a very rare neurosurgical procedure in which one cerebral hemisphere (half of the brain) is removed, disconnected, or disabled. The procedure has been used as a treatment for severely epileptic children.

- Any restriction or loss of blood flow to the brain is a serious problem. A stroke can be caused by either a clot obstructing the flow of blood to the brain, called an ischemic stroke, or a blood vessel rupturing and preventing blood flow to the brain, called a hemorrhagic stroke.

- Stroke victims who are suffering from a diminished blood flow to all or part of the brain exhibit three classic symptoms that everyone should learn and be able to recognize: facial drooping, arm weakness, and speech difficulties. These, plus the fourth action item, time, form FAST, the acronym used as a mnemonic to help detect and enhance responsiveness to stroke victim needs.

- While strokes can be treated if the victim is given prompt medical attention, to reduce your chances of having an ischemic stroke, make sure you control your weight, get plenty of exercise, don't smoke, and eat a healthy diet, all of which can reduce the buildup of dangerous plaque in your arteries.
- Traumatic brain injury (TBI) can be life threatening. According to the Centers for Disease Control and Prevention, traumatic brain injury is a major cause of death and disability in the United States. TBIs contribute to about 30% of all injury deaths. Effects of TBI can include impaired thinking or memory, movement, sensation (e.g., vision or hearing), or emotional functioning (e.g., personality changes, depression).
- The number one cause of TBI is accidental falls. The second leading cause is being struck by or against an object. Motor vehicle crashes are the third overall leading cause of TBI-related visits to the ER, hospitalization, and death.
- If head injuries are repeated over time, the person's condition can morph into chronic traumatic encephalopathy (CTE), a degenerative disease found in people who have suffered repeated blows to the head—most notably professional athletes participating in contact sports and who have experienced repeated brain trauma, such as concussions, as well as blows to the head that do not produce concussions.
- Stay safe by wearing a seat belt and using child seats, wearing a helmet when riding a bike, limiting alcohol and drug use, and slip-proofing your house—especially as you get older. If you have a child who plays contact sports, pull them off the field if you suspect they've suffered a concussion or even a severe blow to the head.

6. How Chemicals Affect Your Brain— And Your Decisions

In the previous chapter, we discussed how your brain is protected from the rough-and-tumble outside world by your cranium, a rigid enclosure that ordinarily does a very good job of keeping your brain safe and snug. We also discussed how your brain, thus encased, must be provided with a steady and uninterrupted flow of oxygen, glucose, and other vital nutrients, which are delivered 'round the clock by the two major arteries that enter the skull from the base through your neck.

We also saw how the protective lining that cushions the brain from the hard skull is composed of three membranes collectively known as the meninges.

The Blood-Brain Barrier

The brain is a sensitive and highly specialized organ and extremely selective about the materials it will accept for use in its daily functions and for growth. In other words, the brain cannot tolerate just any random molecule or cell that happens to be in the blood to enter its space. For this reason, the brain is further protected by the blood-brain barrier (BBB), a highly selective semipermeable membrane barrier separating the circulating blood from the brain and extracellular fluid in the central nervous system. Formed by brain endothelial cells, the blood-brain barrier allows only the passage of water; some gases, including oxygen; certain molecules crucial to neural function, such as glucose and amino acids; and lipid-soluble molecules.

This last category is critically important. Lipids are a group of biological molecules that include fats, oils, and some steroids. They are built from fatty acids bonded to a wide range of other compounds. "Lipid-soluble" refers to the ability of a chemical compound to dissolve in fats, oils, lipids, and some solvents. Lipophilic substances tend to dissolve in other lipophilic substances, while *hydrophilic* ("water-loving") substances tend to dissolve in water and other hydrophilic substances. Almost all lipids are insoluble in water. They are known as *hydrophobic* molecules because they are repelled by water.

For example, ordinary cooking oil is a lipid. You can pour some of it into water and stir it all day, and it will never dissolve; but if you add butter to cooking oil and stir it up, it will dissolve because both are lipids.

Lipids include fatty acids; fats and oils (triglycerides); phospholipids (the main constituents of cell membranes); prostaglandins, thromboxanes, and leukotrienes (structurally related natural hormones); and terpenes (the largest and most diverse class of natural products, the majority of which are found only in plants).

Steroids are lipids. These include cholesterol, estrogen, testosterone, bile salts (found in human intestinal bile), and cortisol (a lipid hormone produced in response to stress).

Vitamins are also commonly classified as either water-soluble or fat-soluble. Water-soluble vitamins, such as vitamin C, are not stored by the body, and their dietary levels need to be relatively high. The lipid-soluble vitamins are stored in fat cells and may accumulate to toxic levels if consumed in large quantity. These vitamins include vitamins A, D, E, and K.

Lipids are essential for vertebrate life. They are important in building cell membranes, storing energy (as a part of fat cells), bodily insulation, cell-to-cell communication, growth, sexual development, regulating metabolism, and immune defense.

Compounds and elements that can pass through the blood-brain barrier do so by passive diffusion as well as the selective transport of molecules, such as glucose and amino acids, which are crucial to neural function.

The blood–brain barrier maintains biochemical homeostasis in the central nervous system by regulating the passage of nutrients, molecules, and cells from the blood to the brain. While many pathogens can't penetrate the BBB, some do. Despite its highly restrictive nature, certain bacterial pathogens are able to gain entry into the central nervous system, resulting in serious disease. To breach the barriers protecting the brain, extracellular pathogens must cross a monolayer of tight junction-expressing endothelial or epithelial cells. The limited number of pathogens capable of crossing these tight barriers and invading the meninges suggests these pathogens display very specific attributes.

Bacterial meningitis is among the top ten causes of infectious disease-related deaths worldwide, with up to half of the survivors left with permanent neurological disabilities. The World Health Organization estimates there are 1.2 million cases of bacterial meningitis per year, of which 170,000 are fatal, with permanent neurological aftereffects occurring in up to half of all survivors. Although a wide range of bacteria can cause disease in humans, only a limited number of pathogens are isolated from the central nervous systems. The most prevalent cause of meningitis varies depending on geographic location, socioeconomic status, age, vaccination availability, and overall health status of the individual.

How do you avoid getting meningitis?

Because a wide variety of bacteria and viruses can cause meningitis and these bacteria can spread through ordinary activities such as coughing, sneezing, and kissing, or sharing eating utensils, a toothbrush, or a cigarette, hiding in a germ-proof room is obviously not the solution. Instead, practice everyday good hygiene.

Wash your hands. Careful handwashing is the number one way to prevent the spread of infection. Teach your children to wash their hands often, especially before eating and after using the toilet, spending time in a crowded public place, or playing with animals.

Don't share drinks, foods, straws, eating utensils, lip balms, or toothbrushes with anyone else.

When you need to cough or sneeze, cover your mouth.

Prepare food properly. Keep cold foods cold and hot foods hot. Reduce your risk of listeriosis by cooking meat, including hot dogs and deli meat, to 165°F (74°C).

By staying healthy, you'll be doing your brain a big favor—and lowering your risk of meningitis!

Vaccines are also available. There are several, each targeted at a different bad bug. Two of them are Haemophilus influenzae type b (Hib) vaccine and Pneumococcal conjugate vaccine (PCV13), both of which are routinely given to children in the United States as well as some adults.

Please give your children the vaccines that your physician recommends! The old myth about vaccines being connected to autism has been totally disproven. Vaccines are safe and effective, and can save lives—perhaps even your own.

Drugs the BBB Keeps Out—And Those It Lets In

The function of the blood-brain barrier is to admit necessary or acceptable molecules while denying entry to a long list of substances the brain doesn't want. Keeping out what's bad is just as important as welcoming what's good.

Pharmacologists—biologists who are concerned with the study of drug action—talk about "drug distribution." This doesn't mean the shady guy on the street corner; the term refers to how a given drug will disperse throughout the body and be either accepted or rejected by various organs. As the *Merck Manual* explains, after a drug is absorbed into the bloodstream, it rapidly circulates through the body. The average circulation time of blood is one minute. As the blood recirculates, the drug moves from the bloodstream into the body's tissues.

Each drug will find greater acceptance in some tissues than in others. Drugs that dissolve in water (water-soluble drugs) tend to stay within the blood and the fluid that surrounds cells (interstitial space). Drugs that dissolve in fat (fat-soluble drugs) tend to concentrate in fatty tissues. Other drugs concentrate mainly in only one small part of the body (for example, iodine concentrates mainly in the thyroid gland) because the tissues there have a special affinity for and ability to retain that drug.

Drugs penetrate different tissues at different speeds, depending on the drug's ability to cross membranes. For example, the antibiotic rifampin, a highly fat-soluble drug, rapidly enters the brain, but the antibiotic penicillin, a water-soluble drug, does not. In general, fat-soluble drugs can cross cell membranes—and the BBB—more quickly than water-soluble drugs.

For any drug to affect the central nervous system (brain and spinal cord), it must first cross the blood-brain barrier. All drugs that pass the blood-brain barrier are at least somewhat lipid-soluble, and the more lipid-soluble they are, the faster they affect the CNS. Heroin and morphine are almost identical in molecular structure, but the two acetyl groups attached to heroin improve its lipid-solubility and increase its potency twofold when compared with the same dose of morphine.

The compounds the BBB keeps out include most of the pharmaceutical drugs that your doctor has prescribed for you for some bodily ailment. The BBB treats most pharmaceutical drugs as foreign molecules and doesn't let them pass. More than 95% of medicinal drugs show poor penetration of the BBB and a lack of useful activity in the brain. A high proportion of large molecule drugs do not cross, which encompasses all the products of biotechnology, including recombinant proteins, monoclonal antibodies, and RNA interference drugs. This has been a major issue for the treatment of diseases, such as brain cancer, which might be treatable by delivering drugs through the bloodstream to the tumors.

It has been known for years that nonsteroidal anti-inflammatory drugs (NSAIDs), such as aspirin, ibuprofen, and acetaminophen, provide relief from fever, pain, and inflammation through their action on cyclooxygenase (COX) enzymes. (These are enzymes that produce prostaglandins, which are hormone-like substances that participate in a wide range of body functions, such as the contraction and relaxation of smooth muscle, the dilation and constriction of blood vessels, control of blood pressure, and modulation of inflammation.) There are three types of COX enzymes—COX-1, -2, and -3. These enzymes produce prostaglandins, which, in turn, promote inflammation, pain, and fever.

Why many NSAIDS work is unknown. We do know that unlike other NSAIDs, acetaminophen is capable of crossing the blood-brain barrier, allowing it to reach concentrations in the brain sufficient to inhibit COX-3. All these lines of evidence strongly implicate COX-3 as the target of acetaminophen action and partly explain the long-standing mystery of why acetamino-phen is often more efficacious against headache and fever than some of the other NSAIDs.

An early strategy for crossing the barrier was to make drugs more lipid-soluble. This allowed them to penetrate the lipid-loving endothelial cells in the brain, but there was a downside: If you make something lipophilic, it'll penetrate every organ and cell in the body. Consequently you must use large amounts, be-cause most of what you administer will end up somewhere else besides the brain, and if the drug can have a bad side effect on another organ or tissue, the bad side effect will occur.

By the way, as you age, the blood-brain barrier may become less effective, allowing increased passage of compounds into the brain. This is another reason why you should be careful with your prescriptions as you get older!

Drugs of Abuse

Everyone knows what "mind-altering" drugs can do. The very term "mind-altering" would serve as evidence that recreational drugs—the kind that society says people abuse—are able to pass through the blood-brain barrier and have some sort of disruptive effect on the normal everyday functions of the brain.

In general, this is true, because most drugs of abuse, including alcohol, cocaine, marijuana, and many opioids, are lipophilic.

As you build your Three Pillars of Life, I'm not going to preach to you about whether or not you should ever smoke pot or drink alcohol. If you do it legally, that's your business. I hope you use these drugs responsibly and not as an escape from some larger problem in your life.

You should definitely not break the law by buying or consum-ing any illegal drugs!

Whatever you choose to do—or not do—you should know

how these substances affect your brain, both in the short term and long term.

First, let's look at what may be the worst and most dangerous drug on the planet: nicotine.

Nicotine addiction is the single largest preventable cause of morbidity and mortality in the Western World. In the United States and other countries, cigarette smoking remains a leading cause of preventable disease and premature death. On average, 435,000 people in the United States die prematurely from smoking-related diseases each year; overall, smoking is linked to one in five deaths. The chance that a lifelong smoker will die prematurely from a complication of smoking is approximately fifty percent. Smoking is no longer seen as just a bad habit; it's a substance addiction problem. The pharmacological aspects of nicotine show that this horrible compound has a broad distribution in the different body compartments, due mainly to its highly lipophilic characteristic. The lipophilic nature of nicotine results in high solubility in membrane lipids and fast passage through the blood-brain barrier directly into the brain.

If you want to have a healthy brain—not to mention healthy lungs and healthy heart—and you smoke cigarettes, the most powerful thing you can do to build your Three Pillars of Life is to *quit smoking right now.* Not tomorrow or the next day. Quit *now*, and if you relapse, quit over and over again until your brain is free of this horrible substance.

Caffeine is a lipophilic molecule that crosses the blood-brain barrier. It shares structural similarities to adenosine, which binds to receptors on the surface of cells in the central nervous system and blocks the release of dopamine, a molecule that when released into the bloodstream decreases fatigue and increases spontaneous behavioral responses. But when caffeine binds to those same cells, it *facilitates* the release of dopamine, making you feel more energized. There is also some evidence that caffeine improves long-term memory formation, which means drinking all that coffee as you study for final exams may actually be helping you remember!

Alcohol is slightly lipophilic and can diffuse across the brain endothelial cell membranes of the capillaries, with the concentration gradient to get into (or out of) the brain. Once in the brain, alcohol interferes with brain cell functions to cause intoxication.

THC, the primary active ingredient of marijuana, is highly lipophilic and easily crosses the blood-brain barrier. It rapidly penetrates into fat tissues and other highly vascularized tissues; this tissue distribution is followed by its slow redistribution from the deep fat deposits back into the bloodstream. This is why traces of THC can be present in your blood days after consumption—so if you need to take a drug test for work, be sure you give the THC from the joint you smoked at least a week to seep out of your fatty cells. Some heavy pot smokers have reported THC being detected in their urine ninety days after their last smoke!

Cocaine is a crystalline tropane alkaloid that is obtained from the leaves of the coca plant. Unlike most molecules, cocaine has pockets with *both* high hydrophilic *and* lipophilic efficiency, violating the normal rule of hydrophilic-lipophilic balance. This causes it to cross the blood-brain barrier far more quickly and efficiently than most other psychoactives.

Opioids: Fentanyl, Heroin, Oxycodone

Opioids are substances that act on opioid receptors in the brain to reduce pain. Opioids include opiates, which are drugs derived from opium, including morphine and heroin. Other opioids are semi-synthetic and synthetic drugs, such as hydrocodone, oxycodone, and fentanyl.

Opioid addiction has become a serious health crisis in the United States.

Public health officials have called the current opioid epidemic the worst drug crisis in American history. Opioids—both legal, such as prescription oxycodone and hydrocodone, and illicit drugs, such as street fentanyl and heroin—killed more than 33,000 Americans in 2015. Half of those deaths involved prescription narcotics.

Nearly two million Americans are addicted to prescription opioids, and three out of four new heroin users start with prescription drugs, which is why opioid prescribing practices are a concern for public health officials.

Because they're both derived from opium, heroin and morphine are almost identical in molecular structure, but the two acetyl groups attached to heroin improve its lipid-solubility, thereby increasing its potency twofold when compared with the same dose of morphine. Heroin is highly lipophilic and has a high permeability through the blood-brain barrier. Consequently, heroin crosses the BBB at a rate more than one hundred times faster than morphine.

Fentanyl is a synthetic opiate painkiller that is much stronger than morphine or heroin—in fact, it's fifty to one hundred times more powerful than morphine. Fentanyl will give a similar result as morphine, oxycodone, or heroin, with symptoms including fatigue, nausea, vomiting, sleepiness, warmth, itchiness, and tendency to nod off. All opiates suppress breathing, which is how they lead to death when too much of the drug is taken. When fentanyl is combined with another drug that suppresses breathing, such as alcohol or benzodiazepines, this combination can also result in death.

The effects of morphine last longer than fentanyl because once morphine *enters* the central nervous system it has a more difficult time *exiting* the cellular lipid barrier (blood-brain barrier). Because morphine is not very lipid-soluble, it takes a long time to cross the blood-brain barrier, both going into and out of the brain. It is this retention in the central nervous system that makes morphine longer acting than fentanyl. This produces what you might call a "slow-in, slow-out" drug. When compared with lipid-soluble drugs, morphine is noted to be slower in onset. Fentanyl, on the other hand, is lipophilic and crosses the blood-brain barrier rapidly in *both* directions; it is a "fast-in, fast-out" drug. Consequently, fentanyl acts quickly and has a short duration of action because of its lipid solubility.

The problem with opioids is that most people can't use them just once and put them aside. Opioids are addictive. They create artificial endorphins in the brain, which initially produce warm, good feelings in the user; but over time, opioids condition the brain to stop the natural production of these endorphins. Once that happens, the only way an opioid user can experience positive feelings is by using the drug in question. This process is the reason why opioids are so addictive.

When the body stops producing its own endorphins, the person feels sick and depressed. For these individuals, taking the opioid—say, oxycodone—is no longer about the positive feelings that were felt the first few times they took the drug. Now, the opioid use has become about avoiding negative feelings and symptoms. When this "switch" occurs (that is, *achieving good* transforms into *avoiding bad*), the person has become addicted to opioids.

When an opioid addict stops taking the drugs they have been abusing, withdrawal symptoms occur almost immediately and can include anxiety, restlessness, suicidal thoughts, stress, depression, lack of sleep, and other debilitating effects. Because of the potentially serious nature of withdrawal and the likelihood of the user returning to the opiate in question during this time, it is crucial that professional help is sought for the opiate addict.

If you suffer a painful injury and your doctor prescribes an opioid painkiller, be extremely careful and take only the *bare minimum* you need to function. These drugs are highly addictive and will quickly destroy your Three Pillars of Life.

Hallucinogens

Because they naturally occur in mushrooms, cacti, and a variety of other plants that early humans would have experimentally eaten, hallucinogenic substances are among the oldest drugs people have used. Many cultures worldwide, both ancient and modern, have endorsed the use of hallucinogens in medicine, religion, and recreation to varying extents, while other cultures—particularly modern industrial nations—have regulated or condemned their use.

Hallucinogens, such as lysergic acid diethylamide (LSD), psilocybin, peyote, N,N-dimethyltryptamine (DMT), and *ayahuasca,* aren't designed to relieve pain, and hence have no "practical" medical value. They're designed to alter your perception of consciousness and change reality into something different.

In the United States, they're all illegal.

To take the example of LSD, according to the Controlled Substances Act of 1970, it's Schedule I, which means it's illegal to manufacture, buy, possess, process, or distribute without a license from the Drug Enforcement Administration (DEA). By classifying LSD as a Schedule I substance, the DEA has ruled that LSD meets the following three criteria:

1. It is deemed to have a high potential for abuse.
2. It has no legitimate medical use in treatment.
3. There is a lack of accepted safety for its use under medical supervision.

Such drugs as opioids can kill you by suppressing your breathing, an involuntary life-sustaining function. Except in massive doses, a hallucinogen such as LSD doesn't do this. There are no documented deaths from its chemical toxicity; most LSD deaths are a result of *behavioral* toxicity—that is, people doing risky things while tripping.

LSD is not addictive, and physical withdrawal symptoms are not typically experienced when chronic use is stopped.

LSD is derived from ergot alkaloids, a naturally occurring fungus that infects rye, Achnatherum robustum ("sleepy grass"), and other grains. It takes a very tiny amount to affect the brain. A typical dose of LSD ranges between 75 and 150 micrograms (millionths of a gram). This is about three thousand times less than the amount of aspirin in a regular-strength tablet.

As Michael Fichman wrote in his Bryn Mawr College research paper "LSD—Origins and Neurobiological Implications," the structure of LSD is similar to that of serotonin, the molecule principally responsible for determination of mood. While not particularly lipophilic, enough of it passes through the blood-brain barrier to have an effect: "A C14 marking of ingested LSD shows that about 10% of LSD molecules ingested by a subject pass through the blood brain barrier and bind to serotonin receptors in the hypothalamus. The hypothalamus is part of the limbic system, which has a diverse array of functions associated with homeostasis, movement, and more importantly, emotion and organization of responses. Once the LSD molecule binds to the serotonin site, it alters the responsiveness of the subject's neurotransmitters. A hallucinogen produces the sensory distortion known as hallucination by lowering the threshold at which nerves produce a response signal. This means that neurons normally requiring a large chemical stimulus to produce a signal, which is then sent to the brain, produce signals at the slightest chemical prompting. This increased volume of neuron activity and signaling means more sensory information is being sent to the brain than it can handle."

Basically, hallucinogens, such as LSD, remove many of the filters that prevent our brains from being overwhelmed by sensory information, producing an overload that can lead to the creation of nonreality-based sights and sounds. Such an effect can be dangerous for someone who has psychological issues. LSD abusers with a personal or family history of psychosis or other severe psychiatric disorders are thought to be at greater risk of having a "bad trip" or developing other psychological problems. Long-term side effects are known by the clinical terms "persistent psychosis" and "hallucinogen persisting perception disorder" (HPPD).

Unlike a compound such as nicotine, about which absolutely nothing good can be said, hallucinogens, including LSD, have been shown to have some clinical value when used in a controlled setting. As Dr. Robin Carhart-Harris, et al., wrote in "The paradoxical psychological effects of lysergic acid diethylamide (LSD)," published in *Psychological Medicine*, research on a group of twenty healthy volunteers revealed that while LSD elicited psychosis-like symptoms acutely, it improved psychological well-being in the mid to long term. "It is proposed," wrote the authors, "that acute alterations in mood are secondary to a more fundamental modulation in the quality of cognition, and that increased cognitive flexibility subsequent to serotonin 2A receptor (5-HT2AR) stimulation promotes emotional lability during intoxication and leaves a residue of 'loosened cognition' in the mid to long term that is conducive to improved psychological wellbeing."

These findings and others suggest that a brain that's too "uptight," to use a classic 1960s expression, could benefit from some "loosening up." As Dr. Carhart-Harris told *The Huffington Post*, "There's probably a sweet spot to the balance of thinking between flexibility on the one hand—the ability to be adaptive and creative—and then on the other hand, to be able to focus and be organized. Maybe to some extent, that's what normal waking consciousness is like when you're healthy—you inhabit this spot. Maybe psychedelics push you a little bit towards the pole of more flexibility, more creativity."

Yet, if your mind is *too* flexible, you may run the risk of psychosis; as he said, "Ideas are being entertained that don't have a firm anchorage in reality or logic."

Since LSD and other hallucinogens are illegal, I will not advocate that you try them unless you want to volunteer for a controlled clinical study; but their use for thousands of years speaks to the human desire to push boundaries and experiment, even with our own brains. As you Train Your Brain for Success and build your Three Pillars of Life, hopefully you can find that "sweet spot" between rigidity and imaginative thinking that will provide both the ability to be creative and the focus necessary to make your dreams a reality.

Headaches

Because your head is a complex structure supported by many muscles and laced with miles of blood vessels and nerves, and the home of several key sensory organs, all of which can malfunction, headaches are a common ailment.

Your brain can't feel pain directly, but it sure can feel the pain of the surrounding nerves! Most headaches happen in the nerves, blood vessels, and muscles that cover a person's head and neck. These muscles or blood vessels swell, tighten, or go through other changes that activate the surrounding nerves. These nerves send a rush of pain messages to the brain, which causes a headache.

The word "headache" is actually an oversimplified catch-all term for a host of possible problems. According to the National Headache Foundation, there are twenty-four distinct types of headaches, caused by wide range of triggers, including allergies, caffeine withdrawal, depression, eyestrain, fever, hangovers, hypertension, sinus infections, and tumors.

Ninety percent of all headaches are tension headaches. They are caused by an emotional response to stressful events and involve the tightening or tensing of facial and neck muscles. Pain is mild to moderate and feels like pressure is being applied to the head or neck.

Migraine headaches can cause severe throbbing pain or a pulsing sensation, usually on just one side of the head. They are often accompanied by nausea, vomiting, and extreme sensitivity to light and sound. Migraines are thought to involve abnormal functioning of the brain's blood vessels. If untreated, a migraine usually lasts from four to seventy-two hours. The frequency with which headaches occur varies from person to person.

Most headaches are treated with rest in a quiet, dark room; hot or cold compresses to your head or neck; small amounts of caffeine; and over-the-counter medications, such as aspirin, ibuprofen (Advil, Motrin IB, others), and acetaminophen (Tylenol, others). Nonsteroidal anti-inflammatory drugs (NSAIDs), including aspirin and ibuprofen, block the COX enzymes and prostaglandins that are naturally produced by the body to promote therapeutic inflammation, pain, and fever. As a consequence, ongoing inflammation, pain, and fever are reduced.

As for acetaminophen, scientists aren't certain how it works—just that it does!

You should seek medical treatment for *any* headache that seems unusual, persistent, or severe. You should seek treatment if you experience any additional or concurrent symptoms, such as confusion, dizziness, fever, nausea, slurred speech, stiff neck, and vision problems—basically anything that tells you that your headache is more than a temporary annoyance.

Summary

- The brain is protected from unwanted substances by the blood-brain barrier (BBB), a highly selective semipermeable membrane barrier that separates the circulating blood from the brain and extracellular fluid in the central nervous system. Formed by brain endothelial cells, the blood-brain barrier allows only the passage of water; some gases, including oxygen; certain molecules crucial to neural function, such as glucose and amino acids; and lipid-soluble molecules.

- The blood-brain barrier admits lipids, a group of biological molecules that include fats, oils, and some steroids. They are built from fatty acids bonded to a wide range of other compounds.

- For any drug to affect the central nervous system (brain and spinal cord), it must first cross the blood-brain barrier. All drugs that pass the blood-brain barrier are at least somewhat lipid-soluble (lipophilic), and the more lipid-soluble they are, the faster they affect the CNS.

- Most prescription drugs aren't lipophilic and don't reach the brain. More than 95% of medicinal drugs show poor penetration of the blood-brain barrier and a lack of useful activity in the brain. Unfortunately, many dangerous and addictive drugs, including heroin, morphine, fentanyl, alcohol, cocaine, marijuana, and nicotine are lipophilic, and pass through the blood-brain barrier into the brain tissues.

- Opioids are addictive because they create artificial endorphins in the brain, which initially produce warm, good feelings in the user. But over time, opioids condition the brain to stop the natural production of these endorphins. Once that happens, the only way an opioid user can experience positive feelings is by using the drug in question. In a sense, the opioid addict isn't trying to feel *more* pleasure than an unaddicted person, just *some* pleasure, which, due to the lack of natural endorphins, isn't there.

- Certain bacterial pathogens are able to gain entry into the central nervous system, resulting in a serious disease called meningitis. The best defense is good hygiene. Wash your hands. Don't share drinks, foods, straws, eating utensils, lip balms, or toothbrushes with anyone else. When you need to cough or sneeze, cover your mouth. Prepare food properly, keeping cold foods cold and hot foods hot. Vaccines are also available, each targeted at a different strain of bad bacteria.

- Caffeine is a lipophilic molecule that crosses the blood-brain barrier and facilitates the release of dopamine, making you feel more energized. There is also some evidence that caffeine improves long-term memory formation.

- Hallucinogens, such as lysergic acid diethylamide (LSD), psilocybin, peyote, N,N-dimethyltryptamine (DMT), and *ayahuasca,* work by removing many of the filters that reduce the flood of sensory information pouring into the brain. This produces an overload that can lead to the creation of non-reality-based sights and sounds.

- Headaches are not a pain in the brain itself (because the brain can't feel pain) but a symptom of a problem elsewhere in the head, neck, or body. Most headaches are resolved with rest and over-the-counter pain relievers, but if a headache is persistent, unusual, or severe, call your doctor!

7. Learning and Memory

Aside from directing the activities of all parts of your body, from the beating of your heart to your decision to scratch an itch and the ensuing choreography of muscle movements to accomplish this important task, one of the most useful things about your brain is its ability to learn new information and store it for long periods of time—often for your entire life.

Learning is the acquisition of knowledge or skills through experiences, study, or being taught. The ability to learn is exhibited in animals with very tiny brains, so it's not exclusive to humans or even to vertebrates, but we can say with confidence that the human brain, because of its size and complexity, is at the top of the class regarding learning.

It's facilitated by an actual physical process. The neurons in your brain are composed of several parts, including the dendrites, the branched projections of a neuron that act to propagate the electrochemical stimulation received from other neural cells to the cell body. As you learn, these brain fibers grow. The fibers connect your brain cells to one another at contact points called synapses. The larger your brain fibers grow and the more brain cells they connect, the more information can be stored in your brain.

Here's the catch: Brain fibers can only grow from existing brain fibers. In other words, to learn new knowledge and Train Your Brain for Success, you must build on information that is already stored in your brain. For example, when a baby says her first word, such as "mama," that first stored success becomes the foundation for the addition of new bits of information about words and language.

For creating stronger, faster connections in the brain, it's essential to practice the skill or information that you wish to fully master. A baby who says "mama" should be encouraged to say it again and again, and build her vocabulary with new words and phrases. Regular practice—whether it involves learning how to eat with a fork, playing the piano, or solving a calculus problem—causes your dendrites to grow thicker and coat themselves with a fatty layer. With enough practice, these thickened brain fibers will eventually form double connections to one another.

Memory is the faculty of retaining information to be retrieved in the future. Memory comes in two broad forms: short term (STM) and long term (LTM). As a general rule of thumb, all memories start as short term, with only some eventually becoming long-term memories.

Short-term memory is like your email inbox. You have immediate access to the emails, but unless you process them quickly and delete some, the inbox gets full and no more new emails can come in. On the other hand, your long-term memory is your folders in your inbox. You place the information you find relevant in these folders, and you can access them for later use.

Learning and memory go hand in hand, since learning involves converting short-term information into long-term memory. Many things we think we have learned soon become forgotten or were never properly learned in the first place because they were never stored as long-term memory. This is why so many times someone teaches you something and although you understand it at that moment, when you try to recall that piece of information it is gone. A good example is when you take a course on how to operate a particular software, such as Photoshop. You go through the course and the required steps, they make sense, and you can do it properly. But after completing the course you don't touch Photoshop for a while, so when you eventually open it you find you have to relearn everything because you haven't repeated what you learned over and over again, and the neural connections were lost.

Think of a neural connection in your brain as starting out like a faint path you've made by walking through a field. If you don't use the path regularly, it will soon disappear, but if you keep walking on the path, it will start to become permanent. If you use it a lot, you might pave it over and make it into a road. If you frequently drive on the road, it will become a highway and last a lifetime.

An effective way to create a long-term memory is with a feedback loop that tells you if you have learned something or not. The key is to test yourself and see if you have actually understood the information. For instance, after you learn something new, can you explain it in your own words? Can you repeat the operation without having to do it again? If the feedback you get from your own testing is positive, you can move to the next piece of information. If it is negative, you need to revise and relearn.

Two processes occur with LTM: First, a repeated stimulus or information from STM is stored. Second, to retrieve that information, you must recall it by memory or recognize it from seeing it before. The main point is that repetition is key for remembering.

Another very important point is forgetting. Although this might sound like something bad, it is actually a good thing. If we didn't forget, our brains would be filled with unimportant information, which would make it harder to absorb new information and make sense of it. Forgetting allows us to prioritize.

There are exceptional cases where the human brain has exhibited the ability to transfer a vast amount of short-term memories into long-term storage. Hyperthymesia is the condition of possessing an extremely detailed autobiographical memory. People with hyperthymesia remember an abnormally vast number of their life experiences. They can recall almost every day of their lives in near perfect detail as well as public events that hold some personal significance for them. Recollection occurs without hesitation or conscious effort. Memories recalled by hyperthymestic individuals tend to be personal, autobiographical accounts of both significant and mundane events in their lives.

But this condition doesn't make you "smarter," and the few known individuals with hyperthymesia—about twenty-five worldwide—don't perform tasks involving reasoning better than anyone else. Hyperthymestic abilities can have a detrimental effect on cognitive capacity because the constant tsunami of memories is like watching an action movie while you're trying to do your income tax return: it's just not helpful. Hyperthymestic people have said they "get lost in remembering," which can make it difficult to attend to the present or future because they're permanently living in the past.

Focus and Concentration

Focus is putting all your effort, resources, and attention into one problem. Concentration is putting all your attention into the problem you are currently working on. Both are key as you Train Your Brain for Success.

Focus is a concentrated form of attention, and "paying attention" is directing your attention to whatever requested it.

Focusing requires greater effort, bringing precise attention to the problem at hand. When we focus, we are directing our minds from random thoughts to a specific thought or actions.

A focused individual's mind is aware of where he or she is, who they are, and why they are there. It means that they are "focused" on the specific task at hand and not letting their mind wander off to other thoughts. For example, a race car driver needs to be highly focused not only on his or her car and its operation but also on the surrounding pack of cars and how the race as a whole is unfolding. The driver needs to keep seeing the big picture even as he or she steers their car into a turn at two hundred miles an hour.

In social sciences, **concentration** is referred to as the ability to pay selective attention to something while ignoring other things. Controlling one's attention is the ability that we refer to as concentration. We cannot concentrate on an object or activity unless we pay selective attention to it. Concentration is an ability that can be improved with practice.

What is the difference between "attention" and "concentration"?

The process of focusing for any length of time on an activity or object is referred to as concentration. For example, while reading an article, your concentration may be divided: if there are two people arguing nearby, however, you are still focused on reading the article. Unlike focus, concentration is not merely a choice of "yes" or "no." There can be various degrees of concentration. Focus, on the other hand, is a fundamental aspect of willpower, which is like a switch that can be turned "on" or "off"—either the person is focused or they are not.

It is a fact that focus is volatile and shifts from one thing to another very frequently. If we are in a room that is noisy, we find it hard to make sense of what a person is saying to us; but when we focus and become selective in our perception, we find that it becomes easier to catch the voice of the person who is talking to us. This requires focusing on one sound and ignoring all other sounds as useless. When students are taking notes and also listening to what their teachers are teaching, they are focusing their attention simultaneously on two activities, as they hear and then start writing after making sense of what they hear. In daily life, there are many examples of situations where we need to pay attention to several activities, which requires switching back and forth from one activity to another.

Both concentration and focus are very important cognitive abilities characteristic of human beings. Most of human behavior and actions are a result of what has been learned, as there is not much besides sleeping and breathing that a person does without learning. Human learning is a result of paying attention to what is being taught as well as making use of our senses. We need to focus our attention on something to learn about it. This is much like focusing the spotlight of a torch in the dark to make sense of the environment.

Deep Learning Isn't Easy!

Our primitive minds were designed not for conscious, deliberative thinking but for quick action, which is why thinking is slow and requires effort. It's an uncertain process, and we tend to rely on past habits and memories to guide our actions.

Like learning how to play a musical instrument, struggle and confusion are a normal part of deep and transformative learning. We tend to avoid this because it requires effort, and we also misinterpret this as a sign that we are not good at the chosen task, but you have to understand that the more complex and difficult the task, the more likely you will be creating stronger connections for your brain to remember. As Daniel T. Willingham wrote in his book *Why Don't Students Like School?: A Cognitive Scientist*

Answers Questions About How the Mind Works and What It Means for the Classroom, "People are naturally curious, but we are not naturally good thinkers; unless the cognitive conditions are right, we will avoid thinking." And, "Curiosity prompts people to explore new ideas and problems, but when we do, we quickly evaluate how much mental work it will take to solve the problem. If it's too much or too little, we stop working on the problem if we can."

Cognitive load is the amount of mental effort being used by your working memory. The more cognitive load you're carrying, the harder it is to learn because—just like your home computer—your brain capacity is full.

How do we calculate cognitive load? The more distraction you have, the more cognitive load. Here's the formula:

Effective load (what you want to focus on) + ineffective load (what distracts you) + task difficulty load = cognitive load

For instance, if you live in a dangerous, violent neighborhood where there's lots of stress, your cognitive load is higher—even if you're doing nothing but sitting on your front porch.

Attention is key in learning, but it's not as easy as one may think. Even if you pay conscious attention to the information presented to you, you can learn either a little or a lot; it depends on if you can meaningfully link the new information with past information and experiences. (As you'll recall, new brain fibers can only grow from existing brain fibers.) It is a dual communication between short-term memory and long-term memory. The act of moving short-term memory into long-term memory is called *active learning*.

Time is also a factor in learning. You must give time for information to be processed by your brain. Long-term memory is achieved when new information is meaningfully linked to already existing knowledge in your memory. The more you process and think about something, the more enduring and retrievable that information is because it generates a lot of talk between your short-term and long-term memory.

If a piece of information isn't meaningful and you don't process it long enough, it doesn't matter how attentive you are because it will not be converted into long-term memory. It's also important to note that short-term memory is limited in time and capacity, which means it can be overloaded.

Here's a story that illustrates this point. I was in college, during final exams, and I had been studying several subjects for a few weeks. To be honest, I was overloaded with work. My semesters usually consisted of up to twenty-eight credits, while the average full-time student takes up to sixteen, but I had been handling the course load for a few years, and I seemed to be doing okay. It was the afternoon before my final exam in molecular biology (this course was my favorite, and in fact one of my degrees is in molecular biology). I was studying hard, but all the information I was reading was not getting into my brain! I would read a paragraph, I would pay attention to my book, but nothing was sticking in my memory. Going to the next page, the same thing would happen. I would read it carefully but retain nothing.

I would take a break, come back, and the same thing would happen. I was so frustrated! This had never happened to me before in my life, and I was a straight-A student who was comfortable studying. I just couldn't understand what was going on.

The next day I took the exam. When the grades came back, for the first time in my college career, I didn't receive an A. It was a B.

Years later, after learning more about the brain, I realized that my brain had been temporarily full. My short-term memory had reached its capacity. Because a lot of what we learned for our exams in school was purely intellectual and unrelated to any real-life experience, it didn't get sent into my long-term memory. It hadn't been processed long enough or repeated enough for it to stick. This is why many students cram for an exam, take the exam, and two days later they can't remember anything because they were only able to store all the information in the short-term memory portion of the brain.

The most powerful learning occurs from an inside-out process, which means we connect new information with previous knowledge. If there's no previous knowledge, the new information will seem random and without context. When given the new information, the brain will shrug and say, "What's the point of remembering this? It doesn't *mean* anything."

If you're looking for the Holy Grail of learning, I hate to disappoint you, but it does not exist. Learning requires time and experience, and there are no shortcuts.

At this point, the relevant question is, "Do we have or do humans have the capacity to learn faster and more effectively?" Yes, we do. Take, for example, savants, or some cases of autism, where a person can read a book and memorize every single word or people who can recite the number *pi* up to fifty thousand characters, but those superpowers, as we may call them, invariably come at the expense of other cognitive processes, such as their ability to be conventionally social with other people.

People have used many techniques to improve short-term memorization, such as mnemonics. You can also use mind maps, which are a great tool to help you learn and remember faster and be able to link bits of information together.

Motivation

Consider the following story that reveals how the brain learns.

In college, I knew a student I'll call Fred. He was nice but a bit of a slacker. His grades were just good enough to keep him off academic probation. In the old days, they called guys like Fred "gentleman C scholars." Like a true gentleman C scholar, Fred did just enough work to get by. He actually did pretty well in

English and history, and in those subjects he occasionally broke through with a solid B.

His worst subject was math. Fred was terrible at math. He'd sit in calculus class, and whenever the teacher called on him, you'd think he was waking up from a nap. As for studying math, Fred complained that it just seemed totally pointless. "Why am I studying this nonsense?" he would say at study hall. "I don't see the point." He even asked our calculus professor why he needed to study it (the class was a requirement), and the professor told him that studying math was beneficial because "it teaches you how to think." Fred replied that he already had plenty to think about, and calculus wasn't helping.

Fred managed to graduate. I lost track of him, and then I ran into him a few years later. He was wearing a very expensive tailored suit and a gold wristwatch. I asked him what he was doing. He said that he worked on Wall Street as an analyst for a big mutual fund. His job was to analyze corporate balance sheets, determine their profitability, and recommend investments.

"Wow," I said. "I'm impressed, but doesn't your job require a lot of math? I remember you as a guy who slept through math class."

"Yeah, I hated it," he said with a grin. "Now I *love* math. To be more exact, I love crunching numbers. Do you know why? They aren't just abstract symbols. They *mean* something, and if I figure them out, I get *paid*."

"Yes, I can see that you get paid—you're doing very well!"

"But it's not just the money," he added. "I really love my job. It's fun. I feel like I'm making a difference for my clients. I'd be doing this even if no one paid me."

"Say, do you gave any good stock tips?" I asked.

He laughed. "Call my office and we'll make an appointment." We chatted for a few minutes, and then he told me he had to catch his plane. He was headed for Cancun for a two-week vacation.

Fred is a classic example of the power of motivation in human learning. On Wall Street, he had the same brain he had in college, but his college brain wasn't motivated. He saw no value in studying math. When he got hired at the mutual fund, a lightbulb ignited in his brain. He saw the purpose behind learning math and the satisfaction that would come. So he threw himself into it with amazing intensity.

Motivation is a key factor in learning. In fact, it may be the most important thing, but learning takes effort and often involves emotional frustration and the willingness to accept setbacks. When you learn something—whether it's how to read a corporate balance sheet, speak a foreign language, or kick a soccer ball into the goal—you need to exert effort and endure the pain of repeated failure until you've mastered it.

Why, then, do people persevere in the presence of discomfort to achieve learning? Here are the answers.

Material reward is commonly used to influence motivation, but the problem with material reward—a cash bonus or a new car if you hit your sales goal—is that it increases performance only for a short time. If we reward an employee for doing well and we do it every week with the same reward, eventually he or she will become numb to that reward, and it will have no more effect. Consequently, you either have to keep rewarding them with different or better things or just use it as a short-term booster to ignite motivation. Rewards can also be useful for boring tasks, but if there is an alternative to a reward, then use that alternative.

Praise is another motivator, but like material rewards there can be a dulling effect if used indiscriminately. It also needs to be delivered quickly; there is no benefit in praising an employee during an annual performance review for a task he or she completed months earlier, and many educators argue that in the last few decades the use of praise for small children has been excessive, such as handing out trophies for "participation." Those children who really excel feel the praise they've received has been cheap or insincere. Many researchers suggest that members of the "overpraised" millennial generation now expect to be praised for everything they do.

Peer acceptance is a powerful motivator. Let's say you're going on a fishing trip. You're a newbie, and your companions are all experienced anglers. I guarantee your brain will be highly motivated to learn about fishing so that you'll be respected by your peers and be able to participate in their discussions about fishing.

Being in a learning environment provides motivation. This often starts with the family. In some families, parents set the pace by being lifelong learners themselves, which sets the example for their children, who grow up assuming that learning is something that you just do every day. Parents can also encourage their children to learn by exposing them to new and interesting things, such as taking them to museums. I was one of those lucky children who grew up in a household where learning new things was considered a normal thing to do. Thanks to my parents, I was naturally curious and extremely motivated to learn. When I was eight, I built my first remote-control car. My dad was an electronics engineer, so he taught me the basics of electronics, and we also had the tools in the house to do carpentry work. I built my little car out of wood, bought a motor, connected some cables and batteries, hooked up some buttons, and I had my first car. I acquired the knowledge to do this because in our household it was just the normal thing to do. No one thought about material rewards or praise. Thanks to my parents, I was naturally motivated by my curiosity, which came from within. Almost everything that I've done in life has been that way. There are things I want to do, and I just go ahead and learn and do them.

Autonomy motivates. This is having the sense of control and feeling that you are learning under your own direction, which is why many people fail in school. It's not because they're stupid; it's because they're told to learn things they don't want to learn, and they don't see the *value* in learning. Remember that learning takes effort, and you'll gladly expend the effort if you see the value in it. This was the case with my friend Fred, who dove into learning math purely as the result of his own decision. When I was in high school, I did not like most of what was taught in history, mainly because it wasn't taught in a way that was fun. It seemed boring and irrelevant.

But when history was about wars, I was totally into it!

Purpose is important. To really get excited about learning something, you have to know the relevance of what you're learning and its application to your life. This is another problem schools have—they too often teach a lot that to the student has no visible purpose and no application in real life. Like my friend Fred, I went through this myself; for example, I had to take math and algebra and then Calculus I, II and III. If Calculus II was painfully irrelevant to my life, you can imagine how I felt about Calculus III.

Once you have the necessary motivation, what are the best strategies to learn more effectively?

1. Retrieving

You can train yourself to retrieve information more effectively from your long-term memory back to your short-term memory. For example, after you're done studying or reading something, put away all your notes or your books and try to recall the most important ideas that you just read. Do this without looking at the book or the notes. Even if you fail to remember anything, it's okay. Go back, read it again, and try to do the retrieval practice. By struggling to retrieve a memory, you make those memories stronger, and trying to reconstruct them without looking at the information, you create a different retrieval pathway in your brain to find that memory.

By searching for that memory, you also activate related information, which makes it easier for future retrieval. Retrieval practice is also a good way of knowing what information we miss, so then we know we haven't really grasped that important piece of information.

2. Pacing

As I learned when cramming for exams, if you continually shove information into your memory pipeline, it quickly backs up, and you'll experience memory overload. To learn effectively, you need to take breaks. This allows your brain to catch up and send some memories—the new information you've taken in—to your long-term memory storage in the limbic system, which includes the hippocampus, the amygdala, the cingulate gyrus, the thalamus, the hypothalamus, the epithalamus, the mammillary body, and other parts of your brain. Sleep is the best break, during which your brain is busy processing the sensory input from the day, but you also need to take breaks every few hours.

During your breaks, you can use retrieval techniques. Each retrieval happens in a different context, and each time you practice you create a new pathway to that memory.

The opposite of this is when you're trying to overstudy or cram. As I mentioned earlier, when we try too learn too quickly— such as the day before the big exam—your brain has no time to reinforce all the new information you've been pouring into it.

3. Interleaving

Research suggests that you shouldn't study one idea, topic, or type of problem for very long. Instead, you should change subjects often. Interleaving is the process of pacing yourself and switching between different topics. For example, you might have to study math, biology, and physics, so you decide you're going to study each one for forty minutes. Interleaving means you alternate, so you say I'm going to study twenty minutes of math, then twenty minutes of biology, then twenty minutes of physics, and then after taking a break going back again for twenty minutes of math and continuing as before. This technique has been shown to reinforce learning.

Studying like this may seem harder than studying one type of material for a long time, but it's shown to be more helpful in the long run. Make sure you spend enough time on each subject; switching too often can start looking like multitasking, which you definitely don't want to do. (I'll talk about multitasking in the next section.)

4. Elaborating

When you learn something, if you can put it into context it has more meaning and it's easier to remember. Elaboration also involves making connections among ideas you are trying to learn and connecting the material to your own experiences, memories, and day-to-day life. It also involves explaining and describing ideas with many details.

For example, let's say you're studying the attack on Pearl Harbor. The date was December 7, 1941. You've been told this brought the United States into World War II, but is that all? It sounds like a random event from more than seventy years ago! The date seems meaningless, but if you elaborate, it becomes easier to remember. Ask yourself *why* did the Japanese attack? Was it just random nastiness?

No, it wasn't just random nastiness. In the 1920s and 1930s, Japan was seeking to expand its influence and control over parts of Asia and the Pacific. To do this, it had an increased need for natural resources including oil, minerals, and steel. This is easy to understand.

The United States was a competitor and also wanted these natural resources. In response to Japanese aggression, the U.S.

government placed restrictions on doing business with Japan. Japanese assets in the United States were frozen. In 1939, President Roosevelt moved the U.S. Pacific Fleet from California to Pearl Harbor. This move was seen as a threat by Japan. Military leaders and politicians in Japan saw a war between the U.S. and Japan as inevitable, with the solution being to attack first, which the Japanese did. Plus, many in the Japanese military command believed that after Pearl Harbor the United States would negotiate a peaceful settlement.

The point to all of this is that if you know the context of what you're learning—that the U.S. and Japan were confronting each other over resources and influence in the Pacific—then the event becomes much easier to remember because it's linked to other memories.

Multitasking

In our culture, people often express admiration for those who can "multitask." They say, "It's amazing how Susan can juggle so many responsibilities at once! Handling emails, reviewing the budget, planning the meeting, training the new hire, overseeing the product launch—all in the same morning!"

Susan may, in fact, be a jack of all trades and master of none.

Although by multitasking we think we're doing several things at once, it's a powerful and destructive illusion. Earl Miller, a neuroscientist at MIT and a world expert on divided attention, says that our brains are "not wired to multitask well . . . When people think they're multitasking, they're actually just switching from one task to another very rapidly. And every time they do, there's a cognitive cost in doing so." Even though we think we're getting a lot done, ironically, multitasking makes us demonstrably less efficient.

When people say they're multitasking, they're really *task*

switching. While there are some people who can task switch better than others, the moment you do task switching you lose focus from the task at hand. Your brain is not able to perform high cognitive load functions at one time because when you switch to a new task, you're presenting your brain with a new goal with a new set of rules to follow to complete that task. This means your brain has to use a lot of its energy to do routine "back office" work to adapt to the new task, and the more complicated the task, the more complex the rules and goals. Research has shown that it actually takes less time to do two tasks consecutively than try to multitask and do two things at once by switching back and forth.

Here's a good example.

Say the numbers "12345678910" as fast as you can.

Now say the letters "ABCDEFGHIJ" as fast as you can.

Now mentally combine the first letter with the first number, and say the new list as fast as you can, without looking at it: "A1 B2 C3 D4 E5 F6 G7 H8 I9 J10." I'll bet you get quickly bogged down as your brain switches back and forth and works to combine two familiar memories. This is what happens when you're trying to do two tasks at the same time. To try to adapt to the different rules and goals, your brain slows down.

Fixed vs. Growth Mind-sets

Consider mind-sets. The pioneer in this concept is Carol Dweck, the Lewis and Virginia Eaton Professor of Psychology at Stanford University. She talks about fixed or growth mind-sets, and I want to include them in this learning and memory chapter because mind-sets influence how we learn. A person with a fixed mind-set believes that he or she is not good at something, so they don't even try or make the effort to be better at it. They believe that you have to be "talented," and that you're born with it; so when they try and it doesn't work out for them, they give up. By giving up, they are not going to learn because they're not even trying, and thus a vicious circle is created. As we know, learning requires hard work, thinking, and practice. Innate "talent" is generally irrelevant.

People with fixed mind-sets run from errors, thus ensuring there will be minimal brain activity. People with growth mind-sets embrace and learn from their mistakes, which ensures that there will be increased brain activity; and this increased brain activity leads to learning.

People with fixed and growth mind-sets have different answers to different questions that they think about, such as:

Question	Fixed Mind-set	Growth Mind-set
Am I prepared enough?	No.	I've done my homework, and now is the time for action!
Will people like me?	No.	I will treat everyone with fairness, dignity, and respect. If they don't like me, that's their problem.
Do other people have the same problems as I do?	No.	Of course everyone has problems. Who cares? I'm going to succeed!
Am I intelligent enough?	No.	I'm just as smart as the next guy!
Do I love my job?	No. I hate it and only work for the paycheck.	I love what I do and cannot wait to get to work every day!

Certain noncognitive factors affect learning. To change your mindset from a fixed to a growth mindset, it's important to understand or to be mindful of the noncognitive factors.

Here are five noncognitive factors that affect learning:

1. **Your ability and competence grows with your effort.** This mindset refers to your own ability to realize that when you put focused effort into something you can achieve greater learning.

2. **A sense of belonging to a community or a group.** For example, when students are in environments where they do not feel welcome, such as if they're being bullied at school or being segregated for their choices, learning becomes harder because they lack a sense of belonging. This directly affects us in the most primitive way. Humans are designed to work in groups; considerable research supports our tendency to act as groups rather than individuals. When we worry about belonging, it increases stress, increases our cognitive load, and lowers our productivity and engagement.

3. **Finding value in what you do.** Growth mind-sets find value in everything they do, whether it has a negative or positive impact. They understand the value of every experience. Mistakes are actually chances to learn. People with growth mindsets understand this clearly. People with a fixed mind-set do not and blame others or themselves.

4. **Knowing you can succeed.** Understanding you have the power is important in learning. People with a fixed mindset tend to believe that they are not good at something, so they fail or give up when much effort is needed.

5. **Meaningful learning requires struggle, confusion, and mistakes.** As mentioned earlier, the harder the task, the more likely you'll learn.

As you Train Your Brain for Success and build your Three Pillars of Life, your ability to focus, learn, and remember are critically important. It's how you learn new skills and gain deeper insight into life. Every person who has a healthy brain should look at learning as a lifelong activity.

Here are fifteen tips to boost your learning potential.

15 Tips to Enhance Your Brain's Cognitive Potential

1. Set Up Rituals and Follow Your Rules

There is nothing worse for your focus and productivity than not having a clear goal and small rituals for the things you do. Set up rules to deal with such things as email or social media accounts. For instance, set a schedule to check and respond to emails two or three times per day, and do not deviate from that.

Pay attention to your environmental stimuli. If you are too cold or too hot or there are too many noises or people around, this will have a detrimental effect on your daily activities.

2. Set Realistic Deadlines and Goals

Set goals that make sense. I can't tell you how many times I have seen people set goals for themselves that are impossible to accomplish. The longer you take to accomplish a goal, the more likely you will be discouraged from keeping at that task. Set mini- or micro-goals: if you have one big goal, divide it into smaller goals. The more goals you achieve, the more your brain gets excited and craves to do more. Finally, set up deadlines so that you do not wait for the last minute to finish a task, which not only can be frustrating but also might jeopardize your results.

3. Increase Your EQ and Discover Yourself

Remember that your EQ—your "emotional IQ"—is the source of your success. Try to understand other people, and try to be in their shoes. Be empathetic. You must be open-minded and understand that there are many points of views and solutions to situations. You must also understand and know yourself. You will not be able to master your EQ if you are not aware of your virtues and flaws.

4. Reward Yourself

Rewarding yourself is one of the most important things you can do to keep going and stay excited. It does not have to be a monetary reward; it can be anything, such as playing an hour of video games, going to the movies with a companion, or eating a candy bar after reading your book chapter. The brain craves rewards; as I mentioned earlier, reward bias is the most important bias we have. Take advantage of this key characteristic of your brain.

5. Avoid Clutter and Be Organized

Nothing is more frustrating for your brain than not knowing where things are or where to begin. Try to keep a neat environment around you. Although you might think that keeping things neat requires more energy than throwing things around, the truth is that eventually the energy required to counteract that entropy is a lot greater than being organized.

6. Prioritize and Understand What Needs Your Focus

In tip number two, I mentioned that you need to set realistic goals. This tip is about which goals should be set in what order. A general rule of thumb is to start with the most complicated task first when your brain is not exhausted or overwhelmed. As your day progresses, you can do the easier tasks, such as checking emails or making phone calls. Remember that you need to focus on one task at a time. It is a myth that we can multitask.

7. Outsource When You Can

This tip might not be very useful for the person who is just starting a new business with limited funds. Sometimes you have to be the CEO, sales guy, CFO, admin assistant, and reception-ist. As your company grows, start delegating the simple tasks to other people. You can then focus on those tasks from tip #6 that really need your attention.

8. Do Not Multitask

Multitasking on complicated tasks is almost impossible. Yes, you can do simple things simultaneously, such as knitting while you watch television, but you can't do two complex tasks at the same time, such as trying to solve a math equation while you read the recipe for how to bake a cake. Your brain can't handle that. The more complex the situation, the more focused it has to be; hence, it cannot focus on a second task. Multitasking is why sometimes you do not remember where you put your car keys. When you put those down, you were most likely focused on something else, and your brain did not register where you left your keys.

9. Take Breaks

Taking breaks gives your mind a moment to be cleared, es-pecially when you are stuck on a task or problem. Go out, take a walk, listen to music, or watch TV. Do something to get your mind off the project. If you work your brain constantly without breaks, it will become fatigued.

10. Establish Different Learning Styles

One of the biggest problems people have is that they have a hard time remembering important information, but the brain learns in many different ways, and you must establish your most ideal learning method. By doing so, you will learn how to learn more effectively. Many techniques can help you absorb more information more effectively, such as flashcards, mnemonics, mind mapping, summarizing, and chunking. Pick a few, try them, and see which one works best for you.

11. Be a Mentor or a Teacher

Although teaching people should go under tip #10, I decided to make this one a tip on its own because this is the most powerful way to learn effectively. If you get into the habit of teaching people what you know, you will be amazed at how much you start remembering. It's equally important to surround yourself with the right mentors and teachers. I have seen too many people give up on a career because they had terrible mentors or teachers. Most teachers are highly capable, but you've probably had one whom no one seemed to understand—and his or her failure to connect discouraged you from learning the subject. On the other hand, you've probably had a teacher whose enthusiasm and desire to teach made the subject interesting. Mentors are a great way to acquire valuable information, tips, and knowledge, but you must make sure you pick the right ones.

12. Understand We Are Visual

I can't emphasize enough how important visual inputs are to humans. Use imagery and videos to learn and teach: they are the most powerful tools we have. Twenty-five percent of our brain power is dedicated to processing visual information. That is a lot of brain power! Use it to your advantage. I, for instance, love learning with diagrams or watching an educational video with pictures. Use PowerPoint effectively—avoid as much text as you possibly can.

13. Ask Lots of Questions

Growing up, I never felt embarrassed to ask any questions in school, and this gave me a great edge. Many people are terrified and scared to look dumb in front of a class if they ask a "bad" question. You must get over that fear. The more you ask, the more you will understand. In fact, mentors love to be asked questions; that is why they are mentoring you. They want to transfer all their knowledge for you to be successful. Take advantage of this, especially when you meet an expert on the field you are in.

14. Learn by Hands-on Experience

Unfortunately, most schools don't have the necessary resources and time to allow students to touch and see the things they learn about. Learning by doing is perhaps the oldest and most effective learning strategy in the world. The minute we're born we imitate what our parents and siblings do. It is just the simplest form of learning. Imagine playing basketball only from watching online training videos—I don't think you would be an all-star! While learning from an online video can be useful, the minute you have the chance, apply those learning tips yourself. Make your own website, build your own tree house, or try selling a product to someone yourself.

15. Exercise Your Brain

This one is crucial for your development, survival, and success. I don't mean to exercise your brain by just solving puzzles or playing brain-training games. Exercising your brain means applying the tips above; it means *challenging yourself* by doing new and unfamiliar things and exercising your body, which also helps your brain. Exercising your brain means not leading a sedentary life, being open to new ideas, thinking outside the box, and embracing new relationships. It means understanding it's OK to fail and learning from those mistakes rather than punishing yourself for them.

Exercising your brain is the source of your well-being and success.

Summary

- While the ability to learn is exhibited in animals with very tiny brains and is not exclusive to humans or even to vertebrates, we can say with confidence that because of its size and complexity, the human brain is at the top of the class when learning something.
- Learning involves the actual growth of dendrites, the branched projections of a neuron that act to propagate the electrochemical stimulation received from other neural cells to the cell body, but brain fibers can only grow from existing brain fibers. To learn something new, you must build on information that is already stored in your brain. For example, when you first learn that 2 + 2 = 4, you then build on that piece of retained information to understand that 25 + 25 = 50.
- Memory is the faculty of storing information to be retrieved in the future. Memory comes in two broad forms: short term (STM) and long term (LTM). In general, all memories start as short term, with only some being converted to long-term memories.
- One of the keys to long-term memory is repetition. Think of a song that you play on the piano. The first time you play it you either read the sheet music or carefully pick out each note by ear. The notes are unfamiliar, but as you play them they go into your short-term memory. If you don't play the song again for a few days, you'll forget how it goes, but if you play it every day, eventually you'll have it memorized—that is, the pattern will be moved to your long-term memory.

- Hyperthymesia is the very rare condition where someone has an extremely detailed autobiographical memory. People with this condition remember an abnormally vast number of their life experiences, which they often find annoying.
- Thinking and learning are slow and require effort. Like learning how to play a musical instrument, struggle and confusion are a normal part of deep and transformative learning.
- Concentration and focus are very important cognitive abilities characteristic of human beings. We need to focus our attention on something to learn about it, and human learning is a result of paying attention to what is being taught as well as making use of our senses. As you Train Your Brain for Success and build your Three Pillars of Life—health, relationships, and wealth—your ability to focus, learn, and remember are critically important.
- Here are fifteen tips to boost your learning potential:
1. Set up rituals and follow your rules.
2. Set realistic deadlines and goals.
3. Increase your EQ and discover yourself.
4. Reward yourself.
5. Avoid clutter and be organized.
6. Prioritize and understand what needs your focus.
7. Outsource when you can.
8. No multitasking.
9. Take breaks.
10. Establish different learning styles.
11. Be a mentor or a teacher.
12. Understand we are visual.
13. Ask lots of questions.
14. Learn by hands-on experience.
15. Exercise your brain.

8. *Sweet Sleep!*

"We are such stuff as dreams are made on, and our little life is rounded with a sleep."

— Shakespeare, *The Tempest*

Ah, sleep! It refreshes the soul and rests the body. Most of us love our sleep and are unhappy when we're deprived of it.

It is amazing to think that we spend nearly a third of our lives fast asleep. That means that by the time you turn sixty, you will have spent *twenty years* snoozing! While much of the science behind sleep is still undiscovered, if our body and mind wants us to sleep for such long periods, it must be an important part of our lives. Think of our distant past when humans were hunters and barely had a safe shelter. Hundreds of predators wanted to taste us for dinner. Staying asleep eight hours every night would make us very vulnerable to those predators, yet we managed to sleep.

Among mammals, the desire and necessity for sleep is ubiquitous, but the amount varies widely from species to species. Dogs sleep an average of ten hours a day, while cats sleep over twelve hours. But do you have a horse? It sleeps only about two hours a night, and does this in a series of short mini-sleeps. What does a horse do during the rest of the night? Basically, it just stands around, pondering the meaning of life. (I just made that up. I do not know what goes through a horse's mind while it stands there under the starry skies.)

Other mammals needing minimal sleep include elephants (three to four hours a night), giraffes (two hours, taken in short chunks), deer (three hours), and walruses, which can go up to eighty-four hours straight without sleeping.

Some creatures can put half their brain to sleep while the other half stays awake. This is called unihemispheric sleep ("uni" meaning "one"). The phenomenon has been observed in birds and aquatic mammals. The reasons for the development of uni-hemispheric sleep are likely that it enables the sleeping animal to receive and respond to stimuli—threats, for instance—from its environment. It can enable a bird to remain aloft while sleeping—the common swift, for example, often stays airborne for months without touching either the earth or the sea. It can also help aquatic mammals, such as the bottlenose dolphin, which needs to surface to breathe. To "sleep," the dolphin shuts down half its brain; after approximately two hours, the animal will reverse this process, awakening the rested half of the brain while resting the active side. This pattern is often called catnapping. In this way, one half of the brain is always conscious enough to direct the animal to swim to the surface to take a breath.

Among other mammals, humans are capable of micro-sleep, which means falling asleep for just a few seconds. A micro-sleep is a temporary episode of sleep or drowsiness, which may last for a fraction of a second or up to thirty seconds. In behavioral terms, micro-sleeps manifest as droopy eyes, slow eyelid-closure, and head nodding. In electrical terms, micro-sleeps are often classified as a shift in electroencephalography (EEG) during which 4–7 Hz (theta wave) activity replaces the waking 8–13 Hz (alpha wave) background rhythm.

While micro-sleeps often occur as a result of sleep deprivation, normal non-sleep-deprived individuals can also experience them during monotonous tasks. Micro-sleeps become extremely dangerous when they occur in situations that demand constant alertness, such as driving a motor vehicle or working with heavy machinery. People who experience micro-sleeps often remain unaware of them and believe themselves to have been continuously awake or to have temporarily lost focus on the job at hand.

If you are sleep deprived and find yourself nodding off behind the wheel, you owe it to yourself and your loved ones to change your daily schedule and *get more sleep*. It may be a matter of life and death.

Sleep is primarily a function of the brain, so it's expected that without a brain that's developed enough to actually sleep, an animal won't sleep. Cnidarians (jellyfish, hydra, coral) never sleep. Sponges never sleep. Plants, bacteria, and fungi do not sleep. (Those nasty bacteria that are lodged in your bronchial passages, causing your sore throat and cough? They're busy 24/7!)

Arthropods (crustaceans, arachnids, insects) don't sleep; they enter a metabolic slowdown state called torpor, which is a state of decreased physiological activity in an animal, usually signified by a reduced body temperature and metabolic rate. The term can refer to the extended time a hibernator spends at low body temperature, or it can refer to a shorter period of low body temperature and metabolism, as in the animal's "daily torpor." Animals that undergo daily torpor include birds and some mammals, including many marsupial species, rodent species (such as mice), and bats.

How Much Sleep Do You Need?

There is no real formula as to how much sleep we actually need. Sleep demands vary from person to person, and many factors influence the need for sleep, such as age, pregnancy, environment, and drugs. Consider the age factor: most infants require about sixteen hours of sleep, yet adults are fine with an average of eight hours. That is half the time needed by an infant. Despite eight hours being the average sleep time, some adults need just five hours every day to feel ready and energized, while others, like myself, need about nine or ten hours.

Is lost sleep recovered? In the long term, no. When your body is deprived of sleep, you generate "sleep debt," and like any other debt you might accumulate in life, you have to pay it back. The more you accumulate sleep debt, the worse it is for your body and mind. We believe we can function at our peak level on less sleep, but that's not true, and considerable research supports this fact. If you live a life of constant sleep deprivation, then you live a life of constant impairment. Your judgment is affected, reaction times slowed, mood soured, body chemicals thrown out of balance, and much more. You might think you're OK, but you're not. It is like a drunken person saying they are fine to drive. They think they are, but we all know it is not the case.

When I was a graduate student, we would attend a few seminars every week to see what other scientists were doing and keep up to date with new advances in science. During my four years of school, I would fall asleep quite often, within five minutes of the speaker talking. I used to believe they were boring, but I was completely sleep deprived, and my body would shut down the first moment it could. Being in a room with dim lights was not the best place to fight sleep. If you fall asleep that easily as I used to, you are sleep deprived.

Stimulants, although effective in the short term, in the long run will not help you. Caffeine is the most popular antisleep stimulant, but if you keep accumulating sleep debt, caffeine or any other stimulant will eventually have no effect on you. Your brain can't be tricked for too long.

The effects of not sleeping can be strong enough to cause

death. Experiments with rodents show that a normal rat, whose life span is about three years, will die if entry into the REM stage of sleep is deprived for five weeks; and rats that are deprived of all sleep stages (one through five) will only live only three weeks. The effects are worse than being food deprived!

Sleep is controlled by our brains. There is a line of thought that I greatly concur with that suggests that neurons need time to repair themselves and get rid of by-products and toxins generated during a normal day. If we do not rest, these neurons accumulate too much toxicity, deplete all their energy, and begin to malfunction. This in turn creates drowsiness, reduces the amount of concentration and logical thinking, increases stress hormone levels, affects motor control and mood, and impairs your memory. Depending on the amount of debt you generate, it can lead to hallucinations, short-term paranoia, and accelerated aging.

How long can a human being survive without sleep?

Scientists aren't sure.

In 1965, a teenager named Randy Gardner established the record for the longest a person has ever voluntarily gone without sleep, staying awake for 264 hours (about eleven days) when he was seventeen years old. (Remember that rats that have been totally deprived of sleep die in twenty-one days. Randy was pushing the limit but probably in no danger of death.) This was for a school science fair project. When Gardner finally went to sleep and woke up fourteen hours later, he seemed to have suffered no ill effects. Testing showed that Gardner appeared to have fully recovered from his loss of sleep, with follow-up sleep recordings taken one, six, and ten weeks after the fact showing no significant differences. While no long-term psychological or physical effects were observed, recent research has shown that your cognitive abilities are diminished by sleep deprivation during the period of the event—that is, while you're awake and sleep deprived. Twenty-four hours of deprivation impairs your cognitive abilities up to 30% and up to 50% for forty-eight hours. They are restored after sufficient sleep.

The time line for death due to sleep deprivation remains elusive. In contrast, if you are deprived of food, oxygen, or water, scientists can give you an exact time line showing what will happen to you during the period of deprivation. It's measurable and certain. For example, if you are deprived of water, you will probably die within three days and certainly within ten days. The physiological changes leading to death by dehydration are well known, but sleep is much more mysterious. No one really knows the limits to which a human can go without sleep because sleep is something the brain *does to itself*, and after certain point it will be implacable in its effort to put itself to sleep.

This suggests that while your brain may not *require* the sleep you give it, it desperately *wants* it, which is an interesting thought. Why would your brain want what it doesn't necessarily need?

My recommendation is to sleep as much as your body tells you. I know this can be a challenge for people with regular jobs and children (especially babies!), but whenever you can, forget the clock and sleep as much as you can. Generally, most healthy people can't sleep too much. At a certain point, your brain wakes up, and that's it—you're awake, and the idea of staying in bed feels unpleasant. If you or a loved one sleeps excessively because you just don't want to get out of bed, you may be suffering from depression, and I urge you to seek the services of a qualified mental health professional. You deserve to be able to wake up refreshed and looking forward to the day ahead!

Sleep 101

The human sleep cycle can be divided into five stages: stages 1 through 4, and REM (rapid eye movement). Stage 1 is our lightest sleep phase. It's when we're falling asleep, and we drift from sleep to wake stages. In this stage, it's very easy to be awakened, and we often experience involuntary muscle contractions.

During stage 2, our muscle activity and our brain activity slow down with some bursts of rapid waves called sleep spindles.

During stages 3 and 4, our bodies are inactive, and we experience extremely slow brain waves called delta. Stages 3 and 4 are the stages of very deep sleep. These are the stages where we do not hear our alarm clocks and when people sleepwalk or children have night terrors. If you are awakened at this stage, you will feel disoriented and typically not remember what happened for a few minutes.

The fifth stage is REM, the last in the cycle. It's characterized by rapid breathing, rapid eye movements (hence the acronym, REM), increased heart rate, male erection, and temporarily paralyzed limbs. When we're awakened from this stage, we tend to describe bizarre visions: our dreams.

The whole cycle takes between 90 and 110 minutes, which means that we typically go through three to five cycles per night. We tend to stay in stages 3 and 4 about 20% of a sleep cycle. Toward the end stages of sleep, the REM stage gets longer.

Our sleep-wake cycle is controlled mainly by a milieu of chemicals called neurotransmitters. They do this by acting as signals to a select group of neurons in our brains. Some of these neurotransmitters include serotonin, dopamine, GABA, and norepinephrine. These chemicals turn on and off groups of neurons that control the wake-sleep cycle.

Other chemicals are also involved in the sleep cycle. For instance, adenosine (a purine nucleoside) has been shown to increase levels in our bloodstream, causing drowsiness. Adenosine is then broken down while we sleep.

Your Circadian Rhythm

Are you a morning person—asleep by ten o'clock and awake and alert at the crack of dawn?

Or are you a night owl and hit your stride after sunset, when everyone else is winding down?

Your natural comfort level with when you like to wake up and go to sleep is a function of your circadian rhythm—the physical, mental, and behavioral changes that follow a roughly twenty-four-hour cycle, responding primarily to light and darkness in your environment. A circadian rhythm can be found in most living things, including animals, plants, and many tiny microbes. The term "circadian" comes from the Latin *circa*, meaning "around" (or "approximately"), and *diēm*, meaning "day."

The study of circadian rhythms is called chronobiology. Your circadian rhythm is determined by your biological clock, which are groupings of interacting molecules in cells throughout the body. A "master clock" in your brain coordinates all the body clocks so that they are in synch.

The master clock that controls circadian rhythms consists of a group of nerve cells in the brain called the suprachiasmatic nucleus, or SCN, which contains about twenty thousand nerve cells and is located in the hypothalamus, an area of the brain just above where the optic nerves from the eyes cross. The SCN takes visual information on the length of the day and night (or more precisely, light and dark) from the retina, interprets it, and transmits it to the pineal gland, a tiny structure shaped like a pine cone and located on the epithalamus. In response, the pineal secretes the hormone melatonin, which makes your body feel tired.

While semiautonomous, your master clock is influenced by your environment. When it's dark at night, your eyes send a signal to the hypothalamus that it's time to feel tired. Your brain, in turn, sends a signal to your body to release melatonin.

That's why your circadian rhythm tends to coincide with the cycle of daytime and nighttime and why you experience jet lag when you fly across many time zones, such as from New York to Honolulu. Suddenly, it's dawn in Honolulu and the day is just beginning, but your biological clock says it's midafternoon New York time. It takes the master clock a few days to reset itself to the new time zone.

Other physiological changes that occur according to a circadian rhythm include heart rate and many cellular processes, including cell metabolism, oxidative stress, endoplasmic reticular stress, epigenetic modification, immune and inflammatory responses, hypoxia/hyperoxia response pathways, autophagy, and regulation of the stem cell environment.

Health problems can result from a disturbance to the circadian rhythm that also affects the reticular activating system, which is crucial for maintaining a state of consciousness. Research suggests a reversal in the sleep/wake cycle may be a sign or complication of uremia, azotemia, or acute renal failure of the circadian clockwork and/or misalignment of the circadian timing system with the light/dark cycle, which might be important in the development of metabolic disorders, such as obesity and diabetes, which are associated with lifestyle and genetic factors.

The drugs you take—whether legal or illegal—can disrupt your central circadian pacemaker. Individuals suffering from substance abuse often display disrupted rhythms that can increase the risk for substance abuse and relapse. It is possible that genetic and/or environmental disturbances to the normal sleep and wake cycle can increase the susceptibility to addiction.

If you've ever wondered why many teenagers seem chronically sleepy, it's because of the sudden shift in their master clocks. One of the many changes in the body during puberty is closely related to how they sleep. There's a shift in the timing of their circadian rhythms. Before puberty, the typical child gets sleepy around 8:00 or 9:00 p.m. When puberty begins, this rhythm shifts a couple of hours later, and the teenager wants to go to sleep at 10:00 or 11:00 p.m.

The natural shift in a teen's circadian rhythms is called "sleep phase delay." The need to sleep is delayed for about two hours. At first, teens may appear to be suffering from insomnia and will have a hard time falling asleep at the accustomed time, but while they begin going to sleep later, they still need an average of nine hours of sleep at night. Suddenly, this can create a problem when they have to wake up at 6:30 a.m. to get to school by 7:30 or even 7:00 a.m. If a teen goes to bed at 11:00 p.m. and is up at 6:00 a.m., that's only seven hours of sleep, which for an adult might be acceptable but is tougher on a teenager. If they go to bed late, they will be unable to get the sleep they need, and they'll drag through the day.

Parents must remind their teens to never drive when feeling tired—it can be just as bad as being intoxicated. Auto accidents related to drowsy driving take the lives of more than 1,550 people every year. These crashes are most often caused by young people under the age of twenty-five. Their lifestyle choices make them more likely to be driving when they are sleepy.

With some extra parental prodding, teens can adjust to the new sleep schedule of their bodies.

A key strategy that parents must use to get their children to sleep on time is to ban all electronic devices, particularly phones, from the bedroom at night. (This advice is good for anyone who wants to care for their brain and get a good night's sleep!) Your bed is for two things: sex (when you're old enough to legally make the choice) and sleep. When it's time to go to sleep, turn off the TV and put away the phone. As you Train Your Brain for Success, give it the sleep it needs and deserves!

As You Sleep, Your Brain Keeps Busy

Although sleep was long thought to be a passive process, we know with certainty that our brains are very active during our sleep phases. One of the greatest discoveries about sleep is that our brains consolidate memories and boost our learning abilities during sleep. The popular phrase "sleep on it" is not far-fetched from reality. Many people have had eureka moments during sleep, such as in the case of Dimitri Mendeleev, a scientist whose greatest discovery was the periodic table of elements. This idea came to him one afternoon while taking a nap. According to the story, Mendeleev had been listening to his family as they played chamber music. He grew tired and, upon excusing himself, went to bed and drifted off to sleep listening to the music.

Mendeleev dreamed a vision of the basic elements of the universe flowing together in a manner akin to the progression of a musical sequence, orderly and beautiful. He awoke and outlined from his dream every element in order. This sequence became known as the periodic table of elements.

Another extremely important function of sleep is the flushing of toxins from your brain. When we sleep, toxins flush from our brain through our spinal cord. This means that if you are constantly sleep deprived you are accumulating more toxins in your brain than you should.

The key question here: If sleeping can boost our memory and learning considerably, why don't we encourage sleeping more? It seems that the only people taking advantage of this fact are preschools, where they provide time for all children to take naps. No wonder children are so clever!

Let's take this a step further. Why don't companies adopt a system to encourage sleeping? Lack of sleep costs the United States $100 billion per year in sleep-related accidents. Why do we only take naps in kindergarten? We know children need it, and we force them to sleep in the afternoon. Our reality, though, is that we *all* need it, not just children. Some agencies understand the value of a nap and having a good night's sleep. At its headquarters, Google has areas dedicated for napping and getting a good rest. The aviation industry understands the importance of having a sharp mind, and most airports have a lounge where pilots can take naps between flights. A NASA study has shown that a twenty-six-minute nap improved a pilot's performance by 34%, and another study has shown that a thirty-minute nap before staying up all night can prevent a significant loss of performance during that night. Considering all the downsides of not sleeping, would you fly on an airplane if you knew the pilot hadn't slept the night before? Would you undergo major surgery with a doctor who is constantly sleep deprived? No. It is crucial for your well-being and your own sanity to get a good rest as often as you can. If you are a business owner, perhaps you would consider allowing employees some free time to allow them to rest. In the end, having more productive employees can only benefit you.

As you build your Three Pillars of Life, getting plenty of shut-eye is an important part of the process! Here are my tips for giving your brain a good night's sleep.

Sleeping Tips

1. Schedule Sleep

Try setting a schedule. Whether you are a late sleeper or an early bird, try to maintain a set schedule. Your body likes routine.

2. Keep it Dark!

Your sleep cycle is affected by light. Avoid watching TV or reading on your iPad while you are in bed. The light from the screens affects your sleep. Also try to keep your room as dark as you can.

3. Exercise

Exercising every day helps you get better sleep. Make sure you do not exercise right before you go to bed or you might end up with the opposite effect.

4. No Drugs That Disrupt Sleep

Avoid caffeine, alcohol, and other drugs. They reduce your sleeping ability and affect REM stages.

5. Relax!

Try relaxing before you go to bed. A warm bath and soothing music are ideal. Read a book or meditate. This calms your body, and your brain activity slows down, which makes it easy to sleep.

6. Get Comfortable

Maintain a comfortable room temperature, and sleep on a comfortable mattress and pillow.

7. Take a Nap

Whenever possible, take a nap in the afternoon. Napping is a natural process that most people need. Who knows, you might discover the next great thing!

As you Train Your Brain for Success and build your Three Pillars of Life, sleep is a great asset, both to rejuvenate your body and to facilitate the formation of memories. Research shows that various sleep stages are involved in the consolidation of different types of memories, and being sleep deprived reduces your ability to learn. In a process called consolidation, while you sleep, you strengthen memories and "practice" skills learned while you were awake. If you are trying to learn something, you can learn it to a certain point with practice, but while you sleep, the process of consolidation makes you learn it better—and requires no effort from you! Now that's a pretty good deal!

Summary

- Sleep is a critical part of our lives. Despite eight hours being the average sleep time, some adults need just five hours every day to feel ready and energized, while others, such as the author of this book, need about nine or ten hours.

- If you live a life of constant sleep deprivation, you live a life of constant impairment. Your judgment is affected, reaction times slowed, mood soured, body chemicals thrown out of balance, and much more. When we sleep, toxins flush from our brain through our spinal cord. This means that if you are constantly sleep deprived you are accumulating more toxins in your brain than you should.

- The human sleep cycle can be divided into five stages: stages 1 through 4, and REM (rapid eye movement). The last in the cycle, REM, is characterized by rapid eye movements, rapid breathing, increased heart rate, male erection, and temporarily paralyzed limbs. When we're awakened from this stage, we tend to remember our dreams.

- While we're able to force ourselves to stay awake, often for extended periods, the effects of not sleeping can be strong enough to cause death.

- Your natural comfort level when you like to wake up and go to sleep is a function of your circadian rhythm—the physical, mental, and behavioral changes that follow a roughly twenty-four-hour cycle, responding primarily to light and darkness in your environment.

- As you Train Your Brain for Success and build your Three Pillars of Life, getting plenty of shut-eye is an important part of the process. Here are seven tips for giving your brain a good night's sleep:
1. Schedule sleep.
2. Keep it dark!
3. Exercise.
4. No drugs that disrupt sleep.
5. Relax!
6. Get comfortable.
7. Take a nap.

9. Alzheimer's Disease and the Aging Brain

As Americans turned the corner from the twentieth century to the twenty-first, we began to think seriously about an issue of demographics that's affecting our nation: An estimated seventy-six million baby boomers—people born between 1946 and 1964 and who represent the largest single age group in the nation—are heading toward retirement and old age.

If you were born in 1946, the beginning of the baby boom, you reached your seventieth birthday in 2016.

If you were born in 1964 at the tail end of the baby boom, in 2016 you turned fifty-two years old. For you, retirement is no longer some far-off event but something looming on the horizon.

For most baby boomers growing up in the 1960s, the idea of "old age" meant golf, grandchildren, apple pie, and rocking chairs, perhaps ending with a vaguely unpleasant stay in a nursing home before being carried away to the family plot. For baby boomers, however, this tolerable and traditional vision of one's "golden years" has been supplanted by something truly horrifying: the possibility of a sort of living death, whereby your mind loses its connection with your past and even your present, and for years, even decades, you exist as a hollow imitation of your former self, wholly dependent on your family or unfamiliar health care providers to help you complete the basic bodily tasks of a three-year-old child.

Alzheimer's disease—perhaps the same illness that people in the old days called "getting senile"—has become a serious health issue for millions of baby boomers and their families. It's a progressive disease that's the most common cause of dementia—a group of brain disorders that cause the loss of intellectual and social skills.

Its name can be traced back to 1901, when German psychiatrist Alois Alzheimer described a condition of dementia in a fifty-year-old woman he called Auguste D. He followed her case until she died in 1906, when he first reported publicly on it. During the next five years, eleven similar cases were reported in the medical literature, some of them already using the term "Alzheimer's disease." For most of the twentieth century, the diagnosis of Alzheimer's disease was applied only to individuals between the ages of forty-five and sixty-five who had developed symptoms of dementia. Then in 1977, a conference on Alzheimer's concluded that the clinical and pathological manifestations of presenile and senile dementia were nearly identical, which eventually led to the diagnosis of Alzheimer's disease as being unrelated to age.

In Alzheimer's disease, brain cells degenerate and die, causing a steady decline in memory and mental function. Changes in brain function happen when abnormal deposits of proteins form amyloid plaques (clusters of protein fragments) and tau tangles (twisted strands of another type of protein), causing neurons to stop functioning and die. As Alzheimer's disease progresses, these plaques and tangles tend to spread through the cortex in a predictable pattern. Over time, the brain physically shrinks— a brain from someone with Alzheimer's is measurably smaller than it was when the person was healthy. The cortex shrivels, damaging areas involved in thinking, planning, and remembering. Shrinkage is especially severe in the hippocampus, an area of the cortex that is most important in forming new memories. Ventricles, the fluid-filled spaces within the brain, grow larger.

The death of neurons eventually leads to problems with basic bodily functions, including swallowing and mobility. This puts the person with the disease at risk for dehydration, poor nutrition, falls and infections, and blood clots. The disease can contribute to such conditions as pneumonia and heart failure.

Alzheimer's disease most commonly affects older adults, but it can also affect people in their thirties or forties. When Alzheimer's disease occurs in someone under the age of sixty-five, it is known as early-onset (or younger-onset) Alzheimer's disease. About 5% of people with Alzheimer's disease have the early-onset form. Many of them are in their forties and fifties when they begin to show symptoms.

The rate of progression varies. People who have been diagnosed with Alzheimer's live an average of eight years, but some patients may survive up to twenty years. The course of the disease depends in part on the person's age at diagnosis and if they have other health conditions.

As of this writing, an estimated 5.5 million Americans of all ages have Alzheimer's disease. Of those, an estimated two hundred thousand individuals are under age sixty-five and have early-onset Alzheimer's. Among all people age sixty-five and older, one in ten—or 10%—has Alzheimer's dementia. Because of the growing number of baby boomers who are turning sixty-five, in the United States, particularly among the increasing ranks of the very elderly, the number of new cases of Alzheimer's and other dementias is projected to soar.

According to the Alzheimer's Association, the disease has ten warning signs:

1. **Memory loss that disrupts daily life.** This includes forgetting recently learned information and important dates or events. Someone with Alzheimer's disease may experience mild confusion and difficulty remembering.

2. **Challenges in planning or solving problems.** The person may experience changes in their ability to develop and follow a plan or work with numbers. They may have trouble following a familiar recipe or keeping track of monthly bills.

3. **Difficulty completing familiar tasks at home, at work, or at leisure.** The person may have trouble driving to a familiar location, managing a budget, or remembering the rules of a favorite game.

4. **Confusion with time or place.** The person may lose track of dates, seasons, and the passage of time. They may have trouble understanding something if it is not happening immediately. Sometimes they may forget where they are or how they got there.

5. **Trouble understanding visual images and spatial relationships.** This is distinct from having normal age-related vision problems, such as cataracts.

6. **New problems with words in speaking or writing.** The person may have difficulty following or joining a conversation, or they may stop in the middle of a conversation and not know how to continue.

7. **Misplacing things and not having the ability to retrace their steps.** They may put things in unusual places or lose something and be unable to review recent events to find it.

8. **Decreased or poor judgment.** For example, they may use poor judgment when handling money and give large amounts to scammers or telemarketers. They may become less attentive to grooming or keeping themselves clean.

9. **Withdrawal from work or social activities.** The person may avoid being social, give up hobbies, or stop following a favorite sports team.

10. Changes in mood and personality. The ordinarily cheerful person can become confused, suspicious, depressed, fearful, or anxious, either at home or at work.

A key to detecting the onset of Alzheimer's is that these changes will occur with greater frequency and consistently over time. For example, everyone misses a bill payment once in a while or misplaces the car keys, but someone who is beginning to show symptoms of Alzheimer's will make these mistakes more frequently and at an increasing rate. Later symptoms include severe mood swings and behavior changes; deepening confusion about time, place, and life events; suspicions about friends, family, or caregivers; difficulty speaking, swallowing, or walking; and severe memory loss.

Causes, Prevention, and (Someday!) a Cure

Human beings are afflicted with many scary diseases, and we can take some comfort in knowing that against even terrible diseases, such as cancer, we can take *action*. We may not be able to cure them, but at least we know we're capable of giving them a good fight, and sometimes we win!

The truly scary thing about Alzheimer's disease is that there is no cure. There is no proven program of prevention. Anyone and everyone who gets Alzheimer's faces an irrevocable decline and early death. To date, there have been no exceptions. A diagnosis of Alzheimer's is a death sentence, with the end coming either quickly or slowly.

To find a cure for any disease, you have to know its causes, and unfortunately the causes of Alzheimer's are still unclear. About 70% of the risk is believed to be genetic, but opinions vary.

The Mayo Clinic says, "Less than five percent of the time, Alzheimer's is caused by specific genetic changes that virtually guarantee a person will develop the disease."

The National Institute on Aging says, "The causes of late-onset Alzheimer's, the most common form of the disease, probably include a combination of genetic, lifestyle, and environmental factors. The importance of any one of these factors in increasing or decreasing the risk of development Alzheimer's may differ from person to person."

The Alzheimer's Association says, "Scientists have identified three genes with rare variations that are believed to cause Alzheimer's, and several genes that increase risk but don't guarantee that a person will develop the disease. Investigators worldwide are working to find additional risk genes. As more effective treatments are developed, genetic profiling may become a valuable risk assessment tool for wider use." Other risk factors include a history of head injuries, depression, or hypertension.

Prevention Magazine—a popular publication—has talked about "Five surprising causes of Alzheimer's disease." According to the magazine, they are:

1. **The use of anti-anxiety medications.** A study published in the *British Medical Journal* followed 1,796 Canadians with Alzheimer's disease and 7,184 healthy controls for six years and found that taking benzodiazepines for more than three months was associated with up to a 51% increase in Alzheimer's disease.

2. **Repeated head injuries, particularly from sports.** This is according to Brian Giunta, MD, Ph.D., a psychiatrist and neuroscientist at the University of Southern Florida. Many other researchers share this opinion.

3. **You're regularly sleep deprived**, which can speed up the development of Alzheimer's disease, according to a study published in the *Neurobiology of Aging.*

4. **You're lonely.** A study in the *Journal of Neurology, Neurosurgery, and Psychiatry* identified links between loneliness and the development of dementia.

5. **You have diabetes in your brain.** According to neuroscien-

tist Suzanne de la Monte, MD, of Brown University, Alzheimer's disease is a metabolic disease that affects the brain. She reasons that since brain cells use glucose as fuel, and insulin tells these cells to take up glucose from the blood, then if brain cells developed insulin resistance, the cells would starve.

With no clear cause, theories abound. Hopefully, in the near future scientists will be able to more accurately determine the causes of Alzheimer's disease and then work in the direction of a cure. In the meantime, what can you do to protect yourself from Alzheimer's?

Unfortunately, there are no scholarly reports on the subject because researchers don't know scientifically what you can do to prevent a disease for which there is no certain cause and no cure. But fear not—the popular press is full of ideas. Probably none of them are harmful, and many are just common sense pointers of how you can keep your brain healthy.

The website Seniorlifestyle.com suggests that you avoid the insecticide DDT. That's good advice for anyone!

Foodmatters.com says you should have a life purpose, and that if you have a life purpose "zestfully pursued," you'll avoid dementia despite those physical impairments. There are many real life examples, they say, of people managing well as they keenly continue to pursue their life adventures, especially adventures that require mental focus and activity. Again—good advice for anyone!

They also claim that a doctor's husband had entered late stage Alzheimer's. After taking a tablespoon of coconut oil twice daily, after a month and a half he was almost completely recovered. The doctor said that metabolizing medium chain triglycerides (MCTs) produces ketones, which dissolve brain plaques and tangles. The website also recommends combining curcumin with vitamin D3 to "prevent or reverse Alzheimer's," and avoiding cookware and deodorants that contain aluminum.

You only need to go online to find dozens of such purported preventative measures against Alzheimer's and even claims of cures, but sadly, none of them have clinical validity, and you should not take them as representing accepted courses of treatment.

But what can you do?

You can keep your brain healthy, challenged, and engaged, and as you build your Three Pillars of Life, remain grateful for the blessings of this life even as you strive to reach a higher level.

Research is making slow but steady progress. The Alzheimer's Association reported that several conditions known to increase the risk of cardiovascular disease, including high cholesterol, diabetes, and high blood pressure, are linked to a higher risk of developing Alzheimer's. Some autopsy studies show that as many as 80% of people with Alzheimer's disease also have cardiovascular disease.

In addition, there is the question of why some people whose brains develop the ubiquitous Alzheimer's plaques and tangles do not progress into full-blown Alzheimer's. Some researchers believe that vascular disease may eventually lead them to an answer. Certain autopsy studies suggest that when the brain is free of vascular disease, plaques and tangles may be present in the brain without causing symptoms of cognitive decline. More research is needed to better understand the link between vascular health and Alzheimer's.

Indeed, much current evidence links brain health to heart health. Your brain is nourished by one of your body's richest networks of blood vessels. Every heartbeat pumps roughly 20% of your blood to your head, and your brain cells consume much of the nutrients and oxygen your blood carries. Therefore, the performance of your heart is critically important to your brain, and whatever you do to your heart will be reflected in your brain health.

It follows that regular physical exercise may be a beneficial strategy to lower the risk of Alzheimer's and vascular dementia. Exercise directly benefits brain cells by increasing blood and oxygen flow in the brain. Because of its known cardiovascular benefits, a medically approved exercise program is a key component of any overall wellness plan.

There's also increasing evidence that *using* your brain may help keep it healthy. As *The New Yorker* reported in July 2016, something called "speed of process" training may be beneficial. This is a specific type of cognitive training that challenges the brain to retain short-term memories and link them together.

As Dan Hurley wrote in the article "Could Brain Training Prevent Dementia?," the person being tested looks at a computer screen. Then, "For the briefest instant, two images appear—one in the middle, one on the periphery. Then the computer prompts you to identify them. Was the central image a tiny car or a little truck? Where along the edge did the second image appear? The more accurate you get, the more fleetingly the pictures appear, the more similar the car and truck get, and the more distracting the background becomes. That is speed-of-processing training. It is always one step ahead of you, yet virtually everyone gets faster and more accurate with practice." Research suggests that people who take this type of training—which, they note, shares many characteristics with the skill set needed to drive a car—are less likely to develop Alzheimer's.

Damage Done By Sensory Deprivation

I've touched upon the growing belief that exercising your brain may help lower your chances of getting Alzheimer's disease. This belief is bolstered by its opposite: It's a fact that when the brain is deprived of sensory input or intellectual stimulation, its health suffers, and the entire organism—the person—can decline and even suffer an early death.

And when your brain is deprived of sensory input, guess what? Out of desperation, it proceeds to manufacture its own.

Here's a very simple example.

Charles Bonnet Syndrome (CBS) is a common condition among people who've lost their sight. It causes people who've lost much of their vision to see things that aren't really there—medically known as having hallucinations. It's named for Charles Bonnet (1720–1793), a Swiss naturalist and philosopher and the first person to describe the syndrome. These visual hallucinations can take many forms, ranging from simple shapes and lines to detailed images of people and landscapes. They may seem authentic, such as seeing a chair in a room that is actually empty, or clearly imaginary, such as a ten-foot-tall Easter bunny. Most frequently, while people will often see patterns or simple shapes, as CNIB reports, there are many accounts of more complex hallucinations, including:

- Little men holding umbrellas at the end of the bed
- Women in red dresses sweeping the floor
- Cloakroom tickets lining the walls and ceiling
- Soldiers marching down the street

By some estimates, as many as 30% of adults with vision loss are affected by CBS, although actual numbers are difficult to determine, since few people who experience these symptoms are likely to discuss them with family members, friends, or physicians.

CBS is sometimes referred to as "phantom vision" syndrome and is often compared to "phantom limb" syndrome in which an individual can continue to receive sensations—and even feelings of pain—from a limb that has been amputated.

The greater the extent of sensory deprivation, the more the brain will try to correct the situation.

One study of intentional sensory starvation was done in the mid-1950s at McGill University in Montreal when Donald O. Hebb, a professor of psychology, set out to study how sensory isolation affects human cognition. Undergraduate student volunteers were recruited to do nothing but lie on a comfortable bed in a lighted cubicle twenty-four hours a day for six weeks.

The volunteers were deprived of normal sensory input. Their eyes were covered with translucent plastic goggles, their heads were cradled in a foam rubber pillow that covered their ears, while the steady hum of an air conditioner and fan masked other sounds. Their arms were encased in soft tubes that kept them from touching anything with their hands. These conditions were maintained around the clock except when the volunteers were being tested, fed, or had to go to the bathroom.

Hebb hoped the experiment would last for six weeks, but the volunteers began to quit after just a few hours. The longest-lasting volunteer served for six days before bailing out. None could tolerate even the low level of sensory deprivation they experienced in the experiment.

In 1957, Woodburn Heron, one of Hebb's collaborators, wrote "The Pathology of Boredom," a *Scientific American* article about the experiences of the subjects. "Nearly all of them reported that the most striking thing about the experience was that they were unable to think clearly about anything for any length of time, and that their thought processes seemed to be affected in other ways." They reported hallucinations of sight, sound, and feeling. "The subjects had little control over the content" of their visions, wrote Heron. "One man could see nothing but dogs, another nothing but eyeglasses of various types, and so on."

How about a practice that's becoming increasingly common in our nation's prisons—solitary confinement? This is keeping a prisoner in a small cell, sometimes for up to twenty-four hours a day, without access to any common activities that prisoners elsewhere in the prison might engage in. The evidence strongly suggests that when the human brain is deprived of normal, everyday intellectual and social stimuli, it begins to malfunction. As *Frontline* reported in 2014, Stuart Grassian, a board-certified psychiatrist and a former faculty member at Harvard Medical School, interviewed hundreds of prisoners in solitary confinement. In one study, he found that roughly a third of solitary inmates were "actively psychotic and/or acutely suicidal." Grassian concluded that being solitary can cause a specific psychiatric syndrome, characterized by hallucinations; panic attacks; overt paranoia; diminished impulse control; hypersensitivity to external stimuli; and difficulties with thinking, concentration, and memory. Some inmates lose the ability to maintain a state of alertness, while others develop crippling obsessions.

Prisoners often adjust to solitary confinement by becoming withdrawn. In a study of inmates at California's Pelican Bay State Prison, psychologist Craig Haney found that prisoners become acutely passive. Haney, a professor at the University of California at Santa Cruz, attributed this loss to the near total lack of control that prisoners have over their day-to-day lives in solitary.

He also found that prisoners in solitary often "begin to lose the ability to initiate behavior of any kind—to organize their own lives around activity and purpose." The results are chronic apathy, lethargy, depression, and despair.

Dr. Haney told *Frontline*, "We are, in ways that we take for granted, social beings, social creatures. We depend on each other for not just stimulation but for a sense of self. A grounding in a social community just in our interactions with other people, how other people react to us, our ability to influence the world by having meaningful interaction and communicating with other people, all of these things are intrinsic to what it means to be a human being. And when you take that away from people, many people are destabilized by it. They begin to question their existence."

The negative effects of isolation can begin in infancy. As Darcia Narvaez, Ph.D., wrote in her article for *Psychology Today* entitled "Can Isolated Babies Become 'Real' Human Beings?," human babies have evolved to expect—and need—nearly constant physical contact while the brain is rapidly developing. Early life requires constant physical presence of other humans, intensive personal care, and responsive social interaction. Frequent physical touch stimulates and grows the baby's sense of self and place. Babies expect to engage frequently in sensitive, responsive face-to-face social "conversations." These experiences build the foundation for social skills that are necessary in adult social life. When human interaction is missing or minimized, a baby will not develop the same social brain as a baby who receives sensory stimulation.

It can be said that while the brain requires tangible substances, such as water, oxygen, and glucose to function, the intangible stimuli of interacting with other people and the environment are equally important. Without such stimulation, while your brain may not literally die—oxygen and glucose can keep it alive—it will malfunction and become not much more useful than an actual three-pound blob of fat.

Speaking of brains that lack stimulation, let's look at a subject that's long been an area of both medical and popular fascination—the brain that slips into a coma, sometimes for years, and then "awakens" and returns to consciousness. Coma is a state of unconsciousness in which a person fails to respond normally to painful stimuli, light, or sound; cannot be awakened; lacks a normal wake-sleep cycle; and does not initiate voluntary actions. A person in a state of coma is described as being comatose.

To determine what insult needs to be done to the brain to go into coma, you have to first establish what parts of the brain are necessary for wakeful consciousness. For a person to maintain consciousness, two important neurological components must both function:

1. The cerebral cortex—the gray matter that forms the outer layer of the brain.

2. The reticular activating system (RAS).

Injury to either or both of these components is sufficient to cause a patient to experience a coma.

A coma can last for hours, days, or weeks. The fascinating question is not why the brain goes into a coma—that's often fairly obvious—but what mechanism brings the patient back into consciousness?

On July 13, 1984, a pickup truck driven by Terry Wallis, who lived in the Ozark Mountains of Arkansas, skidded off a small bridge. The truck was found upside down in a dry riverbed after Wallis smashed into a railing fence and fell twenty-five feet. He was found unconscious and was immobilized but breathing. He was twenty years old.

Within a year of the accident, his coma stabilized into what doctors call a minimally conscious state, but doctors believed his condition was permanent. Medically, a minimally conscious state (MCS) is a disorder of consciousness distinct from a persistent vegetative state. Unlike a persistent vegetative state, in which the patient shows absolutely no response to stimuli, patients with MCS have partial preservation of conscious awareness. They show some responsiveness to outside stimuli—they move a finger or flutter their eyelids. Despite these small responses, patients who are comatose or minimally conscious are incapable of giving informed consent, which is required for participation in clinical research.

For nineteen years—a world record—Terry Wallis existed in this condition, unable to be roused yet showing signs of brain activity. His mother, Angilee, visited him nearly every day and talked to him. He never woke up.

On June 11, 2003, he awakened from his minimally conscious state and began to speak; when a nurse asked him who the lady walking toward him was, he replied "mom." He believed that he was still twenty years old and that the year was still 1984. As *Time* magazine reported, "Using cutting-edge imaging techniques, scientists were able to examine how Wallis's brain had effectively grown new connections—rewiring itself during his long period in the dark—and glean new insight into how the brain works and heals."

Indeed, as *My Multiple Sclerosis* reported, brain scans showed that his right temporal lobe was damaged and withered. There are two temporal lobes, sitting just behind each ear, and both are responsible for storing memories. But despite having one functioning temporal lobe, Walls couldn't make any new memories because his frontal lobes were badly damaged in the crash. They process experience and turn it into memory.

As a result, when Wallis woke up, he assumed he could stand up and walk because he remembered doing these things, but his damaged brain couldn't manage the task. His understanding of himself and the world around him never got updated.

A functional MRI scan (fMRI) scans the brain as it thinks, giving a picture of its different systems at work. Scientists wanted to see Wallis's brain while it listened to his mother's voice, which might reveal what happened to give him back his speech. The scan revealed the expected, normal language system. In other words, just as Angilee had suspected, Terry had been capable of speech all along, but some unknown factor had kick-started his brain.

To try to find out the source of Wallis's rare return to consciousness, a team led by neurologist Nicholas Schiff, of the Weill Medical College of Cornell University in New York, used a new variation of magnetic resonance imaging called diffusion tensor imaging (DTI). As reported by the *MIT Technology Review*, they discovered that a large area in the back of Wallis's brain appeared to have more fibers than normal (fibers are collections of CNS axons having a common site of origin and a common destination), all oriented in the same direction. This suggested that new pathways had grown to connect different brain structures. This unusual pattern encompassed a part of the brain known as the precuneus, which is involved with episodic memory, visuospatial processing, reflections upon self, and aspects of consciousness.

Eighteen months after the first scan, Wallis had improved even more. He could move his previously paralyzed lower limbs, a recovery that was "as unexpected as him recovering speech," said Nicholas Schiff. When the researchers imaged his brain a second time, they found that the unusual area in the back had normalized, while another region, in an area that regulates movement, seemed to have grown more connected.

While doctors knew that throughout its life the brain could reorganize itself by forming new neural connections—a phenomenon called neuroplasticity—it was believed that this didn't happen with comatose or minimally conscious patients. The surprising case of Terry Wallis showed that in many cases the amazing brain, even when its very existence is threatened, is often capable of working "behind the scenes" to repair itself and resume its role as the commander-in-chief of your body.

The Proven Value of Exercise for Good Health

Exercise is a miracle drug. Everyone in the world should be taking high doses of exercise. The more often you take this form of treatment, the more effectively you'll Train Your Brain for Success, and the longer and healthier your life will be. You will sleep better, your mood will be better, age slower, you will feel better, and most of your chronic illnesses will disappear. You will even make more money in the long run!

Unfortunately, in the United States, we often wait until we're sick to address our health. The government spends very little on preventive medicine programs, which in the long run would create a significant decrease in health costs. Take, for example, my story of coping with ADHD and OCD. The cost for those brain scans was well over $3,000, and no insurance would cover it. It was out of pocket. I am lucky and able to afford it, but many people can't. Can you imagine how many peoples' brains might have problems like I did, and I had no idea for years! Imagine how much money we could save if we caught those problems in time!

I am not a politician, so I will not sit here and write about the health care system because it is not the scope of this book, but I do want to emphasize the importance of preventive medicine, and exercising is just that. Considerable scientific literature shows that several diseases respond strongly to exercise, which can reduce blood pressure, lower heart attack risks, and improve diabetes. The opposite is also true. Other literature indicates that people with sedentary lifestyles have a higher risk for several types of cancer, hearts disease, and early death.

Your brain greatly benefits from exercise. Studies have shown that it can help reduce anxiety, memory loss, and depression more effectively for people who exercise than those who have these conditions but do not exercise. In fact, research shows that exercise is the most effective way to prevent Alzheimer's disease and slow its progression.

People used to be much more physically active, just as they still are today in many areas of the world, such as Okinawa, where people have exceptionally long life expectancies. Part of the reason that people's exercise habits have declined started in the twentieth century with the rise of the office worker, treatable medicine, and the booming of organized professional sports.

Eventually, exercise and sports were a focus for people who were endowed with the ability to compete. All of a sudden the world was full of observers of those who exercised. Even studies back in the '50s and '60s and up until not too long ago were all focused on athletes and how to improve their performance and abilities to succeed in organized sports.

I believe part of the problem is that we are not educating people enough on the benefits of exercise. We have seen how schools have been cutting physical education classes from curriculums or reducing them to almost nothing, which partly accounts for increases in obesity rates. In high school, I was lucky to attend a military school where the exercise regimen was extensive and just as important as the academic course load.

This may have been another reason why our school achieved such high academic achievement compared with regular schools. Exercise has been linked to better memory and quicker learning. It is astounding to see educators deciding to cut PE classes from a curriculum. Such actions make you wonder how they were able to obtain their education credentials in the first place! I would much rather cut off a history class (sorry, history teachers) than a physical exercise class. The cost-benefit calculation between those two classes would be so great that it would be easy to decide which one to cut off. Yes, understanding who we are and where we came from is important but not as important as building resilience, reducing the risk of obesity and heart problems, and increasing your memory! .

Although this difference is still present today, there has been a major turn in history and awareness to focus on all individuals and the benefits of exercising.

Exercise Benefits Your Brain

Considerable anecdotal evidence indicates that better brain health—and possibly a greater resistance to Alzheimer's—is linked to physical exercise.

As you may well know, exercising reduces the risk of developing heart disease, stroke, and diabetes. Perhaps those are your overall goals, but the most important part of your body is your *brain*. Exercising has numerous effects on the brain, involving a wide variety of structures and neurons. For instance, thirty minutes per day of aerobic exercise improves certain cognitive tasks as well as affecting gene expression in the brain. It also augments neuronal plasticity.

Long-term effects of exercising include improved neurogenesis (the ability to create new neurons and connections between neurons throughout a lifetime) and synaptogenesis (the formation of synapses between neurons in the nervous system). It reduces overall stress and improves several forms of memory, such as spatial and working memory.

Thanks to a protein called *brain derived neutrophic factor*, or BDNF, regular exercise improves blood flow to the brain, which, in turn, increases the growth of new blood vessels and brain cells. When we exercise, BDNF synthesis is increased by activating mechanisms of gene expression. These mechanisms are not completely understood, but it's clear that increasing your concentration of BDNF is beneficial for your brain. It helps restore and protect your brain cells.

This is also why exercise might be linked to living longer. A recent study has shown that the end caps of our chromosomes called *telomeres* are protected by a molecule called *nuclear respiratory factor 1* that is activated when we exercise, thus delaying their shortening and prolonging our age. The shorter your telomeres, the older biologically you are.

Exercise also might help prevent such diseases as Alzheimer's by reducing inflammation, which promotes the buildup of protein plaques that contribute to the disease.

It produces endorphins, which are neurotransmitters that make you feel good and help minimize stress and discomfort.

Many people turn to exercise for weight loss, which is one of the main reasons why people *give up* exercising. When you exercise for weight loss, your body uses all sorts of mechanisms to *protect you* from losing weight. In fact, many people *increase weight* at first when they exercise due to the repairing mechanisms used to retain water and fix damaged tissue. You can also gain weight as your muscles grow, which is certainly better for you, but when you look at the bathroom scale you believe there's no progress.

And once you lose a certain amount of weight, the body wants to be stable at that weight, meaning you need to work extremely hard and consistently to shave off those next five or ten pounds.

Exercise alone is *not* the best way to lose weight. If you really want to lose weight, consider your eating habits and food choices.

Regular exercise is *indispensible* for overall health, which is why you should exercise. If you exercise, you will live a longer and healthier life, and you will more easily achieve your Three Pillars of Happiness.

Aerobic Exercise

The best kind of exercise is aerobic. "Aerobic" means physical exercise that uses oxygen to adequately meet energy demands during exercise. In plain terms, it's exercise that makes you *breathe hard*. Examples of aerobic exercise are medium to long distance running/jogging, swimming, cycling, and walking. It includes sports that require sustained running, such as tennis, soccer, and basketball. In contrast, such exercises as weight lifting, while valuable for building muscle strength, are not considered aerobic.

Research has shown that people who perform aerobic exercise regularly have greater scores on cognitive function tests, including attentional control, cognitive flexibility, memory capacity, and processing speed. Students from elementary to college level have been shown to improve cognitive performance that helps improve academic performance. In people over the age of fifty-five, just walking thirty minutes a day reduces the risk of getting Alzheimer's and improves overall quality of life.

A study with twins, where one of the twins was active and the other sedentary for at least three years, showed that the sedentary twin had started to develop insulin resistance, had less endurance, more body fat, and less gray matter in the brain areas responsible for motor control. This shows that DNA alone is not the only reason why some people might develop certain conditions. Identical twins have identical DNA, but over time exercise has shown to affect one more than the other.

Research has shown that aerobic exercise induces hippocampal growth, which is involved in memory and learning. Even if you simply walk every day, the effects are tremendous. I have a walking treadmill at the office and try to walk on it at least two or three miles a day. It took a few days to get used to it, but it really works. Those days that I come home and am tired and don't feel like doing a workout, I don't feel guilty because I've already walked three miles.

You must make exercising a habit. For this to happen, you must enjoy it. Find out what you really like to do that can get you excited, and do that. You don't have to run on a treadmill or lift weights every day.

Our bodies were designed to move, not live a sedentary life as many people do today. As recently as one hundred years ago, people in America worked with their bodies, not sitting at desks and answering phones or writing computer code. They went out and found food, cultivated their crops, and built their own homes. They didn't have to think about exercise. All day was exercise for them. We were strong and fit. I remember when I was younger that I was always fit: I never had to worry about my physical state because I was always doing things. I was a gymnast, swimmer, martial artist, break dancer (yes, I did that too), salsa dancer, paintballer—you name it and I was doing most of those things every week. Many children and young adults are like that—they just do something without thinking about it.

As I got older and my responsibilities grew, I stopped doing almost all those things—and sure enough, I started gaining weight, feeling down, and lacking energy. In the past few years, I've had to force myself to work out and be proactive to reverse those feelings and get back on track. It is not as easy, since I loved doing those things and I don't love walking just to walk, but I know better, and I understand that it needs to be done.

How much is enough exercise?

Researchers say the ideal amount is 150 to 180 minutes per week, or about 2.5 to 3 hours per week. It's not a burdensome amount, and it's better to exercise a half hour every day than try to cram two hours of exercise into just one day. Also, it does not have to be intensive workouts. Moderate exercising, for example, fast walking for half an hour is enough to give your heart and brain what they need.

If you're short on time, a study by Martin Gibala has shown that 10 minutes of *high intensity intervals* has the same effect as 50 minutes of regular exercise. The results from his studies showed that the 10-minute workout, which consisted of three peaks of 20 seconds as hard as you can and then three minutes in between of normal intensity exercise, had the same results in heart function and blood sugar level control as the 50-minute counterpart subjects. This is great news, since the number one reason why people neglect working out is time. So imagine that you can achieve the same results in 10 minutes on a treadmill doing high-intensity workouts as you can with a 50-minute average run.

If your goal is to keep in tip-top brain shape, those guidelines will work just fine. Here are some examples of moderate exercises or activities you can do, which I hope you might be doing already:

1. Fast walking
2. Tennis
3. Ping pong
4. Dancing
5. Swimming
6. Stair climbing or going up hills
7. Yoga

You just have to make sure that your heart is pumping and that you get somewhat of a sweat going. If you have a hard time motivating yourself, see if you can join a class or get a gym partner; or, if you can afford it, hire a personal trainer, dance instructor, or tennis coach.

As you Train Your Brain for Success and build your Three Pillars of Life, you'll find that exercise improves your memory and thinking through both direct and indirect means. The benefits of exercise come directly from its ability to reduce inflammation and insulin resistance, and by stimulating the release of growth factors—chemicals in the brain that affect the health of brain cells, the growth of new blood vessels in the brain, and even the abundance and survival of new brain cells.

Indirectly, exercise reduces stress and anxiety and improves your mood and sleep. It increases heart rate, which pumps more oxygen to the brain.

Many studies have suggested that the prefrontal cortex and

medial temporal cortex—the parts of the brain that control thinking and memory—have greater volume in people who exercise versus people who don't. Aerobic exercise has been linked with increases in mental speed, attention, and cognitive flexibility.

Summary

- For millions of baby boomers and their families, Alzheimer's disease has become a serious health issue. It's a progressive disease that's the most common cause of dementia—a group of brain disorders that cause the loss of intellectual and social skills.

- In Alzheimer's disease, abnormal deposits of proteins form amyloid plaques (clusters of protein fragments) and tau tangles (twisted strands of another type of protein), causing neurons to stop functioning and die. As the disease progresses, these plaques and tangles tend to spread through the cortex in a predictable pattern.

- As of this writing, an estimated 5.5 million Americans of all ages have Alzheimer's disease. Because of the growing number of baby boomers who are turning sixty-five, in the United States, particularly among the increasing ranks of the very elderly, the number of new cases of Alzheimer's and other dementias is projected to soar.

- When Alzheimer's disease occurs in someone under the age of sixty-five, it is known as early-onset (or younger-onset) Alzheimer's disease. About 5% of people with Alzheimer's disease have the early-onset form.

- According to the Alzheimer's Association, the disease has ten warning signs:

1. Memory loss that disrupts daily life
2. Challenges in planning or solving problems

3. Difficulty completing familiar tasks at home, at work, or at leisure
4. Confusion with time or place
5. Trouble understanding visual images and spatial relationships
6. New problems with words in speaking or writing
7. Misplacing things and not having the ability to retrace their steps
8. Decreased or poor judgment
9. Withdrawal from work or social activities
10. Changes in mood and personality

- The exact cause of Alzheimer's disease is currently unknown, and there is no cure. Hopefully, scientists will soon be able to more accurately determine the causes of Alzheimer's disease and then work in the direction of a cure.
- To reduce the risk of Alzheimer's disease, keep your brain healthy, challenged, and engaged; and as you build your Three Pillars of Life, remain grateful for the blessings of this life even as you strive to reach a higher level.
- Amazing medical cases, such as that of Terry Wallis, show us that the brain's neuroplasticity—the ability to forge new connections—can take place even over a period of years in a minimally conscious person.
- The performance of your heart is critically important to your brain, so be sure to follow a heart-healthy diet!
- Exercise directly benefits brain cells by increasing blood and oxygen flow in the brain. Regular physical exercise may be a beneficial strategy to lower the risk of Alzheimer's and vascular dementia. Long-term effects of exercising include improved neurogenesis (the ability to create new neurons and connections between neurons throughout a lifetime) and synaptogenesis (the formation of synapses between neurons in the nervous system).

- Exercise also reduces inflammation and insulin resistance, and stimulates the release of growth factors—chemicals in the brain that affect the health of brain cells, the growth of new blood vessels in the brain, and even the abundance and survival of new brain cells.

10. The Care and Feeding of Your Brain

As I've said a few times in this book, the human brain is the most complex and sophisticated object in the known universe.

The amazing thing is that each one of us—all seven billion humans on earth—has one. It's right there in your head. It's what's allowing you to make sense of the peculiar little symbols arranged in lines on this page. Your brain decides when to turn the page and keep reading or put down the book and go to the kitchen for a sandwich.

It's true that some brains work better than others, but barring a birth defect or some other circumstance beyond your control, your brain is just as good as anybody else's. If we survey the range of human achievement, we must conclude that for the most part people whose brains take them high on the Three Pillars of Life are those who *use* their brains. They *work* their brains and try to squeeze out every last bit of potential. In contrast, those who fall behind are often the same people who retreat from learning, think that life is something that happens to them, and are content to just float along, like leaves in a stream. Their brains are rusty or used for nonproductive purposes, such as watching kitten videos on YouTube.

Since you have the most advanced object in the universe, you'll probably want to take really good care of it. After all, it's very valuable, and there's only one per customer. There are no refunds or exchanges. What you have is what you've got.

To stay healthy, your brain needs three things:

1. Protection from injury. We discussed that earlier in the book.

2. Sensory, social, and intellectual stimulation—also discussed earlier in the book.

3. A steady supply of nutrients: water, oxygen, glucose, and various trace minerals and hormones. That's the subject of this chapter.

Your brain demands the nutrients necessary to keep it healthy, and, strictly speaking, it doesn't care where they come from. In the previous chapter, I discussed the amazing case of Terry Wallis, who was in a minimally conscious state for nineteen years. While we don't know exactly how Terry Wallis was kept alive, nourishing the unconscious person generally requires bypassing the normal chewing and swallowing process and at times avoiding the gastrointestinal tract altogether. A nasogastric tube bypasses the mouth and esophagus to deliver liquid nutrition directly to the stomach. The presence of the tube keeps the gastro-esophageal sphincter between the esophagus and stomach open. Because long-term use of a nasogastric tube for feeding almost guarantees aspiration pneumonia, a gastrostomy—a surgical procedure in which a tube is placed connecting the abdominal wall to the stomach—may be performed. The goal is simple: to keep delivering essential nutrients to keep the body alive, the heart beating, and the brain functioning, even at its reduced level.

In everyday life, we certainly don't want feeding tubes. We want to enjoy life and keep ourselves stimulated with the rich variety of foods and experiences the world has to offer. We want to keep building our Three Pillars of Life.

Aside from oxygen, which your brain receives through the involuntary process of breathing, every bit of nourishment your brain receives is from the food you choose to eat. If you eat only doughnuts, your brain will have to survive on the meager nutrition contained in doughnuts. As you probably know, this would not be a good plan. You need to feed your brain with a wide variety of nutritious, wholesome foods.

I know what you're thinking: how come twenty-year-olds are always eating junk food and sweets and doing nothing, but their minds seem pretty sharp?

Here's the answer: While their young minds seem healthy, if they continue on that same course, most of them will die younger than they should. They will develop chronic diseases, and by the time they are eighty will probably have no idea who they are! Having bad habits might seem okay today, but there will be a time where your body will say "Enough!" Your body will shut down; it will not take it anymore. Unfortunately, too often we don't realize this until we're too old, which is why it's extremely important that you educate not only yourself but also your children and grandchildren if you are so fortunate to have them. Their early habits will dictate their future health.

Avoid the Quick-Fix "Diet"

Unfortunately, in the times we now live, with the advances in technology as well as marketing, we are being bombarded by choices, both good and bad. The reality is that most food advertisements and the options we have available are bad. We are living our lives at a fast pace, and a fast pace encourages quick fixes, which come in all shapes and forms. Think of "diets." They were all invented one way or another to quickly get you back into shape or lose a few pounds. A great many diets can be followed, but which one is right for you? Is it the Paleo? Atkins? Mediterranean? The Juicing Diet? And the list goes on. The answer is that all these diets are short-term gimmicks. I—and most nutritionists—believe that no one should be on a "diet." We should simply have healthy eating habits for a lifetime. That is the only true solution.

One reason why diets don't work is that the brain doesn't like abrupt changes. The brain loves long-term patterns and habits. Our brain likes to bounce back to what it knows and likes. This is why many people who were on a diet come back to their normal weight after they stop, and sometimes they even gain more weight. Their brains interpret the reduced-calorie diet as an existential threat, and the response is to want to eat more.

If you change your habits slowly so that the brain is not alerted to the threat of a reduced food supply, you have a much higher chance of success. You're basically conditioning your brain over time. New eating habits have to be introduced slowly to your brain until your brain feels comfortable with them and would feel awkward if you took them away.

We also have to design our eating habits geared toward *better health*, not just weight loss. When you design your life around being healthy instead of just slim, you will naturally lose excess fat.

Taking on the task of being healthy involves not only cutting out carbs or sugar or fat but also your whole body and mind. Once you realize this, you will understand that everything is connected. Your brain is at the top of the pyramid. It will dictate what you do or not do. It is important for you to understand it, learn about it, and figure it out before you can take real action in your life.

Food can change your life as quickly as in a few days. Nutrigenomics is the scientific study of nutrition and genes regarding the prevention or treatment of diseases. Understanding how food works, what it does, and how it affects your body and your brain is essential for your success and losing those pounds you loathe. You also need to understand that food is the number one healer in our bodies. Food contains all the nutrients and building blocks needed to build your proteins, your DNA, your hormones, and your brain. It also contains all the nutrients and minerals that we can't produce ourselves but which are also essential for our survival. Fittingly, these are called *essential* nutrients. Nonessential nutrients are those your body can make by itself, such as alanine, cholesterol, and glycine. Your body makes them from the ordinary foods you eat.

Just Because it's Called "Food" Doesn't Make It Good for You

The mere fact that something is edible doesn't make it a good choice to put into your body and feed to your brain. Thousands of worthless products that we call food are far from it.

Food is actually pretty basic. Except for some of the minerals we need, such as water itself, all our food comes from either plants or animals in two ways:

1. Directly to you in its original form, for example, when you buy a freshly picked ear of corn at the farm stand or supermarket. It's a real, recognizable farm product, with nothing added.

2. In a roundabout way through a factory that has processed it into some other form. This is when you buy a so-called bran muffin that has been sweetened with high fructose corn syrup. It's true that corn syrup is a "natural" product that comes from the same ear of corn you bought in the produce aisle, but it's hidden in the so-called bran muffin, which in reality is nothing more than a fat-and-calorie bomb with a few grains of bran added so that the manufacturer can give it a healthy-sounding name. In

reality, you'd do just as well by eating a doughnut, which probably has less fat.

When given the choice between real food and processed food, always choose real food.

Much of the processed food available at the supermarket is bad for you. Processed food causes inflammation, cancer, diabetes, and cardiovascular diseases. More than 90% of chronic diseases are not caused by your genetic disposition but by epigenetic factors—that is, factors in your environment, such as pollution and processed foods.

Food, Dopamine, and Hormones

Our brains have been hardwired over thousands of years to crave certain foods. This is a mechanism we developed to ensure our survival. Our brain really craves sugar in the form of glucose and with good reason: we need glucose to produce energy to move, talk, digest, fight, and play. Here is the bad part: If you think you can rely on willpower to fight your bad habits, you will not win this battle. Forget about it. Your instinctive brain has much more power than your thinking brain. In fact, your thinking brain is basically controlled by your reptilian brain.

The junk food industry knows this very well and have expert chemists creating irresistible combinations of tastes and texture in their food to make you want more and more every time. In the industry, they call this the "bliss point." It activates the same brain pathways as drugs, such as cocaine! It is a whole conspiracy against our weak brains, and it takes knowledge and willpower to see the truth and say "no" to bad foods. The more educated you are, the more likely you can win this battle.

One key player in this chemical warfare in our brains is a neurotransmitter called dopamine. A neurotransmitter is a chemical molecule released by brain cells to send signals to other neighboring nerve cells. Dopamine is synthesized in several regions of the brain, and one of its main roles is reward and motivation. Dopamine levels have been shown to increase in every type of reward seeking behavior, including the use of stimulants, such as cocaine, which acts on your brain by amplifying its release.

Like cocaine, sugars induce a high spike in dopamine, which activates the reward system and gives you a rush, alters your brain state, leaves you wanting more, and even generates an addiction to it. This addiction, in turn, results in detrimental effects in your body to the point of changes at the DNA level.

Aside from our beloved dopamine, we also have five key hormones that affect our brain chemistry and thus our appetite control: insulin, ghrelin, leptin, peptide YY, and cortisol.

Insulin, which is produced by the pancreas, helps transfer sugar from your blood to your cells. After you eat a bowl of pasta, your digestive system takes the sugar from the food you eat and transfers it to your bloodstream for distribution to your cells. Your blood sugar levels rise, and insulin is released to facilitate the transfer of blood sugar to the roughly 37.5 trillion cells in your body. When we constantly overeat sugar, the cells start building resistance to insulin, which eventually leads to type 2 diabetes.

Ghrelin is the hunger hormone. It is released in the stomach and signals your brain that you are hungry.

Leptin is a hormone produced by the body's fat cells. The more body fat they carry, the more leptin they produce. Leptin's primary target is in the brain, particularly the hypothalamus. Leptin is supposed to tell the brain that we have enough fat stored, that we don't need to eat, and that we can burn calories at a normal rate. Its function is to regulate how much fat we store in our bodies—we always want some but not too much. The levels of leptin go up when you are fat and go down when you are thin. It is often referred to as the "satiety hormone" or the "starvation hormone."

The problem with obese people is that they build a resistance to this hormone effect and stay hungry. There's lots of leptin in the bloodstream, but the brain doesn't recognize it.

This condition is known as leptin resistance. It is now believed to be the main biological abnormality in human obesity.

PYY is released in the colon after a meal and has been shown to help reduce appetite.

Although it's a stress hormone, cortisol influences our eating behaviors during moments of stress. It causes hunger and storage of fat, which is why many people with depression tend to gain weight.

As you can see, many things can influence our behavior and alter the way we feel and eat. We must be careful about what we eat. You should really focus on what you are eating. Studies show that when you eat without paying attention to the food, such as eating while watching TV, you eat more food than you normally would eat if you were focused only on eating.

How do you focus on eating? Eat with your family. Have rituals about eating together. Cook together and enjoy the food together. In my family, unless we go out we have dinner at the table every day. We never sporadically eat at different times. I grew up this way, and I love it. Aside from enjoying your food better, it is also a healthier environment for you and your family. If you are not married and have no children, have meals with friends and colleagues. When I was in college, I always had lunch or dinner at the cafeteria with my close friends or coworkers. If you're alone, sit down at the table and just eat. Use that time to think about your day. Don't watch TV, don't read a book, and don't be on the phone. Just eat. Enjoy your meal.

Here is another trick to eat less: Use a smaller plate. Studies show that the larger the plate you use, the more food you add to it, and hence you eat more. I'm not saying that you should eat dinner on your dessert plate, but I have seen plates that range from nine to fourteen inches in diameter. Get the nine-inch plates!

When you start eating, focus on the healthy foods first. Sometimes you will be full before you finish the less healthy choices. I know it is hard. We all want to start with the dessert if we can, but try it—it works.

While on the subject of portion sizes, over the twentieth century the beverage industry inflated the size of its servings. Back in 1955, the average size of a soft drink at McDonald's was seven ounces. This rose steadily until the 1990s, when a McDonald's large was thirty-two ounces and a 7-Eleven Big Gulp was forty ounces. Soft drinks are carbonated and served cold, so unless you wanted to be sipping a warm, flat beverage, you'd drink it quickly. A Big Gulp Coca-Cola delivers 410 calories and 132 mg of salt into your bloodstream, with zero protein, zero fiber, zero fat. It's like eating 25 spoonfuls of pure granulated sugar and washing it down with water.

Fortunately, in recent years, the soft drink industry has been experiencing declining sales and responded with smaller portion sizes—Coke now offers 7.5-ounce mini-cans and bottles, which consumers are embracing despite their higher price per ounce. The smaller bottle or can is perceived as an automatic portion controller, protecting the drinker from overdoing the intake of sugary carbonated beverages. For many consumers, the smaller option is the better value, no matter what the unit price says.

The Glycemic Index

The glycemic index (GI) was developed to rank dietary carbohydrates based on their overall effect on blood glucose concentration after the consumption of a meal. Foods containing carbohydrates that are quickly digested, absorbed, and metabolized have a high GI (GI 70 or more on the glucose scale) and cause the blood glucose levels to rise higher and stay that way for a longer period. As you can see in the table, high GI foods are highlighted in red. For example, pure glucose has a GI of 100. If you eat table sugar or drink a sugary soft drink, the glucose your bloodstream rises almost instantly, producing a sharp spike. And here's the really bad news: all those calories do *nothing* to relieve feelings of hunger. If you guzzle a 40-ounce Big Gulp, you'll get a whopping 410 calories, and then a few minutes later you'll feel hungry—as if you'd eaten nothing at all. This is because all those calories have been quickly converted to glucose and shoved into your bloodstream, leaving nothing in your stomach but water.

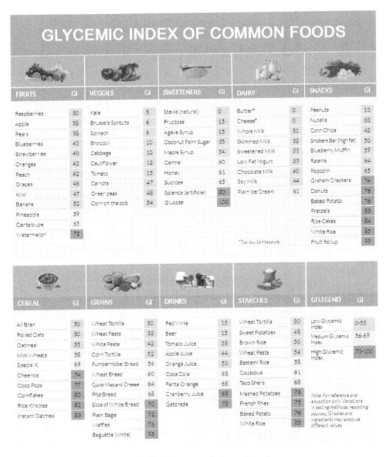

GLYCEMIC INDEX OF COMMON FOODS

FRUITS	GI	VEGGIES	GI	SWEETENERS	GI	DAIRY	GI	SNACKS	GI
Raspberries	30	Kale	5	Stevia (natural)	0	Butter*	0	Peanuts	13
Apple	38	Brussels Sprouts	6	Fructose	15	Cheese*	0	Nutella	33
Pears	38	Spinach	6	Agave Syrup	15	Whole Milk	31	Corn Chips	42
Blueberries	40	Broccoli	10	Coconut Palm Sugar	35	Skimmed Milk	32	Snickers Bar (high fat)	50
Strawberries	40	Cabbage	10	Maple Syrup	54	Sweetened Milk	33	Blueberry Muffin	59
Oranges	42	Cauliflower	12	Carmel	60	Low Fat Yogurt	33	Raisins	64
Peach	42	Tomato	15	Honey	61	Chocolate Milk	40	Popcorn	65
Grapes	46	Carrots	47	Sucrose	65	Soy Milk	44	Graham Crackers	74
Kiwi	47	Green peas	48	Splenda (artificial)	80	Plain Ice Cream	61	Donuts	76
Banana	52	Corn on the cob	54	Glucose	100			Baked Potato	76
Pineapple	59							Pretzels	83
Cantaloupe	65							Rice Cakes	84
Watermelon	72							White Rice	85
						*Too low to measure.		Fruit Rollup	99

CEREAL	GI	GRAINS	GI	DRINKS	GI	STARCHES	GI	GI LEGEND	GI
All Bran	30	Wheat Tortilla	30	Red Wine	15	Wheat Tortilla	30	Low Glycemic Index	0-55
Rolled Oats	50	Wheat Pasta	32	Beer	15	Sweet Potatoes	48	Medium Glycemic Index	56-69
Oatmeal	55	White Pasta	42	Tomato Juice	38	Brown Rice	50	High Glycemic Index	70-100
Mini Wheats	58	Corn Tortilla	52	Apple Juice	44	Wheat Pasta	54		
Special K	69	Pumpernickel Bread	56	Orange Juice	50	Basmati Rice	58		
Cheerios	74	Wheat Bread	60	Coca Cola	63	Couscous	61		
Coco Pops	77	Quick Mac and Cheese	64	Fanta Orange	68	Taco Shells	68		
Cornflakes	80	Pita Bread	68	Cranberry Juice	68	Mashed Potatoes	73	Note: For reference and education only. Variations in testing methods, reporting sources, GI scales and ingredients may produce different values.	
Rice Krispies	82	Slice of White Bread	70	Gatorade	78	French Fries	75		
Instant Oatmeal	83	Plain Bagel	72			Baked Potato	76		
		Waffles	76			White Rice	85		
		Baguette (white)	95						

Table 1. *Glycemic index of foods*

Intermediate GI foods have a GI between 56 and 69. These are highlighted in yellow. They include everyday foods, such as pineapple, raisins, a blueberry muffin, and wheat bread.

Low-GI foods (GI 55 or less on the glucose scale), highlighted in green, have slowly digestible carbohydrates that elicit a reduced glucose response. For example, fructose, the sugar in fruits, has a relatively low GI of 15, which means that while it's still a form of sugar, just like glucose, it takes longer for your body to process it and put it into your bloodstream. A food like kale, which is high in indigestible fiber, has a GI of only 5, which means it takes a long time to digest and makes you feel full longer.

You should refrain from consuming high quantities of high glycemic foods. My advice is to consume a small amount of high glycemic vegetables and eat plenty of low glycemic ones as well as low glycemic fruits, such as berries.

How to Read a Nutritional Label

One of the biggest problems that people have when shopping is that they don't really understand how to read a nutrition label properly. Companies try hard to be as confusing as they can so that you still buy their products. In fact, they're not only tricky in their nutrition facts but also even more so on the main label. I've seen so many products where they will write down something like "all natural," "from natural fruits," "all green," "low fat," "sugar-free"—and the list goes on. But when you look at their nutrition label, that product tells a whole different story.

Make reading nutrition labels a habit. When my wife and I go to the supermarket, we pretty much read every single product before we buy it. I'm not kidding. It does take some time, but I would rather waste an extra five minutes of my time reading the labels than spend ten years at a hospital because of liver failure. I'm not trying to be morbid here, but most of these products are just bad. Take most commercial yogurts, for example. Everybody thinks of yogurt as this awesome, healthy product to eat, yet it is so hard to find a healthy yogurt in the supermarket! In fact, the average flavored yogurt you see at the supermarket contains anywhere between 25 and 35 grams of sugar per serving. You might as well eat a candy bar. Plain, unsweetened yogurt has about 12 grams of sugar from the milk from which it's made.

USE THE NUTRITION FACTS LABEL TO EAT HEALTHIER

Check the serving size and number of servings.

•The Nutrition Facts Label information is based on One serving, but many packages contain more. Look at the serving size and how many servings you are actually consuming. If you double the servings you eat you double the calories and nutrients, including the % DVs.

•When you compare calories and nutrients between brands check to see if the serving size is the same.

Calories count, so pay attention to the amount.

•This is where you'll find the number of calories per serving and the calories from fat in each serving.

•Fat-free doesn't mean calorie-free. Lower fat items may have as many calories as full-fat versions.

•If the label lists that 1 serving equals 3 cookies and 100 calories, and you eat 6 cookies, you've eaten 2 servings, or twice the number of calories and fat.

Look for foods that are rich in these nutrients.

•Use the label not only to limit fat and sodium, but also to increase nutrients that promote good health and may protect you from disease.

•Some Americans don't get enough vitamins A and C, potassium, calcium, and iron, so choose the brand with the higher % DV for these nutrients.

•Get the most nutrition for your calories-compare the calories to the nutrients you would be getting to make a healthier food choise.

NUTRITION FACTS

Serving Size 1 cup (228g)
Servings per Container 2

Amount Per Serving

Calories 250	Calories for Fat 110

	% Daily Value*
Total Fat 12g	18%
Saturated Fat 3g	15%
Trans Fat 3g	
Cholesterol 30g	10%
Sodium 470g	20%
Potassium 700mg	20%
Total Carbohydrate 31g	10%
Dietary Fiber 0g	0%
Sugars 5g	
Protein 5g	
Vitamin A	4%
Vitamin C	2%
Calcium	20%
Iron	4%

*Percent Daily Values are based on a 2,000 calorie diet. Your Daily values may be higher or lower depending on your calorie needs.

	Calories:	2,000	2,500
Total fat	Less than	65g	80g
Sat fat	Less than	20g	25g
Cholesterol	Less than	300g	300g
Sodium	Less than	2,400mg	2,400mg
Total Carbohydrate		300mg	375mg
Dietary Fiber		25g	30g

The % Daily Value is a key to a balanced diet.

•The %DV is a general guide to help you link nutrients in a serving of food to their contribution to your total daily diet. It can help you determine if a food is high or low in a nutrient-5% or less is low, 20% or more is high. You can use the %DV to make dietary trade-offs with other foods throughout the day. The * is a reminder that the % DV is based on a 2,000-calorie diet. You may need more or less, but the % DV is still a helpful gauge.

Know your fats and reduce sodium for your health.

•To help reduce your risk of heart disease, use the label to select foods that are lowest in saturated fat, trans fat and cholesterol.

☐ •Trans fat doesn't have a % DV, but consume as little as possible because it increases your risk of heart disease.

•The % DV for total fat includes all different kinds of fats.

•To help lower blood cholesterol, replace saturated and trans fats with monounsaturated and polyunsaturated fats found in fish, nuts, and liquid vegetable oils.

•Limit sodium to help reduce your risk of high blood pressure.

Reach for healthy, wholesome carbohydrates.

•Fiber and sugars are types of carbohydrates. Healthy sources, like fruits, vegetables, beans, and whole grains, can reduce the risk of heart disease and improve digestive functioning.

☐ •Whole grain foods can't always be identified by color or name, such as multi-grain or wheat. Look for the "whole" grain listed first in the ingredient list, such as whole wheat, brown rice, or whole oats.

•There isn't a % DV for sugar, but you can compare the sugar content in grams among products.

•Limit foods with added sugars (sucrose, glucose, fructose, corn or maple syrup), which add calories but not other nutrients, such as vitamins and minerals. Make sure that added sugars are not one of the first few items in the ingredients list.

For protein, choose foods that are lower in fat.

•Most Americans get plenty of protein, but not always from the healthiest sources.

•When choosing a food for its protein content, such as meat, poultry, dry beans, milk and milk products, make choices that are lean, low-fat, or fat free.

I have divided the nutritional label into several segments so that it is easy for you to understand. Refer to the nutrition label sample image to understand each section in detail.

Serving Size

The nutrition facts label is based on *one serving* (as the company defines it), but most packages contain more than one serving. If you decide to take two servings, you must multiply all the values you are consuming by two. For instance, the serving size for cereal is based on one cup. Most people consume two to four cups of that cereal in a single serving, so if you are having four cups of the cereal, you are consuming four times the calories, fat, fiber, and protein.

Be wary of same-brand products: the serving sizes might not transfer over. You have to look at every package individually.

Calories

Here you can see the number of calories per serving and how many of those calories come from fat. Remember that fat-free does not mean calorie-free. Some have plenty of calories coming from sugars, carbs, and other nutrients.

As mentioned in the serving size, bear in mind the number of servings. In the cereal example, if one serving equals one cup, which equals 100 calories, then consuming four cups equals 400 calories.

Percent Daily Values

These values are important for you to evaluate how a particular food fits into your daily meal plan. It can help you determine if a food is high or low in a particular nutrient. As a general rule, anything under 5% is low, and anything above 20% is high. These values are based on the recommended *daily intake*, not one individual meal or snack, so you have to add the percentages throughout the day to see if you are over or under.

The asterisk (*) after "% Daily Value" is to remind you that the numbers are based on a 2,000-calorie diet. Here's where this gets tricky, and most people don't know this. For example, if you're a small petite girl and your body consumes about 1,000 calories per day, you have to double the % daily value for every serving. On the other hand, if you're a high-performing athlete and consume 3,000 calories per day, you need to reduce the % daily values and consume more to reach your goals. The 2,000-calorie value is just an average. My recommendation is that you have a blood panel to determine your caloric daily consumption. Then you'll know exactly how to do the math on the labels for your body.

Vitamins and Minerals

Labels list the amounts of vitamins and minerals present in the food. Use these levels to see if you are getting sufficient amounts of these micronutrients in your body. Generally, fruits and vegetables are rich in most vitamins and minerals. You can also use the Internet to search for specifications on vegetables and fruits and see their contents.

Fats and Sodium

Your body needs fat, and the fat in foods helps you to feel full longer. Use this portion to see the fat contents and to control your intake of sodium. Consuming less saturated fat, added sugars, and sodium will help prevent chronic diseases. Avoid trans fats or hydrogenated fats: they increase your risk of heart disease. Mono unsaturated or polyunsaturated fats are the best fat choices.

Carbohydrates

This is usually divided into two sections: sugars and dietary fiber. Although there is no percent value for sugar, you can count it in terms of weight (grams) to limit yourself. You want products with low sugar and high fiber content. Remember that sugars come in sixty-one different name varieties, so do not be fooled. Sugars add calories to your diet but no nutrients and do not help you feel full after eating.

Protein

Like sugars, the protein % daily value is not required, but you can see the weight in grams. You should use this number to determine how much protein you are consuming.

Ingredients List

The ingredients list has all the actual ingredients that make up that product. As a general rule, the more names you can't understand when you are reading, the more processed that food is and the more you should stay away from it. The ingredients list is presented in order of weight. If the first item in the list is a sugar, then that product has more sugar, by weight, than any other item in the list.

If any ingredient has its own list of sub-ingredients, they are listed in parentheses. As an example, if the recipe uses packaged tomato sauce, the label would list each ingredient, and then when tomato sauce came up they'd list it something similar to "Tomato Sauce (Tomatoes, water, less than 2% of: salt, citric acid, spice, tomato fiber, natural flavor)." Ingredients that are less than 2% of the total can be listed in any order at the end.

Summary

- As you Train Your Brain for Success, be sure to give it a steady supply of nutrients: water, oxygen, glucose, and various trace minerals and hormones. Aside from oxygen, which your brain receives through the involuntary process of breathing, every bit of nourishment your brain receives is from the food you choose to eat. You need to feed your brain with a wide variety of nutritious, wholesome foods.

- Excess body weight is a growing global problem, and we are bombarded by a great many so-called "diets" that purport to help us lose weight. All these diets are short-term gimmicks. Like most nutritionists, I believe no one should be on a "diet." We should simply have healthy eating habits for a lifetime. That is the only true solution.

- To lose weight, change your eating habits *slowly* so that the brain is not alerted to the threat of a reduced food supply. You will have a much higher chance of success.

- Design your eating habits geared toward *better health*, not just weight loss.

- Nutrigenomics is the scientific study of nutrition and genes regarding the prevention or treatment of diseases. The food you eat is the number one healer in your body. Food contains all the nutrients and building blocks needed to build your proteins, your DNA, your hormones, and your brain.

- Much of the processed food available at the supermarket is bad for you. Processed food causes inflammation, cancer, diabetes, and cardiovascular diseases. When given the choice between real food and processed food, always choose real food.

- Your brain releases a neurotransmitter called dopamine. One of its main roles is reward and motivation. Like cocaine, sugars induce a high spike in dopamine. This activates the reward system, gives you a rush, alters your brain state, leaves you wanting more, and even generates an addiction to it.

- Aside from dopamine, we also have five key hormones that affect our brain chemistry and thus our appetite control: insulin, ghrelin, leptin, peptide YY, and cortisol.

- Insulin, which is produced by the pancreas, helps transfer sugar from your blood to your cells. When we constantly overeat sugar, triggering the release of more insulin, your cells start building resistance to insulin, which eventually leads to type 2 diabetes.

- The glycemic index (GI) was developed to rank dietary carbohydrates based on their overall effect on blood glucose concentration after the consumption of a meal. Foods containing carbohydrates that are quickly digested, absorbed, and metabolized have a high GI of 70 or more. Eat very few of these foods! Intermediate GI foods have a GI between 56 and 69. Low GI foods of 55 or less on the glucose scale have slowly digestible carbohydrates that elicit a reduced glucose response. Your diet should emphasize low and intermediate glycemic foods.

- The federal government mandates nutrition labels on processed foods. At the supermarket, make nutrition label reading a habit. Learn about the numbers for serving sizes, calories, percent of daily values, vitamins and minerals, fats and sodium, carbohydrates, protein, and the ingredients list. Know what you're feeding your brain!

11. Dr. Fresco's Plate

Let's talk about eating with the goal of keeping both your brain and body in tip-top shape.

At the most fundamental level, your brain and body need five specific types of organic and inorganic molecules, which they get through the food you eat. They are:

- Carbohydrates
- Fats
- Proteins
- Vitamins and minerals
- Water

Carbohydrates, fats, proteins, and water represent virtually all the weight and volume of food, with vitamins and minerals making up only a small percentage of the weight.

Some scientists categorize alcohol as a totally separate food type, but since it's not required for sustenance, I'm not going to include it as a food.

Remember we're talking about *molecules*, not the tempting burger on your plate, the five-dollar specialty coffee drink, or the pint of Ben & Jerry's you ate last night. These are merely the consumable forms your food takes when you prepare it and eat it. It's true the food you eat needs to be tasty and tempting, as that's what helps keep your brain engaged and positive, but your bloodstream, which is tasked with delivering nutrients to your brain and all the other cells of your body, *does not care where these molecules come from.* Your digestive tract—your gut—takes the food items you eat and breaks them down into their most basic component parts. This is why a feeding tube jammed down your esophagus, delivering liquid nutrients to your stomach, is just as acceptable to your body's 37.5 trillion cells as a fifty-dollar filet mignon at a fine French restaurant. As long as they get them, your cells don't care where the molecules they need come from.

Having said that, balanced meals of real food are the best way to feed your brain, and you can get most of your nutrients in your daily servings. Too many people don't eat a healthy diet. As Americans, we eat too much sugar, salt, and fat—which happen to be prevalent in processed foods. Although the government tries to educate us by creating the food pyramid and then the food plate, with the goal of more Americans eating a well balanced diet, their formula is not ideal.

To reflect my guidelines, I've created a new plate concept adopted from the government food plate. I call it Dr. Fresco's Plate (*Image 1*). Your meals should consist of lean protein, low-carb vegetables, whole grains, low-glycemic fruits, and water or tea (not sugar-filled tea). Vegetables and fruits are also the main source for most of your micronutrients (vitamins and minerals), many of which we can't produce on our own. Essential vitamins and minerals participate in thousands of chemical reactions that help your body run smoothly. Many vegetables and fruits contain antioxidants and anti-inflammatory compounds that help fight disease. Inflammation has been linked to accelerated aging as well as many diseases, including diabetes, Alzheimer's, dementia, cancer, and cardiovascular disease. Vegetables are great for your health, and the more colorful the variety of vegetables is, the healthier and the more nutrients you are getting.

I recommend that half of your daily plate includes low-glycemic vegetables. About 30% of the plate should be lean protein, and another 20% can be whole grains and/or starchy vegetables, such as carrots or sweet potatoes.

I have not included dairy because you need to limit your dairy consumption. You want to make it more of a treat and use small portions. For instance, if you want to sprinkle some Parmesan cheese on your salad once in a while, it's perfectly fine. Or if you want to drink some milk it's also a good thing—perhaps one glass of milk a day for an adult. Dairy can be a good source for calcium, vitamin D, and potassium, but you must also remember that a lot of dairy products are processed and can include unwanted fats.

Proteins—The Source of Amino Acids

Proteins consist of smaller building blocks called amino acids, which are linked together with chemical bonds. Our gut has enzymes (called proteases) that reduce proteins from thousands of amino acids down to a few short chains of amino acids (called peptides) or monomeric amino acids.

I hate to burst a romantic bubble, but as far as your gut is concerned, the protein that you get from a shark steak versus a bowl of beans and rice is *exactly the same*—they're both nothing more than sources of amino acids. No protein molecule ever goes into the bloodstream and thence to a cell. If you eat a lion, your muscles will not receive "lion protein." They will receive the same amino acids as if you had eaten a piece of turkey, a bunch of fried grasshoppers, or a bowl of beans and rice. From these amino acids, your muscles and other parts of your body will create their own human proteins that look nothing like those of other species.

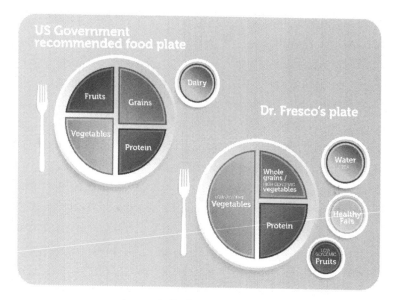

Image 1. *Dr. Fresco's food plate*

Speaking of grasshoppers, insects represent the world's greatest source of food protein. The average bug is around half protein by dry weight, with some insects (such as locusts) up to about 75% protein. They're incredibly easy to raise, without many of the other nutritional problems of factory-farmed livestock, such as overuse of antibiotics, hormones, and grain feed. Insects are also highly efficient in converting food into edible tissue—about twice as efficient as chickens and pigs, and more than five times as efficient as beef cattle.

Insects could be a truly amazing food source in the decades ahead as the human population soars toward ten billion and higher.

Considering amino acids again, some can only be obtained from the foods you eat, and these are called *essential amino ac-*

ids: isoleucine, leucine, methionine, phenylalanine, threonine, tryptophan, valine, histidine, and tyrosine.

It is those essential amino acids that provide jobs for many people selling recipes or protein powders or books about which proteins you should get. All meats, poultry, and fish contain all the essential amino acids (and are called complete proteins). Vegetarians have a slightly more difficult job, as there is no single plant that contains all the essential amino acids, so they must mix foods to obtain them.

One of my favorite vegetable dishes, hummus (a combination of chickpeas and sesame seed paste or tahini), contains all the essential amino acids. Another famous protein source is from the South: beans and rice contain all the essential amino acids. Vegetarians and vegans can easily get all the essential amino acids if they just do a bit of combining.

Fats—the Good and the Bad

Back in the 1970s, nutritional experts announced that fats were bad for you and urged the food industry to cut fats from processed foods. The industry did this, and to compensate for the loss of flavor, sugar was added, generally in the form of corn syrup sweetener. In the ensuing decades, this was revealed to be a huge mistake. Sugar is much worse for you than fat and has been linked to the soaring rates of obesity in the United States.

I include healthy fats as part of my plate. Evidence now shows that we need some saturated fat in our diet, and your own experience will tell you that consuming some fats makes a meal more satisfying and keeps you feeling full longer. In contrast, sugar and the sugar substitutes found in diet soft drinks actually make you hungry! You drink the diet soft drink, and your appetite skyrockets, and so you eat! If you want to lose weight, the last thing you should be drinking is diet soft drinks. They are basically canned poison and will not help you eat less.

Fats are essential nutrients in our diets. They are an important part of a healthy diet, providing essential fatty acids, keeping our skin soft, delivering fat-soluble vitamins, and are a great source of energizing fuel.

It's true that some fats are better than others. Basically, there are two groups of fats: saturated and unsaturated. Within each group are several more types of fats.

The best are the unsaturated fats, which include polyunsaturated fatty acids and monounsaturated fats. Both mono- and polyunsaturated fats, when eaten in moderation and used to replace saturated or trans fats, can help lower cholesterol levels and reduce your risk of heart disease.

Unsaturated fats have been shown to reduce diabetes, heart disease, Alzheimer's, and cancer. These fats include olive oil, avocados, and nuts. Butter can also be part of your healthy fat diet—not margarine or those fake "I can't believe it's not butter" products, but organic butter made from the milk of grass-fed cows.

Most healthy unsaturated fats are either omega-3 or omega-6, the first one being the healthiest choice. These oils are essential, meaning we can't produce them, so we must get them from other sources. Our brain is packed with omega-3 and omega-6 fatty acids, which makes them crucial for a healthy brain.

In the omega-3 world, there are three main types, which is important to understand because many supplements on the market do not provide you with the right ratio of the fats you need. The three most important types are ALA, EPA, and DHA.

ALA is mostly found in plants, while EPA and DHA are mostly found in animal foods, such as fatty fish.

From the three, the preferred ones you should be consuming are EPA and DHA. Salmon and sardines are a great source for these two fatty acids. Although ALA can be useful, our body does not convert it very efficiently. If you are not certain of the sources of fish or you are worried that they might be contaminated with mercury, taking a supplement of fish oil is a good alternative.

Two types of fat should be eaten very sparingly: saturated and trans fatty acids. Both can raise cholesterol levels, clog arteries, and increase the risk for heart disease.

Saturated fats are found in animal products (meat, poultry skin, high-fat dairy, and eggs) and in vegetable fats that are liquid at room temperature, such as coconut and palm oils. Fats that are mostly saturated (such as butter) tend to be solid at room temperature, while fats that are mostly unsaturated (for example, olive oil) are liquid at room temperature.

To be fair, there are many types of saturated fats, and scientists aren't in agreement as to which ones are bad for you and which ones may actually be good for you. Some researchers believe that sounding the alarm about saturated fat may simply be a simplification of deeper problems with our diets. The top three sources of saturated fat for Americans are cheese, pizza, and such grain-based desserts as cookies and cakes. Consuming foods that contain saturated fat might be risky for your health. For example, two slices of pizza with meat toppings at a popular chain not only pack twenty grams of saturated fat but also nearly a thousand calories, more than a day's supply of sodium, and a gram of trans fat. None of that is good for you in those quantities!

Carbohydrates and the Gift of Glucose

Although carbohydrates carry a negative connotation and are often considered the reason for the obesity epidemic in America, they are an absolute must in your diet. Carbohydrates are the main source of the energy your 37.5 trillion cells, including your 100 billion brain cells, need to function. Glucose, a simple form of carbohydrate, is essential for proper brain function. Without it you would not be able to think, daydream, or prepare for an exam. Glucose is also crucial for your muscles to work. It is like the gasoline that runs your car.

Half of the energy required to run your body comes from carbohydrates. The rest comes from fat. Fortunately for us, we have many sources in nature that provide carbohydrates. In fact, my eating recommendations are filled with carbohydrates. At first sight, my plate might resemble an Atkins diet, but it isn't. Vegetables, grains, and fruits are packed with carbohydrates, and that makes up half of my meal plate! The key here is that not all carbohydrates are made equal. The best kinds of carbs to eat are unrefined and unprocessed.

Carbohydrates used to be classified as simple or complex, based on the number of simple sugars in the molecule. Carbohydrates composed of one or two simple sugars, such as fructose or sucrose, were labeled "simple," while starchy foods were labeled "complex" because starch is composed of long chains of the simple sugar, glucose. (See the image for a list of simple and complex carbohydrates). Is this image in my guide?

Complex carbohydrates come in three categories: glycogen, starch, and fiber.

Glycogen is the storage form of energy in our bodies, while starch is the storage form in plants, and both are made up of very long chains of glucose. Our body is equipped with enzymes that break down glycogen from storage and starch to their individual glucose units so that we can use them for energy.

Fiber is different. We need fiber to help lower blood cholesterol, and it also helps maintain the levels of blood sugar in our blood by delaying the breakdown of polysaccharides into their glucose units. Fiber comes from plants, and we are not able to digest it because we do not have the right enzymes to break it down. Fibers can be soluble, which are gradually broken down by bacteria in our gut, or insoluble, which mainly help us with our bowel movements.

Fruits

I've taken fruit out of the main plate and added it as a side option. Fruit has a high content of sugar, mainly glucose and fructose. Despite the popular belief that you can eat all the fruit you want, overdoing fruit consumption can lead to spikes in your glucose levels, which can, in turn, lead to insulin deficiencies. Much of the fruit that is grown today has a lot more sugar than they would have in a natural environment. Try eating a wild-grown apple and you will notice that it is not as sweet as its modern cultivated cousins. For years, humans have been smart to select sweeter fruits. With modern technology, we have also been able to make fruits larger. Now we are left with huge, oversized apples that are sweeter than their genetic predecessors a century ago. Eating lots of sugar also increases your dosage of fructose, which, as you will see in the next section, is not an ideal sugar.

I am not trying to scare you into not eating fruit. I love fruit and I eat some every day. The key is to eat moderate amounts. It's good for your health and provides you with many nutrients that your body needs as well as satisfying those sweet cravings we all get!

Below you'll find a list with some of my recommended healthy foods for all the plate categories (*Table 1*).

LOW GLYCEMIC VEGETABLE LIST	HIGH GLYCEMIC VEGETABLES/WHOLE GRAINS	LOW GLYCEMIC FRUITS	PROTEIN	HEALTHY FATS
Kale	Wild rice	Apples	Beans	Nuts
Spinach	Brown rice	Berries	Lean beef	Avocado
All greens	Quinoa	Plums	Chicken	Olive oil
Mushrooms	Sweet potato	Kiwi	Eggs	Grass fed butter
Broccoli	Yams	Nectarines	Pork	Dark chocolate
Cauliflower	Turnips	Pears	Fish	(preferably no sugar)
Artichoke	Squash		Lentils	Chia seeds
Celery	Pumpkin		Turkey	Full fat yogurt
Asparagus	Carrots			(no sugar)
Cabbage	Green peas			Cheese (in moderation)
Bell peppers	Corn			2% Milk
Green beans				
Cucumbers				
Zucchini				

Table 1. *Recommended foods*

Good Sources of Fiber:
Vegetables—all vegetables
Whole grains, such as quinoa or brown rice
Flax seeds
Legumes, such as beans

Bad Sugar

As mentioned earlier, most of the sugar we consume contains either glucose or fructose. Glucose is essential to our health, while fructose is really not. It's a lot sweeter than glucose, which is why we are very fond of fruit and processed foods.

Here is the problem: processed food. Did you know that 80% of the food in the supermarket has some form of added sugars? And did you know that there are sixty-one different names for added sugars? (*Table 2*)

•Agave nectar	•Corn syrup solids	•Glucose solids	•Mannose
•Barbados sugar	•Date sugar	•Golden sugar	•Maple syrup
•Barley malt	•Dehydrated cane juice	•Golden syrup	•Molasses
•Barley malt syrup	•Demerara sugar	•Grape sugar	•Muscovado
•Beet sugar	•Dextrin	•HFCS (High-Fructose	•Palm sugar
•Brown sugar	•Dextrose	Corn Syrup)	•Panocha
•Buttered syrup	•Evaporated cane juice	•Honey	•Powdered sugar
•Cane juice	•Free-flowing brown	•Icing sugar	•Raw sugar
•Cane juice crystals	sugars	Invert sugar	•Refiner's syrup
•Cane sugar	•Fructose	•Malt syrup	•Rice syrup
•Caramel	•Fruit juice	•Maltodextrin	•Saccharose
•Carob syrup	•Fruit juice concentrate	•Maltol	•Sorghum Syrup
•Castor sugar	•Glucose	•Maltose	•Sucrose
•Coconut palm sugar			•Sugar (granulated)
•Coconut sugar			•Sweet Sorghum
•Confectioner's sugar			•Syrup
•Corn sweetener			•Treacle
•Corn syrup			•Turbinado sugar
			•Yellow sugar

Table 2. *Types of sugars*

The most common food additive is high fructose corn syrup (HFCS). This sugar is the number one cause of metabolic syndrome diseases today. It's nothing other than fructose and glucose, just as you find in fruits or your regular table sugar, commonly called sucrose. The difference is that it is a much longer chain, a complex carbohydrate. It is called "high fructose" because it has slightly more fructose molecules than glucose. This sugar is used in many of the processed foods you see in the supermarket. It's not only a sweetener but also a preservative, and it retains moisture, provides texture, and enhances flavor. This is why companies use this sugar; it is very appealing to our palate—so appealing that we crave it all the time, which is what food companies want. They want you to keep buying their products. Unfortunately, the amount of fructose and glucose that is in these products goes beyond what your body can really handle.

You should consume about fifty grams of total sugar per day, including all carbs. One twelve-ounce can of regular Coca-Cola contains thirty-nine grams of sugar in the form of high fructose corn syrup. If you drink two cans of Coca-Cola, you're basically consuming more than the requirement of sugar per day, and that doesn't include any of the food you might have eaten with the Coca-Cola. Too much glucose can cause a spike in your blood, which affects your insulin sensitivity over time and eventually leads to type 2 diabetes. Fructose, on the other hand, has a lower glycemic index and takes longer to digest, so it does not cause a spike in blood glucose. It can cause fatty liver disease because the excess fructose turns into fat, which can lead to liver failure.

Drinks

The last ingredient of our food plate is drinks. I recommend just water. Plain water. We have tricked our minds to want more than just water. We love sodas, juices, coffee, wine, and beer. I am particularly happy with just water, although I indulge in an occasional soda once in a while.

One good trick you can do to water is add such things as lemon or mint leaves to give it a new flavor. Drink sparkling water if you like the feeling of bubbly CO_2 in your mouth.

In my plate, I suggest teas as well. Herbal teas or green tea are also good drinking solutions. Do not add sugar, though, or you might as well be drinking sodas!

People often ask me about milk, coffee, and wine. Here is my take on those three: limit yourself to one cup per day, maybe two, but just fill your glass with water the rest of the day. Wine over time can lead to brain damage, while coffee can lead to insomnia, anxiety, and a raised heart rate. In fact, you should avoid wine all together if you can. Yes, many will say that the resveratrol in wine has antiaging and antioxidant properties, and you are correct but so do grapes and other foods in nature. Milk contains lots of fat and sugar, which you want to avoid if you are trying to lose weight.

One last alternative is to drink a balanced meal replacement shake, which I go into more detail in the next section.

Alcohol is considered by scientists to be its own food group. Alcoholic drinks are made by fermenting or distilling, or both, natural starch and sugar, producing ethanol. Upon ingestion, it passes quickly into the bloodstream and can penetrate the blood-brain barrier and enter brain cells. Ethanol is a depressant, which in low doses causes euphoria, reduced anxiety, and sociability; in higher doses, it causes intoxication, stupor, and finally unconsciousness.

Meanwhile, your body—mainly your liver—starts to break it down. The body processes and eliminates ethanol in separate steps. Enzymes help to break apart the ethanol molecule into other compounds (or metabolites), which can be processed more easily by the body. Some of these intermediate metabolites can have harmful effects on the body.

Most of the ethanol in the body is broken down in the liver by an enzyme called alcohol dehydrogenase (ADH), which transforms ethanol into a toxic compound called acetaldehyde. Another enzyme called aldehyde dehydrogenase quickly breaks down the acetaldehyde to a less toxic compound called acetate, which is then broken down to carbon dioxide and water, mainly in tissues other than the liver.

Because alcohol is made from sugar or starch, it contains lots of calories. Pure ethanol is 238.21 calories per 1.5 ounces. An ounce of 80-proof hard liquor (gin, vodka, rum, whiskey, or scotch), which is 40% ethanol, contains sixty-four calories. These are "empty calories," meaning they have no nutritional value other than the calories themselves—no protein, no carbohydrates, no fat. Most alcoholic drinks contain traces of vitamins and minerals but not usually in amounts that make any significant contribution to our diet. Accordingly, consuming empty calories is actually worse than consuming nothing because the process of digestion, detoxification, and elimination drains and leeches the body of necessary vitamins and minerals.

In the old days, beer and ale were much lower in alcohol and were a form of liquid food, especially where water supplies were unreliable. Today, however, drinking alcohol is purely recreational, and alcoholic beverages should be enjoyed in moderation and never before or during the operation of a motor vehicle.

Spice It Up!

I've added a small section on spices because most books on nutrition fail to mention them as a source of healthy additives to your diet. Many spices have antioxidant and anti-inflammatory properties. Many also contain vitamins, minerals, and essential oils. Take, for instance, mustard, turmeric, or pepper. They all have health benefits, and most are what make our food taste great!

In this guide, I'm not going to go in detail on each spice, but I will leave you with a list of spices you should try to use when cooking or in a salad dressing. These spices have all been shown to have health benefits (*Table 3*).

SPICES		
1. Curry Powder	6. Rosemary	11. Fennel
2. Oregano	7. Cinnamon	12. Mint
3. Mustard	8. Ginger	13. Sage
4. Curcumin	9. Cumin	14. Garlic
5. Pepper	10. Basil	15. Saffron

Table 3. *Spice you should use daily*

Supplements

About 80% of Americans are taking at least one over-the-counter supplement, which is a very large percentage of people. Unfortunately, most people take supplements without knowing if they need them or not. Many supplements are harmless, but some can be detrimental to your health. I'm not saying that no one should take supplements—it would be hypocritical of me, since I sell my own line of supplements, but many people take supplements for the sake of taking them, because their friend takes them, or their spouse told them to.

You have to get a blood panel to find out your deficiencies. Let me give you a personal example. I had my blood panel done, and my results showed that my level of iron was extremely high. In fact, my doctor recommended that I *donate* blood so that I could get rid of some of the excess iron and to take it easy on the red meat. If I had not done the blood panel, and I had decided to take a multivitamin that, like most, included iron, then I could have damaged my body.

When taken in excess, some vitamins can have toxic effects. For instance, overconsuming vitamin D can lead to overabsorption of calcium and then calcium deposits in your organs, kidney stones, nausea, and vomiting. Overdoing vitamin A can lead to visual changes and skin changes.

Certain supplements are fine as long as you take them in moderation. For instance, taking a daily dose of fish oil pills will most likely never cause any side effects. There are many like these that won't hurt, but you have to make sure the supplement is right for you.

Aside from natural supplements or multivitamins and minerals, millions of people consume protein shakes and meal replacements. Assuming they have the right ingredients, these can be a great source of nutrients, especially meal replacements. These shakes are a great alternative when trying to lose weight or when you are on the run all the time and don't want to be stuck eating junk food on the road. I always tell people that nutritionally almost any protein shake or meal replacement on the market today is a better choice than a slice of pizza or a burger and fries. Most of the shakes I have seen not only have carbs, proteins, and fats but also other important vitamins and minerals. As with everything else, you do not want to overdo it. Take one shake a day, or two if you are training or trying to lose weight.

Summary

- As you Train Your Brain for Success, remember "you are what you eat." In the computer business, they say, "garbage in, garbage out," and the same applies for your brain. Feed it well and you'll get better results! To stay healthy and grow properly, your brain and body need five specific types of organic and inorganic molecules, which they get through the food you eat: carbohydrates, fats, proteins, vitamins and minerals, and water.
- I've created a new dietary concept adopted from the government food plate. On Dr. Fresco's Plate, your meals should consist of lean protein, low-carb vegetables, whole grains, low-glycemic fruits, and water or tea (not sugar-filled tea). Vegetables and fruits are also the main source for most of your micronutrients (vitamins and minerals).
- Proteins consist of smaller building blocks called amino acids, which are linked together with chemical bonds. Our gut has enzymes (called proteases) that reduce proteins from thousands of amino acids down to a few short chains of amino acids (called peptides) or monomeric aminoacids.
- The world's greatest source of food protein could be insects. The average bug is around half protein by dry weight, with

some insects (such as locusts) up to about 75% protein. They're easy to raise and highly efficient at converting food into edible tissue.

- Fats are an essential part of a healthy diet. They provide essential fatty acids, keep our skin soft, deliver fat-soluble vitamins, and are a great source of energizing fuel.

- It's true that some fats are better than others. There are two groups of fats: saturated and unsaturated. Unsaturated fats have been shown to reduce diabetes, heart disease, Alzheimer's, and cancer. Saturated and trans fatty acids can raise cholesterol levels, clog arteries, and increase the risk for heart disease.

- Carbohydrates are the main source of the energy for your 37.5 trillion cells, including your 100 billion brain cells. My eating recommendations are filled with carbohydrates. Vegetables, grains, and fruits are packed with carbohydrates, which make up half of my meal plate. Fiber, which is indigestible carbohydrate, helps lower blood cholesterol and maintain the levels of blood sugar in our blood by delaying the breakdown of polysaccharides into their glucose units.

- Know your sugars! Most of the sugar we consume contains either glucose or fructose. Glucose is essential to our health, while fructose is not. Eighty percent of the food in the supermarket has some form of added sugars, with the most common being high fructose corn syrup (HFCS). This is the number one cause of metabolic syndrome diseases today.

- For drinking, I recommend plain water. While we love sodas, juices, coffee, wine, and beer, I am particularly happy with just water, although I indulge in an occasional soda once in a while. One good trick you can do to water is add such things as lemon or mint leaves to give it a new flavor or drink sparkling water.

- Alcohol (ethanol) is considered by scientists to be its own food group. Upon ingestion, it passes quickly into the blood-stream and can penetrate the blood-brain barrier and enter brain cells. Because alcohol is made from sugar or starch, it contains lots of "empty calories," meaning they have no nutritional value other than the calories themselves—no protein, no carbohydrates, no fat.

- Spices are a source of healthy additives to your diet. Many spices have antioxidant and anti-inflammatory properties. Many also contain vitamins, minerals, and essential oils.

- Dietary supplements can be useful if you take the right kind and in moderation. There are many like these that won't hurt, but you have to make sure the supplement is right for you.

12. Happiness Is All in Your Mind!

In 2008, I visited a small area in the northeastern part of Brazil called Natal. I had a wonderful time meeting lots of people, participating in many fun activities such as snorkeling and ziplining (without a harness—was crazy!), and enjoying good food and the sand and beach.

I was surprised that by U.S. standards most of the local people I met would be considered poor, and yet they seemed very happy.

One man I'll never forget. His name was Tiago. He had a fruit drink stand right on the beach, just a little cart, with an umbrella, and himself just wearing a pair of shorts. I went to the beach almost every day, and he was there with people around him, sharing big laughs and singing. On the second day, I went to the beach to get a drink or at least see what he was selling, since he seemed to have a popular cart. He was selling only one drink, which he made there on the spot with acai fruit. He welcomed me with great enthusiasm, asked me where I was from, and told me that he had the best acai drink in all of Brazil. I bought one. It was delicious. The next day I had to get another one, so I went, but because my scientific nature was kicking in, this time I had questions in my mind and things I wanted to know. The main question I needed answered was why was he so happy? What was his secret? From the outside, his job would be the most boring monotonous job ever. You have a cart, you sell one product, you go home, and the next day you start again.

Now you might be thinking, "Of course he *looks* happy, and he treats you with enthusiasm. It's because he needs to sell you a drink."

This was not the case. You can't pretend day in, day out to be that happy. I see it all day in the United States—people who operate food carts, newsstands, or who drive cabs, who barely smile. No one I have ever seen with such a monotonous low-level job is that happy. And seeing him a whole week like that? It could not have been an act.

I approached him, bought another drink, and since I speak Portuguese I was able to talk with him. I asked him questions, such as what else did he do, where did he live, how old was he, where was his family, did he go to school, what was his goal in life, and why was he so happy?

Although Tiago's answer to being happy was not that clear or elaborate, he said that he loved the beach and meeting people, and that the drinks made him enough money to bring home and enjoy the rest of the day.

It was clear to me that Tiago was onto something.

Not only Tiago but also most of the people in that town were just as happy. It was the same experience I had felt when I went to Amish country for a week with my good friend Tai. Everyone just seemed so happy all the time. Boy, did that make me jealous! Who cares what car I drove, how big my house was, what degrees I had earned, or which expensive hobbies I embarked on? I could *feel* they were much happier than I was, and it made me wonder how I could do that. I had much better tools at my disposal, I had more money, more education, and I was pretty sure a much higher functioning brain—but for what?

Isn't our life's mission to be happy? Isn't everything we do is done so that we can bring joy to our lives and others? We try to make more money so that we can buy more things so that we can buy happiness because that's easy. We get promotions at work, so we feel better and brag, and we tell our friends about all our accomplishments. But in the end I realized that happiness had nothing to do with that. My formula for happiness was so off track it was unbelievable.

I went back to the United States, and while I was happy and excited that I had gone on a trip, now I had a *mission*. I needed to find out what was wrong with my brain. I had all the tools at my disposal to be happy like Tiago, but I wasn't.

After reading many studies on happiness, relationships, and your life purpose, I discovered that I was doing it all wrong.

What was also interesting is that on that trip I was extremely happy all the time as well, and what I learned as you will see in sections below is that experiences, relationships, and a sense of purpose are the key to building a long and happy life.

I believe that happiness is not so much a *trait* but a *talent*. While part of our happiness depends on our genetic traits, and some is due to external factors, much of it is governed by our own attitude and our choices, such as being social, exercising, and setting goals.

What's good is that it's all trainable, and it's all in your brain. You can truly Train Your Brain for Success—and for happiness, too!

Happiness does not have a one-size-fits-all solution. Many books and programs claim that if you follow certain steps you will reach happiness, but the truth is that happiness comes in many colors, shapes, and forms. Everyone is different and so is their approach to life.

Happiness does not only reside within one person. It's also the result of our relationship with the world around us and our social environment. Being happy includes such things as optimism, resilience, sense of purpose, satisfaction, and emotional well-being.

Studies show that people who are more optimistic or have a sense of purpose have a greatly reduced risk of developing major illness, such as diabetes or heart disease.

Applying yourself to something that takes effort makes you happy. We crave challenges, and we're often happier when we are pursuing a goal than actually achieving it. This is why entrepreneurs love starting companies. The challenge of starting something new and the challenges that come with it are more exciting than the daily routine of running the business.

We too often believe that accomplishing things will make us happy, even if we aren't happy now. This is so wrong. The more we try to do and achieve, the further away from being happy we are. We are encouraged all the time to keep up with a coworker, a classmate, or the Joneses. We're used to just checking off to-do lists so that we can achieve the next great thing. This puts our minds into a constant state of stress as we strive to get things done and reach a destination so that we can then be happy. By doing this, we are constantly sacrificing the present moment and foregoing personal happiness.

There's certainly a level of deep satisfaction that comes from accomplishing challenging goals. In fact, I always encourage people to set goals, but the problem is that today we're constantly trying to squeeze every minute to try to achieve something and never stop to think and reflect. Ask yourself: "Am I doing what I want? Am I happy in my work? Is this my purpose?" This level of self-reflection can only be achieved by understanding yourself and how your brain operates, when you are overdoing it, and what stresses you.

Stay in the Moment

When we constantly deny ourselves the time to reflect, we become so accustomed to what our "normal" is that we never truly seek happiness. The true personalized formula for your happiness is slowing down and focusing on what is happening right in front of you in that particular moment. Slow down. Multitasking is the opposite of that, and I know it's counterintuitive because we want to do more so that we can achieve more, but if you look at older, wise, happy people, you can appreciate that they take their time and experience more of the moment. In fact, being more in the moment not only has been shown to make you happier but also more productive. Multitasking and task switching are very counterproductive behaviors that we are all too accustomed to doing.

Imagine the last time you were involved in something you enjoyed or a project you were focused on. Time went faster, you finished more rapidly, you experienced more joy, and you felt you had accomplished more.

A study at Harvard University with more than five thousand adult participants found that on average people spend 50% of their time in the moment, which means that our minds are wandering the other fifty percent. So, consider your twenty-four-hour day. Eight of them are spent sleeping. Of the remaining sixteen hours, during eight of those your mind is wandering! This study also showed that we are happiest when we are in the present moment, making meaning of what's in front of us. For instance, I'm sure while some of you are supposedly playing with your children, you're really checking your phone. I'm guilty as well. For us to enjoy the moment, we have to devote the time to the children and leave that phone behind. That will bring more joy to both you and them.

How can you keep yourself in the present? Here are a few tips to help you stay in the moment:

1. Be self-aware. You must make a conscious effort to catch yourself in the act when your mind wanders while you're doing something. It's not an easy task, but with training you can do it.

2. Put away the gadgets. Phones, messages, music, TV—they can all distract you and disrupt your present moment. Take a break from them, even if it's for thirty minutes while you write a paper or play with your child.

3. Don't obsess so much on self-improvement. Instead, focus on things that are already good about yourself. Thinking of the future and improvements you want to make brings you back to that task-list mentality of just trying to achieve and not enjoy.

4. Try meditation. Research shows that people who meditate regularly have less brain activity in areas involved in their minds wandering.

5. Enjoy the simple pleasures of life. These come from a meal with a friend or family, a walk in the park, watching a butterfly, or enjoying a chocolate bar. Close your eyes if you can, and try to enhance your senses on the experience at hand. This will not only bring you to the moment but also extend the length of that pleasure.

Plan for Happiness

We have forgotten to *plan for happiness*. We constantly plan for meetings, vacations, work projects, house chores, dinner, and the clothing we are going to wear. When was the last time you planned for happiness? Have you ever planned for it? Probably not. Just as no one ever goes to the doctor because their brain isn't deciding correctly. When you were a baby, a toddler, or a young child, happiness was programmed for you. Your parents picked you up, played with you, watched cartoons with you, took you to the park, and gave you hugs and kisses. All things that are part of the joy in life. But once you were on your own, no one was there for you but perhaps your spouse, who is probably in the same boat as you. No one is there to infuse happiness, and now you have responsibilities, work, bills to pay, and children to make happy.

To avoid a happiness deficit, you must give your happiness a priority. You have to make it part of your goal to Train Your Brain for Success—if possible, on a daily basis. You also need to understand what makes you happy. If you are not sure, you need to embark on a mission to figure it out as I did.

Resilience

Happiness is strongly related to how well we bounce back from setbacks in our lives. We can all train to be more resilient, which will help us recover from adverse experiences—and perhaps even learn from them.

Resilience is a set of skills; it's not a personality type or a genetic predisposition.

Experience is the major force in building resilience.

Our brains are wired to quickly react to stressful situations, and thus we get more stressed than we realize. Just sitting in a bus on the way to work can jump-start our stress signals in our brain, with traffic lights, loud noises, sudden stops, people bumping into you, and having to stand the whole ride. Building resilience helps reduce the level of stress. The problem is that even though we are not faced with a hungry bear trying to eat us or a neighboring tribe trying to steal our food and spouse, the same pathways of fear and stress are activated for the smallest things, such as someone honking the horn of a car. Thus, we enter a cycle where the more we activate these pathways, the more our brains become accustomed to it, and it becomes the normal default.

Many of the studies that were done on resilience came after World War II. Many others come from people who had suffered catastrophes, such as hurricanes, tsunamis, and earthquakes.

The more resilient the brain, the quicker the brain returns to its normal baseline. Dr. Dennis Charney, dean of the Icahn School of Medicine at Mount Sinai, says, "Resilient people seem to have the capacity to appropriately regulate the subcortical fear circuits under conditions of stress."

Dr. Richard J. Davidson, Founder of the Center for Healthy Minds at the University of Wisconsin–Madison, may have found the brain's resilience pathway: the prefrontal cortex, which is involved in planning and decision making, to the amygdala, which is where our emotions take place and where we process fear and treats. Thus, the more you can reinforce this circuit, the faster your prefrontal cortex can talk to the emotional part of your brain to shut off the alarm.

Tips for Building Resilience

- Research has found that facing things we fear actually relaxes the fear circuitry, which is why people who watch horror films get less and less scared of scary movies. This is a great technique to help build resilience.
- Having support builds emotional resilience. Few highly re-silient people are strong by themselves. You need support. Even if you're not part of a religion or a community, friends and loved ones are key when life is challenging.
- Physical fitness conditioning also builds resilience. Part of the reason is that working out increases neurogenesis caused by stress damage. This is the process of creating new neurons from neural stem cells. Contrary to popular belief, neurogen-esis continuously occurs in specific regions in the adult brain.
- Try to find meaning in any traumatic experience you ever experienced. Trauma, in and of itself, is horrible and serves

no purpose. Yet, somewhere in the pain can be opportunity. Working with an energy healer to repair and restore your energy empowers you to intentionally leave the bad experience behind and perhaps build a new life.

- Take advice from resilient people. They accept circumstances they can't change and expect that things will get better. Observing and developing the traits of emotionally resilient people is a great way to moderate your reactions and consistently take a more balanced approach to life.

- Don't dwell on the past. Buddha said, "Do not dwell in the past, do not dream of the future; concentrate the mind on the present moment." (Note that he *didn't* say, "Do not *plan* for the future." Planning is good!) Thinking too much about times gone by keeps your mind—and your life—stuck in a repeating cycle. If you habitually ruminate over your earlier life, you may regularly be revisited by feelings of anger, guilt, resentment, sorrow, or shame.

- Recognize your own strengths, which are a mixture of your talents, knowledge, and skills. These are part of what makes you unique as an individual and part of the value you offer to the world. Think about the things you really love to do, and look at the underlying elements that enrich these experiences for you.

Money and Happiness

Since ancient times, many people have sought money and wealth, believing it will bring them happiness.

Others—philosophers and those with a deep understanding of the human condition—have warned that wealth alone does not bring happiness. In fact, Ecclesiastes, one of the greatest books of the Old Testament, is devoted to precisely this subject. This passage was written around 400 BCE: "He who loves money will not be satisfied with money, nor he who loves wealth with his income; this also is vanity. When goods increase, they increase who eat them, and what advantage has their owner but to see them with his eyes? Sweet is the sleep of a laborer, whether he eats little or much, but the full stomach of the rich will not let him sleep." (Ecclesiastes 5:10–12.)

In today's society where we're no longer bartering food for beaver pelts, you need money to pay for food and the necessities of life. The point is, however, that money doesn't *create* happiness. It *reveals* it. Money alone will not turn an unhappy person into a happy person. Conversely, the loss of money will not turn a truly happy person into a bitter one. There's an old saying that says, "The real measure of your wealth is how much you'd be worth if you lost all your money."

Consider the Happiness Dissociation Curve shown below.

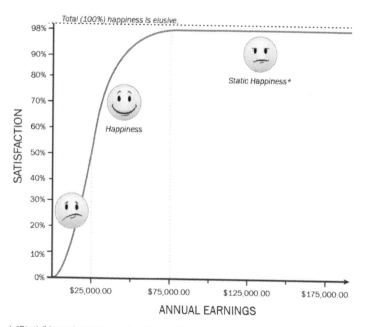

* "Static" here describes no growth: resulting in restlessness or negative happiness.

In the United States today, money, as the chart implies, makes you happy up to a certain point, and then any further benefit curves off. Research suggests that we need a minimum amount of money ($25,000) to meet our most basic needs, and this grants us a baseline level of happiness. Once you exceed $75,000 (again, this is in the United States), the subsequent increases in your happiness are barely enough to register as a difference.

Material possessions have a short-lasting effect. This is called *hedonic adaptation*. We become used to them. The thrill of buying a new Cadillac wears off, and soon you're eyeing a Bentley. Your first two-story house, which seemed so amazing when you moved there from a tiny city apartment, becomes humdrum, and you're soon eyeing the mansion on the hill.

Experiences, on the other hand, have longer lasting effects. With material things, we usually imagine what we will feel when we get them, and we anticipate that satisfaction, but it soon goes away because the moment of satisfaction that you are anticipating will be gone the minute you take possession of that which you coveted.

This is not to say that certain kinds of *dissatisfaction* are not healthy. Over thousands of years, we have developed the ability to be dissatisfied. If that were not the case, we would not have built civilization the way it is today. We would have no electric lights, no vaccines, no airplanes, no smart phones. We would still be living in caves. But this type of dissatisfaction has nothing to do with money. It has everything to do with our desire to make the world a better place.

As you Train Your Brain for Success, moderation is key. For example, watching television makes people happy but only in moderation. Happy people watch TV for an hour a day to relax and be entertained, but research shows that when people watch TV for hours a day their overall level of happiness is lower than that of people who never watch TV.

Buying objects just for bragging rights does not make you happy. If you want to buy a Ferrari because you admire the amazing Italian engineering of a fine automobile, you'll be happy owning it. If you want to buy a Ferrari to show off your wealth, it will make you miserable.

Something very important is to know that research shows an apparent paradox: the things that *are ephemeral* create the most lasting happiness. This is why traveling to a foreign country for a week can bring overall more satisfaction and happiness that buying a new flat screen TV.

Healthy Habits for Happiness

When your brain is happy, you're happy! Here are my tips for keeping your brain happy regardless of the balance in your bank account:

1. Sleep well. People who sleep an adequate amount of time have a better chance of having a more stable emotional brain, which, in turn, benefits decision-making and ultimately your happiness.

2. Exercise often. Exercising boosts endorphins and other hormones related to elevated mood states.

3. Get outside! Research has shown that sunlight can boost serotonin, which is the "happy" chemical of the brain.

4. Eat right. Just like sunlight, many foods promote the synthesis of neurotransmitters, such as dopamine and serotonin. Tryptophan, for instance, is a precursor of dopamine and can be found in leafy green vegetables and poultry.

5. Be optimistic. People who believe tomorrow will be better than today—even if they live in a slum—are happier than people who believe that their best days are behind them.

I realized from the people in Brazil or the Amish that their happiness was completely independent of money or materialistic things. It didn't matter where or how they lived because they had a purpose and the right people to share that purpose with. It depended on the relationships they had with the people surrounding them. In fact, as was confirmed by the Harvard study I discussed in the first chapter of this book, when people ask me what they need to do to be happy, my answer is to have purpose in life and meaningful relationships.

Summary

- Like most people, you probably want to be happy. While part of our happiness depends on our genetic traits, and some is due to external factors, much of it is governed by our attitude and the choices we make with our brains, such as being social, exercising, and having goals. You can choose to Train Your Brain for Success, or let it stay untrained and susceptible to making poor choices.
- Like your personality, your happiness is unique to you. Happiness comes in many colors, shapes, and forms, and everyone is different, and so is their approach to life. Don't emulate others, but seek your own happiness—as long as it's legal and healthy!
- Being happy is good for your health! Studies show that people who are more optimistic have a greatly reduced risk of developing major illness, such as diabetes and heart disease.
- Once your income rises above the poverty line, subsequent increases in your bank account do not produce an equal increase in your happiness. This has been proven by the Happiness Dissociation Curve, which shows that once you get above a comfortable income, having exponentially more money doesn't make you that much more happy.
- Plan for the future and cherish the past, but don't dwell on

either. Keep yourself focused on the present by following these tips:

1. Be self-aware.
2. Put away the digital gadgets.
3. Don't obsess so much on self-improvement.
4. Try meditation.
5. Enjoy the simple pleasures of life.

- We all experience setbacks and disappointments. Your happiness is strongly related to how well you bounce back from them. You can become more resilient, which will help you recover from adverse experiences and perhaps even learn from them.
- Positive dissatisfaction has shown to be a force that motivates us to make the world a better place. Progress is made when you say, "That could be done better than it is now!"
- Here are my tips for keeping your brain happy and focused on your Three Pillars of Life:

1. Sleep well.
2. Exercise often.
3. Get outside!
4. Eat right.
5. Be optimistic.

13. Relationships and Your Purpose

The physical nourishment that you provide to your brain comes to your brain internally through the bloodstream. As we've seen, this internal pipeline delivers a wide variety of substances to your brain that affect it in many different ways, both positive and negative. It delivers life-giving oxygen, water, and glucose, among other nutrients. It also delivers substances that aren't good for you, such as nicotine and powerful opioids. It's up to you to manage this internal supply system so that your brain will operate at its best.

Your brain is also affected by external factors, and their influence can be just as powerful—both positive and negative—as the nutrients that are delivered internally. These external factors shape your emotions, and they influence—or even control—the decisions you make that can lead to either better health or poor health, and even death. While your brain is quite capable of making calculations like a computer, it is not a machine, and it makes important decisions based as much on emotion as on measurable facts.

As you Train Your Brain for Success, everything and anything that your brain perceives can affect the way you feel at a particular moment and therefore the choices you make. Your brain is also hardwired to be responsive to your environment. This is a reptilian survival strategy; in the jungle, an organism that is unaware of its surroundings will soon fall victim to a stealthy predator.

For example, if you're trying to study for an exam and the room you're in is too hot or too cold, or there are external noises from construction or people talking, your brain will not be able to focus as effectively because it is preoccupied with those external environmental factors. You cannot help it—your brain insists on being "tuned in" to your environment, even if it's distracting.

A mother with an infant sleeping in the next room can be engaged in some unrelated activity, and if the infant makes some small sound—a gurgle or a whimper—then the mom, who was not consciously thinking of her child at that moment, will instantly respond.

Human relationships shape our emotions, and their influence on our behavior can be enormous. They take many forms, from intimate and personal relations with family and loved ones to the casual encounter with the teller at a supermarket or the phone conversation with an annoying telemarketer. This is why one of the Three Pillars of Life is relationships. After food, water, and oxygen, nothing is more important to your brain than robust human interaction and, ideally, long-term healthy relationships with other people.

This idea is nothing new! Consider the words of Aristotle, who wrote in the fourth century BCE in his book *Politics*: "Man is by nature a social animal; an individual who is unsocial naturally and not accidentally is either beneath our notice or more than human. Society is something that precedes the individual. Anyone who either cannot lead the common life or is so self-sufficient as not to need to, and therefore does not partake of society, is either a beast or a god."

Conversely, the pain of social rejection can be just as real as the pain from a physical injury. As Emily Esfahani Smith wrote in her 2013 article in *The Atlantic* entitled "Social Connection Makes a Better Brain," a study by social psychologist and neuroscientist Matthew Lieberman, done in collaboration with his wife, Naomi Eisenberger, revealed that social loss and rejection are more painful than we might realize.

Here's how it worked.

Researchers put volunteers in a brain scanner and then had them play a simple Internet video game called Cyberball, in which three people toss a ball around to each other. The volunteers were told that that the other two players in the game were other study participants, when, in fact, they were computer-generated avatars.

When the game began, all three players tossed the ball to each other in turn; but after a while, the avatars ignored the human volunteer and tossed the ball only to each other. The human volunteer was effectively ostracized. Even though it was just a video game in a research study, the research volunteers were sincerely hurt. They felt rejected. When they came out of the scanner, they emphatically told the researchers about how upset they were.

During the game, the researchers tracked the volunteers' brain activity. Their brains processed social rejection in the same way as physical pain. As Lieberman, Eisenberger, and Kipling Williams wrote in their paper "Does Rejection Hurt? An fMRI Study of Social Exclusion":

"Paralleling results from physical pain studies, the anterior cingulate cortex (ACC) was more active during exclusion than during inclusion and correlated positively with self-reported distress. Right ventral prefrontal cortex (RVPFC) was active during exclusion and correlated negatively with self-reported distress. ACC changes mediated the RVPFC-distress correlation, suggesting that RVPFC regulates the distress of social exclusion by disrupting ACC activity."

To the brains of the volunteer game players, social pain felt the same as physical pain—"a broken heart can feel like a broken leg," as Lieberman puts it in his book. The more rejected the participant said he or she felt, the more activity there was in the part of the brain that processes the distress of physical pain.

The measurable effect on the brain of social isolation was reaffirmed in a 2007 study by Lieberman et al. entitled "Neural pathways link social support to attenuated neuroendocrine stress responses." Here, thirty participants completed three tasks in which daily social support, neurocognitive reactivity to a social stressor, and neuroendocrine responses to a social stressor were assessed. ("Social support" is a good thing; a "social stressor," such as a spouse who's an alcoholic, is a bad thing.) Over a ten-day period, participants who interacted pleasurably with supportive individuals showed diminished cortisol reactivity to a social stressor. (This means their adrenal gland produced less cortisol, a damaging stress hormone.) Meanwhile, "greater social support and diminished cortisol responses were associated with diminished activity in the dorsal anterior cingulate cortex (dACC) and Brodmann's area (BA) 8, regions previously associated with the distress of social separation. Lastly, individual differences in dACC and BA 8 reactivity mediated the relationship between high daily social support and low cortisol reactivity, such that supported individuals showed reduced neurocognitive reactivity to social stressors, which in turn was associated with reduced neuroendocrine stress responses." This means that when you're engaged in pleasant social activities your hormones and brain are happier; when you're exposed to "social stressors," such as your spouse being an alcoholic, your brain instructs your body to produce more stress-related hormones, which over a long period of time are not good for you.

Scientists are learning how your brain responds to external emotional input. The amygdala is the emotional gatekeeper region of the brain. It receives information about, say, a potential threat, which produces the well-known fight-or-flight response. Then a few milliseconds later it receives contextual information to help modulate the response. With the help of the decision-making centers in our cortex, we try to rationalize the situation and make the most logical decision possible.

As for human relationships, we may respond irrationally and with intense emotion to either a perceived threat or a perceived attraction. This can occur when we meet someone for the first time or with someone with whom we are in an intimate relationship. Our emotional brain is constantly evaluating facial expressions, responding to positive or negative cues, and hopefully keeping us in tune with the social situation.

Protecting ourselves from danger is an important response to have, but reacting in the appropriate way with others in a particular situation can help us keep our relationships healthy and productive. Early life experiences, including how we were raised and our interactions with friends and family, in addition to genetics and other environmental factors, can affect how this circuitry works.

Relationships have a significant impact on our brains. Even when we are just a few months old, we seek eye contact and warmth from the people that take care of us. This response has been hardwired into our reward-seeking mechanisms, and it triggers the release of specific neurotransmitters, keeping us coming back for more.

Our relationships with others can either be detrimental to our health or a benefit. Research has shown that stressful personal relationships—with your boss, family member, or even a politician who gets you riled up—trigger the release of stress hormones and decreased immune function, while the opposite is true when we are involved in fruitful and positive relationships. A number of naturally produced hormones are important in personal attachment, including oxytocin and vasopressin. Attachment is a genetically valuable force because it's the bond that keeps couples together long enough for them to have and raise children. Oxytocin is a powerful hormone released by men and women during orgasm, and it's called "the cuddle hormone." It's been shown to reduce the level of stress hormones like cortisol. Vasopressin may be released directly into the brain from the hypothalamus and may be important in social behavior, sexual motivation and pair bonding, and maternal responses to stress. This, in turn, reduces anxiety, increases relaxation, and increases trust. Attachment overall makes us feel good not only mentally but also physically, especially when we interact with people who are supportive, positive, and nurturing.

Here is the great news: we are the only living organisms that have the mechanism to deal with situations, either positive or negative, in a way that we can control and alter to our advantage. We have the ability to self-regulate and change the course of actions as we please. We can communicate by talking to others and express how we feel emotionally, and we have the ability to listen to others as well. As a result we can all understand each other's needs, motivation, desires, and frustrations. No other animal on the planet can achieve this.

I'm not saying it's an easy task. I'm sure you've frequently encountered situations that can get out of hand, and you've done or said things that you later regret and which can affect that relationship forever.

The good thing is that you can change and not make the same mistakes twice.

The Four Types of Relationships

I like to divide relationships into four categories: intimate, personal, professional, and temporary.

Intimate relationships include those you have with your parents, children, your family members, and your significant others (girlfriend, boyfriend, spouse).

Personal relationships are those you have with your friends, close coworkers, and business partners.

Professional relationships are those you have with the people at your workplace who are not necessarily your friends, such as your boss or somebody in another division with whom you have professional encounters. It also includes the relationships you have with your lawyer, your doctor, or a sales rep who visits you every month.

Temporary relationships include all other relationships you have with other human beings. This includes the retail salesperson, the stewardess on the flight, the waiter who took your order at the restaurant, or the grandma you helped cross the street.

I will not go into details on each type of relationship in this guide. All the principles behind relationships apply to all four categories. There are certainly differences between the relationships and the way you should handle them, but that's a whole book in itself. I do want you to understand that all four levels of relationships in essence are the same in the sense that people have to trust you and your motives before they will let you into their circle. Even in a casual relationship, you must trust the person you're talking to. To use a simple example, let's say you're on a first date with someone, and that person has invited you to dine at a public restaurant. The date goes well, and you feel you could have a relationship with this person. At the end of the evening, the person says, "Oh dear, I left my credit card at home. Would it be possible for you to pick up the tab?" So you pay the bill. A few days later the same person calls you and asks you to go out again. You hesitate while your brain frantically replays the events of the first date, looking for other red flags. The trust isn't there yet.

So how do we gain trust?

To gain trust, three things need to happen:

1. People have to like you.
2. They have to understand you.
3. You must have the right knowledge.

If people don't like you, your brain's primitive system otherwise known as the reptilian brain ceases to communicate with the rational centers in your cortex and, as a result, no matter what you try to do they will not trust you. This is crucial, and this is what happens, for example, when you meet a sleazy car salesperson. You can tell his intentions are not genuine. No matter what he is trying to sell, you will not buy, and your brain shuts down. The same applies for a politician; if you feel a visceral aversion to them, their policies and promises will mean nothing to you.

The next important factor is that people need to understand you. If your message is not clear, it's too complicated, or too confusing, the same thing happens: Your brain shuts down, or it loses focus and leads to people not trusting you. It's not entirely your fault because you might have the best intentions. The problem is that you are not able to get the message across the way you want to. You need to decide how to make your message or your intentions very clear to the other person.

Finally, you need the right knowledge. You must understand or have a good grasp of what you're trying to convey. This is especially important when you're trying to teach someone or exert your professional authority in a particular topic or field. If a person feels that you don't understand or have full knowledge of what you're trying to explain or teach, it will send a red flag alert to their brain centers, and they will immediately not trust you or anything you say.

Remember also what we learned about cognitive biases. They are crucial to understand so that we can consider our flaws and other people's flaws when relating to them. Cognitive biases can cause a lot of distress in relationships. Consider the stereotyping bias and how by stereotyping you might alienate a person or group of people from your life just by having prejudgmental opinions of them. Biases tremendously affect the way you think and the way you feel: being aware of them and recognizing them when they occur is essential to enhance your relationships with people. It is also a major advantage for you and those you spend time with to know them. Most people don't even know anything about cognitive bias.

One of the most important things in any relationship is empathy, which I discussed earlier in the book. Being an empathetic listener is paying attention to another person with emotional identification, compassion, or feeling. We must seek to understand and feel others' emotions before we can be understood. In layman's terms, being empathetic is basically putting yourself in the other person's shoes. Emotional intelligence (EQ) is highly correlated to empathetic listening. The better you become as an empathetic listener, the higher degree of understanding for others you have, which is an indication of higher EQ.

All these character traits—being likable, able to communicate, and trustworthy, being free from cognitive biases, and having empathy—are created and controlled by your brain. Keeping your brain healthy and well nourished is important to its functioning at a high level and guiding you on your path to the Three Pillars of Life.

Shown below is a list of tips you can apply to enhance your relationships with just about anybody. Just by applying these twelve basic principles you can significantly increase the quality of your relationships.

1. Be aware that positive relationships have a tremendous effect on your brain.
2. Be an empathetic listener.
3. Be knowledgeable.
4. Be likeable.
5. Be genuine.
6. Listen. Give people your undivided attention.
7. Avoid prejudgment. Eliminate all stereotypes and your own personal conclusions.
8. Observe their emotions and body movement; seek patterns.
9. Don't be quick to respond; take your time.
10. Let them know that you understand what they are telling you.
11. Ask questions and seek clarification.
12. Eliminate distractions.

Your Purpose

It's not by accident that this is the concluding section of the book.

If there's one thing you can do to keep your brain healthy and engaged, and which represents the culmination of your Three Pillars of Life, it's to have a *purpose* for what you do every day.

In fact, it's safe to say that without a purpose to inspire and guide you, your Three Pillars of Life will be in constant danger of crumbling.

What does this mean—to have a purpose?

This question has vexed humankind since the dawn of history.

In the old days—and for many people today—the answer has been found in religion and spirituality. For example, in ancient Egypt, your purpose in life was straightforward: You needed to conduct your life in accordance with the wishes of the various gods, including the god who was living on earth, the pharaoh. If you did this, after death your soul would make its way toward the

Hall of Truth in the company of Anubis, the guide of the dead, where it would wait in line with others for judgment by Osiris. Your heart would be weighed, and if it were as light as a feather, you'd be granted eternal life.

In today's world, spirituality is still powerful and still relates to your purpose in life—in fact, a perennial best-seller is *The Purpose-Driven Life* by Christian pastor Rick Warren.

This is not to say that Christians, among others, don't have problems finding their purpose. One of the greatest books of the Bible is Ecclesiastes, in which the protagonist, Solomon, wracks his brain over this exact problem. As he ruminates over his empty life, he says, "This too is a grievous evil: As everyone comes, so they depart, and what do they gain, since they toil for the wind? All their days they eat in darkness, with great frustration, affliction and anger." (Ecclesiastes 4:16–17)

These are difficult and weighty questions, which I'm going to sidestep. The purpose of this book is not to attempt to answer the most profound mysteries of the ages but to help you Train Your Brain for Success and build your Three Pillars of Life. I want to focus on what you can do regardless of your personal faith on a practical, day-to-day basis to develop a sense of purpose in your life.

If there's one thing that everyone can agree on it's that we humans are happier and healthier when we're devoted to something that's bigger than ourselves and which goes beyond satisfying our own immediate materialistic needs.

This is not to say that you should neglect yourself. Far from it! The road to deep satisfaction in life begins with making sure that you're physically and mentally able to make a contribution to the world, and you can't do that if you've got lung cancer from smoking cigarettes or you're loading up your body with sugar or alcohol or opioids. The first step toward fulfilling your purpose—whatever that is—is to strive for good health.

Some people find their purpose in life very early. Mozart began composing music at the age of five. Enrico Fermi was a mathematics and physics prodigy who by age ten was spending his free time studying geometric proofs and building electric motors. At the age of five, Shirley Temple was working as an actress and tap dancer. When she was seven years old, she received a special Academy Award. As an adult, she served as United States ambassador to Ghana and then Czechoslovakia.

Others find their purpose late in life. The artist known as Grandma Moses began painting in earnest at the age of seventy-eight. Colonel Sanders began his fried chicken franchise in his sixties. Leonard Cohen did not release his first album until he was thirty-two years old. Poet Wallace Stevens started writing poetry late in life after a career as an insurance salesman and executive.

Your purpose need not be the same thing as how you make your money.

You may find fulfillment teaching Sunday school every week or raising your children to be responsible, loving adults. You may find fulfillment volunteering at the local hospital or supporting a rape crisis center. You may even find fulfillment working on your Great American Novel that you know will never be a best-seller. The point is that you're dedicating your brainpower to a project or effort that's bigger than your day-to-day worries. By focusing on your long-range goal or an ongoing activity that benefits others, the little things that annoy you during the day will seem less important. If you're serving lunch to people in a homeless shelter, you're not going to be as concerned about your bad hair day. In fact, it's amazing what people can overcome when they have a purpose. We've all heard stories about multiple amputees who have climbed mountains or people from impoverished backgrounds who have achieved great business success. These people didn't allow their present condition to deter them from their ultimate goal.

Your purpose need not be grand or heroic. It can be whatever works for you. As you build your Three Pillars of Life, your purpose, whatever it is, will guide you and keep you on course.

Remember that your brain is the most sophisticated and complex thing in the known universe. One of these amazing devices has been entrusted to you. If you take care of it and make the most of it, your brain can do spectacular things for you!

Summary

- Everyone knows the expression "You are what you *eat.*" It's true—the food you put into your body will either nourish or damage your brain. Equally true is the expression "You are what you *experience.*" Your brain is influenced by external events—not only physical threats but also what happens in your social circle. Make every effort to keep your environment healthy and positive!

- After food, water, and oxygen, nothing is more important to your brain than robust human interaction, including long-term healthy relationships with other people.

- Conversely, the pain of social rejection can be just as real as the pain from a physical injury. Studies, such as the Cyberball game used by Lieberman and Eisenberger, have revealed that social loss and rejection are more painful than we might realize.

- Social rejection can lead to measurable changes in the brain. When you're engaged in pleasant social activities, your hormones and brain are happier; when you're exposed to "social stressors," such as your spouse being an alcoholic, your brain instructs your body to produce more stress-related hormones, which over a long period of time are not good for you.

- We can divide relationships into four categories: intimate,

personal, professional, and temporary. Each is built on trust. You can build trust in three ways:
1. People have to like you.
2. They have to understand you.
3. You must have the right knowledge.

- Empathy is a key to building relationships. Being empathetic means paying attention to another person with emotional identification, compassion, or feeling, and putting yourself in the other person's shoes. Emotional intelligence (EQ) is highly correlated to empathetic listening. Use my twelve powerful tips to strengthen your capability for empathy and significantly increase the quality of your relationships.

- The key to building your Three Pillars of Life is your life's purpose. Your purpose, which can be anything you like that's positive for you and your community, is like the fuel that keeps you going. It allows you to ignore the petty distractions that can mire you down. It gives your life meaning and value. If you feel you have no purpose in life, get out and try different things—you may discover something that makes you say, "This is what I was meant to do!"

Thank You!

Thank you for reading *Train Your Brain for Success*. I hope that I've provided you with useful and actionable information that will help you get the most from your amazing brain, keep it healthy, and live a meaningful and productive life.

If you'd like more information, I invite you to visit Doctor-Fresco.com for more resources and to sign up for our Brain Training Course.